GRANTA

12

Editorial and Subscription Correspondence: Granta, 44a Hobson Street, Cambridge CB1 1NL. (0223) 315290.
All manuscripts are welcome but must be accompanied by a stamped, self-addressed envelope or they cannot be returned.

Subscriptions: £10.00 for four issues; from 30 September 1984, £12.00 for four issues.

Back Issues: £2.50 for *Granta* 3; £3.50 for *Granta* 5 to 10; £3.95 for *Granta* 11. *Granta* 1, 2, and 4 are no longer available. All prices include postage.

Granta is set by Lindonprint Typesetters, Cambridge, and is printed by Hazell Watson and Viney Ltd, Aylesbury, Bucks.

Granta is published by Granta Publications Ltd and distributed by Penguin Books Ltd, Harmondsworth, Middlesex, England; Penguin Books Australia Ltd, Ringwood, Victoria, Australia; Penguin Books Canada Ltd, 2801 John Street, Markham, Ontario, Canada L3R 1B4; Penguin Books (NZ) Ltd, 182–90 Wairau Road, Auckland 10, New Zealand.

Cover by Chris Hyde

ISSN 0017-3231
ISBN 014-00-75658

Published with the assistance of the Eastern Arts Association

---

Contents

Stanley Booth

The True Adventures of the Rolling Stones

Coke
BO-WEEVI

6 December 1969

It's late. The world is black outside the car windows, just the dusty clay road in the headlights. Far from the city, past the last crossroads, we are looking for a strange California hillside where we may see him, may even dance with him in his torn, bloody skins.

As we come out from under a railway viaduct, there is an unmarked fork in the road. The Crystals are singing 'He's a Rebel'. The driver looks left, right, left again. 'He don't know where he's going,' Keith says.

See the way he walks down the street
Watch the way he shuffles his feet
Oh, how he holds his head up high
When he goes walkin' by
He's my guy
When he holds my hand I'm so proud
'Cause he's not just one of the crowd

'Do you—are you sure this is the way?' Mick asks. Turning left, the driver does not answer. The radio is quite loud.

'Maybe he didn't hear you.'

Mick closes his eyes. Certain we are lost, but so tired, with no sleep for the past forty hours. Each moment we feel less able to protest or change direction.

My baby's always the one
To try the things they've never done
And just because of that they say
He's a rebel
And he'll never ever be
Any good
He's a rebel
'Cause he never ever does
What he should.

'Something up ahead here,' the driver says. Parked by the road is a Volkswagen van, a German police dog tied by a rope to the back door handle. The dog barks as we pass. Further on there are more cars and vans, some with people in them, but most of the people are in the road, walking in small groups, carrying sleeping bags, canvas rucksacks, babies, leading more big ugly dogs.

Keith Richards and Stanley Booth, 1969.

'Let's get out,' Keith says.

'Don't lose us,' Mick tells the driver, who says 'Where are you going?', but we are already gone, the five of us, Ron the Bag Man, Tony the Spade Heavy, the Okefenokee Kid, and of course Mick and Keith, Rolling Stones. The other members of the band are asleep back in San Francisco at the Huntington Hotel.

The road descends between rolling dry-grass embankments, the kind of bare landscape where in 1950s science-fiction movies the teenager and his busty girl friend, parked in his hot rod, receive unearthly visitors. But now it is crowded with young people, most with long hair, dressed in heavy clothes, blue jeans, army fatigue jackets, against the December night air that revives us as we walk. Mick is wearing a long burgundy overcoat, and Keith has on a Nazi leather greatcoat, green with mould, that he will leave behind about sixteen hours from now, in the mad blind panic to get away from the place we are lightly swaggering toward. Mick and Keith are smiling: it is their little joke to have the power to create this gathering simply by wishing for it aloud, and the freedom to walk like anybody else along the busy barren path. People are laughing and talking quietly among themselves, but there is little conversation between groups, although it seems that none of us is a stranger; each wears the signs, the insignia, of the campaigns that have brought us, long before most of us have reached the age of thirty, to this desolate spot on the western slope of the New World.

'Tony, score us a joint,' Keith says, and before we have been another twenty steps giant black Tony has dropped back and fallen into stride with a boy who's smoking, and hands Tony the joint saying 'Keep it.' So we smoke and follow the trail down to a basin where the embankments stretch into low hills already covered with thousands of people around campfires—some sleeping, some playing guitars, some passing smokes and great red jugs of wine. For a moment it stops us; it has the dreamlike quality of one's deepest wishes, to have all the good people, all one's family, all the lovers, together in some private country of night. It is as familiar as our earliest dreams and yet so grand and final, campfires flickering like distant stars as far as our eyes can see, and as we start up the hillside to our left, walking on sleeping bags and blankets, trying not to step on anyone's head, Keith is saying it's like Morocco, outside the gates of Marrakesh, hear the pipes....

The people are camped right up to a cyclone fence topped with barbed wire, and we are trying to find the gate, while from behind us the Maysles brothers, filming what will eventually be *Gimme Shelter,* approach across sleeping bodies with blinding blue-white quartz lamps. Mick yells to turn off the lights, but they pretend to be deaf and keep coming. The kids who have been looking up as we pass—saying Hi, Mick—now begin to join us. There is a caravan of young girls and boys strung out in the spotlights when we reach the gate which is, naturally, locked. Inside we can see the Altamont Speedway clubhouse and some people we know standing outside it. Mick calls, 'Could we get in, please?' and one of them comes over, sees who we are, and sets out to find someone who can open the gate. It takes a while, and the boys and girls all want autographs and to go inside with us. Mick tells them we can't get in ourselves yet, and no one has a pen except me, and I have learned not to let go of mine because they get the signatures and go spinning away in a frenzy of bliss and exhilaration, taking my trade with them. So we stand on one foot and then the other, swearing in the cold, and no one comes to let us in, and the gate which is leaning rattles when I shake it, and I say we could push it down pretty easy, and Keith says, 'The first act of violence.'

The Tour: Los Angeles

I woke up under a Wizard of Oz bedspread, magenta and turquoise, with Dorothy and the Straw Man and all the rest of them in a balloon. I showered and dressed, looking out over Los Angeles, invisible under a dense elephant-coloured cloud, and then made my way to the kitchen. I was in a big characterless house on a sunny morning in which I couldn't see the rest of the world around me because of the noxious vapours enveloping it, but I could open the fridge and find bottles of raw milk and whole-grain bread. California. It's ten o'clock.

It's my first full day on the Stones' first tour in the United States for three years, and as I walked back through the house, I passed Jo Bergman, working on the publicity kits for the morning's press conference.

It was, as I would learn, typical of the Stones' manner of doing business that I never knew exactly what Jo did for them, and neither did she, and neither did they. She was born in Oakland, California, and grew up in the United States and England. Jo had spent most of her adult life working for celebrities, and spoke a mix of Hip and Celebrity Code. In an intense breathless rush of pleasure and excitement, Jo spoke a tongue in which words, phrases, entire paragraphs were omitted, and if you didn't know the code or the private affairs of the people being talked about, you could only listen with a game smile and admire the fervent delivery.

I didn't know then that Jo had consulted an astrologer in London who had told her that I would write about the Stones, and that it would cost me everything except my life. She did not know the details—that while writing I would be assaulted by Confederate soldiers and Hell's Angels, go to jail, be run over by a lumber truck on the Memphis-Arkansas bridge, fall off a Georgia waterfall and break my back, have epileptic seizures while withdrawing from drugs—but if she had known, she would not have told me. She didn't tell me about the astrologer until much later.

The press conference was at the Beverly Wilshire Hotel, and Jo and I left early in one of the limousines that were on duty around the clock at all three of the Stones' LA abodes—our place with Charlie Watts and his wife Shirley on Oriole Drive; the Laurel Canyon house where Keith Richard, Mick Jagger and Mick Taylor were staying; and the Beverly Wilshire where Bill Wyman and his girlfriend Astrid Lindstrom, the Swedish Ice Princess, would be until Jo could get them a house together.

We entered the conference-room through a labyrinth of bars and luncheon rooms. Fifty or sixty folding chairs had been arranged in semi-circles before a long table. To the right there was a bar and another table with tea, coffee, fruit salad and little cakes. The press began to arrive. They all appeared to be in their early twenties, most of them carrying notebooks, cameras, and tape recorders, all dressed in the current style, achieved by spending large sums of money to look poor and bedraggled, like a new race of middle-class gypsies.

Around eleven-thirty, three television crews arrived. With one was Rona Barrett, the televised Hollywood gossip, a small woman whose large blonde hairdo was frozen within a layer of spray shellac.

She perched on a folding chair, a cultured pearl among the suede and denim.

At noon the Rolling Stones stumbled into the room in single file like drunken Indians and arranged themselves at the long table. The television cameras started and flash-bulbs popped. The Stones sat and scratched their heads.

With the Stones, sitting next to Keith, was another young Englishman, wearing a burgundy-coloured leather jacket, dark glasses, and piratical dark greasy locks. He was Sam Cutler, a recent addition to the Stones' entourage whose function, other than to carry whatever Keith would not want to be caught carrying, was at the moment unclear.

Finally the flashes stopped and for a long moment there were no questions. No one could think what to ask. The confrontation was enough: three years ago, when the Stones last toured the United States, most of the people here now were teenagers screaming in darkened arenas. The Stones, in the interim, had been arrested, had swapped women, broken up, died, and yet here they were—elbows on the table.

The first questions, fielded by Jagger, revealed only that the Stones' new album, *Let It Bleed,* would be finished and released in about three weeks, and that they had, after all, no serious plans for a record label of their own. 'That's about all we'd get: the label,' Mick said. 'Unless you hire a fleet of lorries and sell the records for half price, there's no point in it.' The meeting, it appeared, would be friendly and dull, without the conflict that once characterized the Stones' encounters with the press.

Someone asked for a reply to the statement by rock and jazz critic Ralph Gleason who had said in his column the day before that 'the price of tickets for your concerts is too high and a lot of people who would like to see you can't really afford it.'

'Maybe we can fix something up for those people,' Mick said.

'A free concert?' someone asked.

Mick said he didn't know and evaded the issue with aristocratic ease: 'We can't set the price of tickets. I don't know how much people can afford. I mean, I've no idea.'

Someone else asked whether the US State Department gave the Stones any trouble or asked them to sign anti-drug statements before allowing them to enter the country. Mick said, 'Of course not, we've never done anything wrong.'

Through the laughter and applause Rona Barret asked, 'Do you consider yourself an anti-establishment group, or are you just putting us on?'

'We're just putting you on,' Mick said.

'Taking you for a ride,' Keith murmured, reptile eyelids drooping.

Mick told a questioner that the Stones hoped to hire Ike and Tina Turner, Terry Reid, B.B. King, and Chuck Berry as supporting acts for the tour, and the question of a free concert returned. These young reporters seemed to suggest—even more strongly than Ralph Gleason—that the Stones had an obligation to a new community, formed largely in the Stones' image. It seemed the sort of thing that the Stones in their independence had never flirted with, and Mick avoided the subject again: 'If we feel that's what's got to be done then we'll do it. I'm leaving that very fluid you notice, I'm not committing meself.'

'And how is Marianne Faithfull?' Rona Barrett asked Mick.

Three days after Brian Jones died, Marianne Faithfull, Jagger's *regulaire* for the past two years, in Australia with Mick to appear in a movie, looked into a mirror and saw not her face but Brian's. Then she took an overdose of sleeping pills. Only luck and prompt medical attention saved her life. After recuperating in Australia and Switzerland, she returned to Mick's house in London, where she was now, feeling neglected.

'She's all right,' Mick said to Rona. 'How are you?'

Rona, undaunted, wanted to know of any plans Mick had to run for public office: 'I'm not feeling very messianic,' he said, laughing.

Other people asked more questions about festivals and free concerts. The subject would not go away. This year the popular imagination had been outraged or delighted, captured anyway, by the pop festivals—mammoth exhibitions of drugs, sex and music. Last year's spectacle had been the police violence in Chicago during the Democratic Party's nominating convention; the year before, the mass media had discovered the widespread use of psychedelic drugs among the young; this year there had been giant music festivals in Woodstock, Hyde Park, Atlanta, Denver, the Isle of Wight, Dallas—where people came without paying, went naked, had sex and took drugs openly, but where there were almost no arrests because there was no way short of war to arrest hundreds of thousands of people. It seemed that the babies after World War Two had grown into a force traditional society might be unable to restrain.

There should be, Keith said about the festivals, 'ten times more of them.'

But someone still wanted to know, What about the prices of tickets to the Stones' concerts?

Mick, Keith, and Sam Cutler began talking at once, stopped together, and Sam said, 'Could I just say this: the prickets—' And Keith kissed him on the cheek.

They were still, after all, the Rolling Stones. Mick made a little speech: 'We aren't doing this tour for money, but because we wanted to play in America and have a lot of fun. We're really not into that sort of economic scene. I mean, either you're gonna sing and all that crap or you're gonna be a fucking economist. We're sorry people can't afford to come. We don't know that this tour is more expensive. You'll have to tell us.'

The questions trailed off, and Mick said, 'Thank you very much, people,' sounding as if he were ending a presidential press conference.

Al Steckler—the promotion man from the New York office of Allen Klein, the group's business manager—Jo, and I then met the Stones in Bill Wyman's suite, where the serious question in the sitting room was whether the Stones would release a single from the new album before the tour started.

Jagger suggested releasing the title track 'Let It Bleed', 'if anybody would play it on the radio.'

'Not with those lyrics,' Jo said.

'Well, they're not just dirty, I mean they're *double entendre,*' Mick said.

'"If you want someone to cream on, you can cream on me," is pretty single *entendre,*' Jo said.

'We also have to decide which press you'll talk to,' Al Steckler said, and named several periodicals that had requested interviews.

'*Saturday Review,* what's that like?' Mick asked.

'Dullest magazine in America,' I said. 'Duller than the *Saturday Evening Post.* Duller than *Grit.*'

'That's all right, then.'

The meeting was short; nothing was settled.

I had dinner with Charlie Watts and Mick Taylor at a trendy, surly restaurant that wasn't much fun, but afterwards we met the other Stones at the Whiskey à Go Go to hear Chuck Berry.

It was on the Sunset Strip, on the corner, and as we entered we passed the remote loungers at the entrance, and went into the darkness, where it was hot and smoky and crowded, a big barn with a small elevated dance floor, the bandstand high in a corner. I sat with Jagger, Keith, and Wyman. Young girls kept walking by our tables, passing maybe six times before they got up the nerve to ask for the Stones' autographs.

Onstage were four white musicians, loud and incompetent. A light show was playing on two walls, one covered with jello-coloured liquid globs and swirls, the other showing salmon leaping up a small waterfall, intercut between scenes from a Japanese movie featuring a giant beast come from the sky to devour the world.

But then a lean, high-cheekboned, brooding black man came on stage, wearing his guitar low, stroking it with obscene expertise, and even Keith's image—Indian, pirate, witch, grinning at Death—reverted to what it had been when he first heard Chuck Berry: a schoolboy in his uniform and cap. For years Keith had been unable to see Chuck Berry in person, because Berry had been in the federal penitentiary for taking a fourteen-year-old Indian whore across a state line for the wrong reasons, but Keith and Jagger had both learned Berry's trademark—his duck walk—from the film *Jazz on a Summer's Day,* which Keith saw fourteen times. Later, when Chuck Berry was out of prison and Mick and Keith were Rolling Stones, they met, and Berry, unlike many of their musical idols, snubbed them repeatedly, so that they respected him even more and were trying to hire him for the present tour.

When Berry's set ended we left the Whiskey (the leaving, like all their arrivals and departures, was swift and dramatic, everyone staring at the Stones as they swept out into limousines at the kerb) and rolled, four carloads of us, down the super-highway toward the Corral, a night club in Topanga Canyon, to hear Gram Parsons and the Flying Burrito Brothers.

Along the miles and miles of highway, we (Charlie Watts and his wife Shirley, Bill and Astrid, two or three others) were talking about music when for the first time on this tour we encountered Wyman's Weakness. Bill told the driver to stop at a gas station, 'Got to go to the loo,' and we rolled on and there was no place open, and Bill again said, 'Hey, you gotta stop somewhere, gotta go to the loo,' and the driver said, 'Doesn't seem to be any place open.' 'Well, stop at one that isn't open,' Bill said, 'just let me out of the car,' and Charlie reminded him that 'It was you got us in trouble like that the time before.'

That was in 1965, the last night of the Rolling Stones' fifth tour of England, as they were heading for London in Mick's Daimler. Before they reached home, Wyman needed to urinate. As their road manager Ian Stewart described the situation, 'Really, if you sit in a dressing room all night, drinking Coca-Cola, go onstage for about thirty minutes, leap about like idiots, drop your guitar to run out into a car in the bloody cold weather, you're just about ready for a quick tiddle.'

Mick turned the big, black car into a service station on the Romford Road in East London. It was about eleven-thirty. According to the station attendant, forty-one-year-old Charles Keeley, 'A shaggy-haired monster wearing dark glasses' got out of the car and asked, 'Where can we have a piss here?' Wyman's behaviour, according to Keeley, 'did not seem natural or normal.' He was 'running up and down the forecourt, taking off his dark glasses and dancing.' Then 'eight or nine youths and girls got out of the car.' Mr Keeley, 'sensing trouble,' told the driver of the car, Mick Jagger, to get them off the forecourt. Jagger pushed him aside and said, 'We'll piss anywhere, man.' This phrase was taken up by the others, who repeated it in 'a gentle chant.' One danced to the phrase. Then Wyman urinated against a garage. Mick Jagger and Brian Jones followed suit further down the road. According to Mr Keeley, 'Some people did not seem offended. They even went up and asked for autographs.' One customer, however, told the Stones their behaviour was 'disgusting.' At this the Stones 'started shouting and screaming.' Eventually the Daimler drove away, its occupants making 'a well-known gesture with two fingers.' The incident finally ended when, some time later, the Stones were ordered by a London court to pay fifteen guineas costs, in spite of Wyman's plaintive statement: 'I happen to suffer from a weak bladder.'

But as he told the story now, while we rolled down the California coast on this pleasurable night, it was different again: 'So I go behind this place, see, and I've got me chopper out, when here comes this bloke waving a bloody electric torch, cryin' 'Ere, 'Ere—'

'He probably had to have a torch to see it,' Shirley said.

We found a gas station and while waiting for Bill we lost the other limousines. None of us knew where the Corral was, least of all the driver, and we raced along the highway looking for spoor. Somebody thought it was down that turning to the right, Is that it, Nah, that place is closed, and then there it was on the left, a little roadhouse, capacity about two hundred, tables and a small dance floor, crowded with rednecks and members of Los Angeles rock and roll society.

We sat at a long table, the Stones gang and their friends and women, drinking pitchers and pitchers of beer, whooping and hollering while the Burritos played 'Lucille' and old Boudleaux Bryant songs—a real rock and roll hoedown. It had been nearly six years since the Stones played in English clubs where sweat condensed on the walls and people swung from the rafters. They were glad to have stopped and gone on to bigger places, but later they missed them, as they had come, since their drug arrests during the last three years, to miss playing itself.

Now, getting ready to go back on the road, it was good to be at the Corral and see all these different types—motorcycle boots, eagle tattoos, lesbian romancers, white English niggers, Beach Boys, Georgia boys—brought together by the music. The night seemed to pass like a dream: one minute all of us were singing along and the next minute it was closing time and we were going out.

1962

Keith Richards: In 1962, the big music among the kids was traditional jazz—some of it very funky, some of it very wet, most of it very very wet. Rock and roll had already drifted into pop like it has already done again here. No good music coming out of the radio, no good music coming out of the so-called rock and roll stars. No good nothing.

Just about the time Mick and I were getting the scene together with a bass player named Dick Taylor, trying to find out who's playing what and how they're playing it, Alexis Korner starts a band at a club in the west of London, in Ealing, with a harmonica player called Cyril Davies, a bourbon-drinking car-panel beater who worked in a junk yard and body shop. Cyril had been to Chicago and sat in with Muddy Waters at Smitty's Corner and was therefore a very big deal. And who happens to be on drums, none other than Charlie Watts. We went down about the second week it opened, and Alexis gets up and says, 'And now, folks, a very fine bottleneck guitar player who has come all the way from Cheltenham to play here tonight'. And suddenly someone's playing fucking Elmore James up there—beautifully—and it's Brian Jones.

So we start talking to Brian, and he's moving up to London with his chick and his baby. His second baby—his first one belongs to some other chick. He's left her and he's really in trouble in Cheltenham. He can't stay there any longer—he's got shotguns coming out of the hills after him, so he's moving up to town.

Alexis Korner: **I met Brian because he came up to me after a concert in Cheltenham and asked if he could speak to me. That's how we got together. He used to show up at the Ealing club on Thursdays and weekends and occasionally play a bit.**

A little later, Mick sent me a tape of some stuff he and Keith had got down—odds and ends of Bo Diddley and Chuck Berry—and he came over to my place. Mick was into the club at Ealing almost from the beginning, standing around waiting to sing his three songs every night.

Mick wasn't a good singer then, just as he isn't a good singer now—in general terms. But it was the personal thing with Mick: he had a feel for belting a song even if he wasn't able to sing it. He has this tremendous personal thing—which is what the blues is about, more than technique. And he had this absolute certainty that he was right.

Keith: In the early summer of 1962, Brian decided to get a band together. So I went round to this rehearsal in a pub called The White Bear, just off Leicester Square by the tube station.

We had one rehearsal which was a bummer, with Stu on piano, Brian, a guitar player called Geoff somebody, and a singer and harp player we used to call 'Walk On', because that was the only song he knew. He was a real throwback, greasy ginger hair. These two cats didn't like me because I played rock and roll. Stu loved it and so did Brian. So Brian didn't know what to do, but eventually decided to get rid of these two cats. Meanwhile I persuaded Mick to come to rehearsal, and the band now consisted of Stu, me, Mick, Brian, and Dick Taylor on bass, no drummer. Piano, two guitars, harmonica, and bass. We got this other pub for rehearsals, Bricklayers' Arms in Berwick Street. We had a rehearsal up there and it was great. It was probably terrible. But it swung and we had a good time. That was virtually home for the rest of the summer.

Brian was living in Howard Square in a basement: very decrepit place with mushrooms and fungus growing out of the walls, with Pat and his kid. One night Mick, who'd been playing a gig with Korner, went round to see Brian, if I remember rightly, and Brian wasn't there but his old lady was. Mick was very drunk, and he screwed her.... This caused a whole trauma. At first Brian was terribly offended—the chick split—but it made Mick and Brian very close. It put them through a whole emotional scene that knitted things together. That's how we began.

'Stu' (Ian Stewart, Stones' road manager who plays piano occasionally): Although we were rehearsing, we still didn't have a name. In those days, it was the thing to open your own club. Korner had started a band at the Marquee Club and he packed the place every Thursday night. Thursday night was also the BBC live jazz broadcast and when they asked Alexis to do it—meaning he had to go to the BBC studio—he asked us if we wanted to fill in for one night. We said Yeah, but we had to think of a name and so, in desperation, we became the Rolling Stones. The Marquee was our first job.

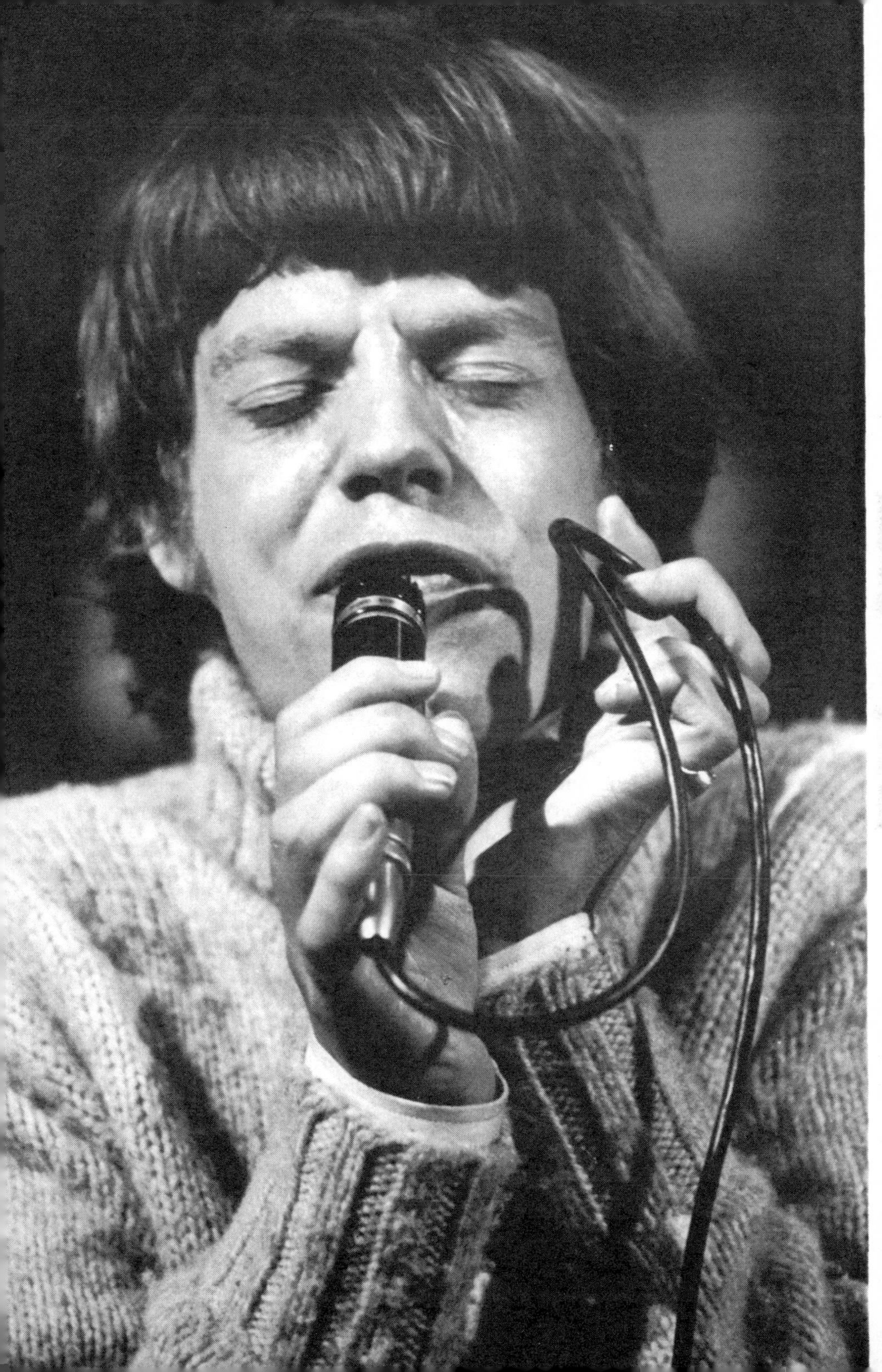

At the start, nobody in England played the music we played. All the others were jazz musicians trying to play the blues, but they had never really heard it. And once having seen the Stones at the Marquee, the people running the scene were one hundred per cent against us, and it was one bloody fight to get anywhere. We tried to open in Ealing on a Tuesday night and for two weeks we got not a soul—not one person would come to Ealing to see the Rolling Stones. We tried Tuesday night at the Flamingo, and it was the same thing. I'll never forget the first time we went down to the Flamingo for an audition on a Sunday afternoon. The Flamingo was a pretty smart place—it was *the* modern jazz club in town—and everybody was going there in their zoot suits. I remember I said to Keith: 'You're not going down to the Flamingo looking like that are you?' He said, 'What ho, Stu, I've only got one pair of fuckin' jeans.'

Keith Richards: Winter of '62 was the tough one. It's down to sello-taping the rips in your trousers. We're completely broke, and this guy arrives, this strange little guy whom Brian used to go to school with. He was about five feet three, very fat, wore thick spectacles. He belonged to the Territorial Army. They all live in tents, get soaking wet, catch colds, learn how to shoot a rifle and at the end they get eighty quid cash. This cat arrives in London fresh from the hills, from his tent. And he wants to have a good time with Brian, and Brian took him for every penny: the guy would do anything for Brian. Brian would say, 'Give me your overcoat.' Freezing cold, it's the worst winter, and he gave Brian this army overcoat. 'Give Keith the sweater.' So I put the sweater on. 'Now, you walk twenty yards behind us.' And off we'd walk to the local hamburger place. 'Ah, stay there. No, you can't come in. Give us two quid.' This cat would stand outside the hamburger joint, freezing cold, giving Brian the money to pay for our hamburgers.

Brian gets him to buy him a new guitar, a new Harmony electric. He pays for everything. In two weeks we've spent all the money so we say, 'See ya, man,' and put him on a train and send him home. He's incredibly hurt, and although he regrets very much being fleeced, he stills comes up to London again later with even more bread, and we fleece him again. Brian and I were really evil to this guy. It ended up with us stripping and trying to electrocute him.

That was the night he finally disappeared. It was snowing outside. We came back to the pad and he was in Brian's bed. Brian for some reason got very annoyed. We had all these cables lying around and Brian pulled out this wire: 'This end is plugged in, baby, and I'm coming after you.' Brian ran after him with this long piece of wire cable that's attached to an amplifier, electric sparks, chasing around the room, and the bloke ran screaming down the stairs out into the street with nothing on, shouting, 'Don't go up there, they're trying to electrocute me.' Somebody brought him in an hour later. He was blue.

The next day the cat split. Brian had a new guitar, and his amp fixed, a whole new set of harmonicas. This was down at Edith Grove in this pad Mick found. Brian's working, just about making enough to keep us from being chucked out of this place, and it's winter, the worst winter ever. Brian and me sitting around this gas fire, wondering where to get the next shilling to put in it to keep the fire going. Collecting beer bottles and selling them back to the pubs, getting three shillings, and going to pads where we knew there'd been parties on, walking in saying 'Hello, how nice, we'll help you clean up,' and we'd steal the bottles and whatever food we could find lying around the kitchen and run for it. It was getting sick, down to picking people's pockets. Around this time, Phelge moves in. Phelge was as horrifyingly disgusting as Brian and myself. You would get home, and he would be standing at the top of the stairs, completely nude except for his underpants, which would be *filthy,* on top of his head, and he'd be spitting at you. You couldn't get mad, you just collapsed laughing. Covered in spit, you'd collapse laughing.

Meanwhile this pad is getting so screwed up. For six months we used the kitchen to play in, and slowly the place got filthy and started to smell, so we bolted the doors and locked them all up, and the kitchen was condemned. I was making tapes at that time—I had a recorder and reels and reels of tape in the bedroom, which was located next to the bog. I used to keep the microphone in the cistern of the bog, and the tape recorder at the foot of the bed. I had reels and reels of tapes of people going to the bog. Chains pulling.

But we're now trying to get this band off the ground and we haven't got any real hope. The Beatles' first record comes out and we're really depressed. It's the beginning of Beatlemania. Suddenly everybody's looking round for groups, and we see more and more being signed. Alexis Korner gets a recording contract, splits from the Marquee Club, and who gets his spot? the Rolling Stones. For just about enough bread to keep alive. We really needed a bass player then. I'm not sure what happened to Dick Taylor. I think we kicked him out, very ruthless in those days. Nobody could hear him because he had terrible equipment and he seemed to have no way of getting anything better. Everybody else had hustled reasonable size amplifiers. The drummer we've got says, 'I know a bass player who's got his own amplifier, huge speaker, plus a *spare* Vox 130 amp'—which at the time was the biggest amp available, the best. And he's got one of those to spare—fantastic. So on to the scene comes Bill Wyman and we can't believe him. He's a real London Ernie, Brylcreme hair and eleven-inch cuffs on his trousers and huge blue suede shoes with rubber soles.

Bill Wyman: They didn't like me, they liked my amplifier. The two they had were broken and torn up inside—sounded great, really, but we didn't know that then. But I didn't like their music very much. I had been playing hard rock—Buddy Holly, Jerry Lee Lewis—and the slow blues things seemed very boring to me.

Keith Richards: We're starting to get a steady scene in London at last, and at one of these gigs we decided to get rid of our drummer and steal Charlie Watts from this other band he was working with, because we were now in a position to offer Charlie twenty quid a week. Then we got that Richmond gig that built up to an enormous scene. In London that was *the* place to be every Saturday night, at the Richmond Station Hotel, on the river, a fairly well-to-do area, but kids from all over London would come down there.

Stu: It was at the Richmond Station Hotel that you really started seeing excitement. The crowds finally started to get up off their backsides and move, and within two months they were swinging off the rafters. The Station Hotel lasted only about ten weeks, because they

wanted to pull the place down, so they moved us to Richmond Athletic Club, which had a very low ceiling, with girders, so of course everyone starts leaping about among them; they're going barmy. I'd love to see all that again.

We were still rehearsing three times a week. Nobody had any money. But there was a thrill about being involved with it all. The Beatles were filling the Albert Hall with screaming kids, there were still Gerry and the Pacemakers and Billy Jay Kramer and that lot, but there was no guts to it. You were aware at the time that you were really starting something.

Charlie Watts: At Richmond we became sort of a cult, in a way. There was so many people that there was no room for Mick to dance onstage and he just used to wiggle his arse, which sort of made.... I don't know, but it sort of created—it was a lovely.... That was really the best time, although predictable, knowing that every time you did a certain set at a certain time everything would explode. And sure enough it always did, and it always ended up in an absolute... gyrating riot.

Glyn Johns, chief engineer at the recording studios of the Independent Broadcasting Corporation, January 1963: I can remember taking the Stones to IBC for the first session and being frightened of introducing them to George Clouston, the guy who owned the studio. I see photographs of them then and they look so tame and harmless, and I can't associate it with the effect they had on people. It was just their appearance, their clothes, their hair, their whole attitude was immediately obvious to you as soon as you saw them playing. It was just a complete *pppprt* **to society and everybody and anything.**

Alexis Korner: At the start it was Brian who was the monster head. Brian was incredibly aggressive in performance. His hair was pretty long, and he had what was almost a permanent pout, crossed with a leer, and he used to look incredibly randy most of the time. He used to jump forward with the tambourine and smash it in your face and sneer at you at the same time. The aggression had a tremendous impact. He was also a very sensitive player, Brian. But I remember

> **him most for his 'I'm gonna put the boot in' attitude. Brian achieved what he wanted by his extreme aggression, and it was extreme—it was incitement: when Brian was onstage he was inciting every male in the room to hit him. Really and truly that was the feeling one got. At the start Brian was the image of aggression in the Stones much more than Mick. Onstage Brian made blokes want to thump him. He would deliberately play at someone's chick, and when the bloke got stroppy, he'd slap a tambourine in his face.**

Stu: Brian could have been killed many times.

6 December 1969

They lock the gate behind us. We are inside, but where are we? A plateau of dusty red clay. The road leads downward again, away from the Altamont Speedway clubhouse. A station wagon meets us in the road and Sam Cutler gets out, phosphorescent from speed and cocaine, and we all get in the wagon and drive to another basin where there are more cars and trailers, scaffolding going up, and a big orange bonfire. The wind whips the fire high, great blasts toward our faces, the people quietly saying hello. Someone hands up a jug of California red wine and Mick drinks, then Keith, holding the jug in both hands, leaning back, and then I drink, thinking of all the people coming to rest around glowing coals on these hills, and if there are this many here now, how many will be here tomorrow afternoon? The Maysles brothers have followed us in another car and once more announce their presence with the bright quartz lights, circling the outside of the crowd so that the light is always shining directly into someone's face.

'Turn off the lights,' Mick says. 'No lights.' They again ignore him, and Mick turns to Ronnie Schneider. 'Tell them no lights,' he says.

'Mick says no lights,' Ronnie shouts. Al Maysles, peering through the camera lens, says 'Sync it,' to his brother David, who hits the microphone with his notebook, and for the moment their film stops. Al, the camera man, the older brother, leaves the business deals, the con artistry, to David, thirty-seven, and now Al is staring at David over his Ben Franklin half-glasses, saying eloquently without words, 'What the hell? Here we are on some godforsaken hillside with these strange people, this Jagger you've got a crush on, spending our own money to make a film about them, trusting them to look after our interests, these people who just skipped the hotel bill in Miami, and now your crooked pansy friend Jagger is telling us to stop? This is crazy!' Al says all this in a quick perplexed palms-up peep over his glasses, camera balanced perfectly on his custom-made shoulder.

A girl brings round a joint, the tiny end of a joint, too small to smoke, and she holds it between her fingertips, tells Mick to open his mouth and blows the smoke into Mick's open thick pursed lips, everyone watching the ritual tableau. Then she does the same for Keith, as Mick walks away, toward the stage rising on the slope.

Away from the fire, it is windy and dark. The production manager is on the stage, the scaffolding for the PA system is growing, and the manager says that it will be finished by dawn, which, we see by his watch, is not far off. We walk behind the stage to the trailer that is to be the Stones' dressing room and shelter in the stormy blast of the day to come, and there we find some of the finer comforts of home, from grass and cocaine to a girl who offers us chocolate chip cookies and is heating coffee in an electric skillet.

Sam Cutler looks at his watch: 'Ten minutes to five,' he says, rolling his eyes like a madman.

Grateful Dead factotum Rock Scully is here, grimy, saying, 'Well, we've got a lot of work to do.'

'A cold shower and a few laps around the quad, lads,' Keith says.

Mick is talking to a radio interviewer: 'I think the concert's just an excuse. It's for everyone to come and have a good time, to get together and talk to each other and sleep with each other and ball each other and get really stoned and have a nice night out and a good day. It's not like just coming to hear the Grateful Airplane and the Rolling Dead—'

Los Angeles

Al Steckler, the Stones' promotion manager had come out from New York for the first big show, and I rode to the LA Forum with him and Michael Lydon, the rock reviewer from *The New York Times.* We parked and walked down a slanted ramp to the backstage area, passing a broadly smiling helmeted policeman.

The Forum had been used that afternoon for an ice hockey game, and the first show had been delayed while they covered up the ice. It was really just a basketball gym, and the mood was unsettling—ice underfoot, cops everywhere, You can't stand here, You can't do this, You can't do that. I retreated backstage, where manager Allen Klein and Al Steckler were having an argument with a Forum staff man, who said, 'I'm more worried about crowd control than anything else.'

'I'm not,' Klein snapped. Behind them four different varieties of uniformed police were standing around eight large trunks labelled 'Riot Helmets', 'Gas Bombs', and 'Masks'. It was disturbing, and I walked out front, where B.B. King was having trouble starting his set because his voice microphone wasn't working. A young black man who worked for B.B. came out from backstage, and said, 'Come on back here for a minute.' We strolled past the cops and war-gear to B.B.'s dressing room—nobody there—and into the bathroom—also vacant—where he carefully unfolded a piece of tinfoil. 'Hey, man,' he said, 'this *here* shit is *her*oin, you don't do this shit, do you?'

Four light brown sniffs on a shiny knifeblade, and we waltzed out of the bathroom. Better insulated against the cops, I listened to the rap B.B. had developed for the flower crowd: 'Laze and gennlemen, if we just had more love, we wouldn't have no—wars.' (Applause.) 'Than kyou—And if we had more love, we wouldn't have no—jails.' (Clap, clap, clap.) 'Than kyou'—and so on.

B.B. stopped talking, was quiet for a moment, played eight searing bars of blues, and sang, '*When I read your letter this morning, that was in your place in bed.*' The crowd, white city people, hooted and hollered, and for the moment even the cops seemed to stop harassing bystanders.

B.B.'s set was followed by the Ike and Tina Turner Revue, and while they played I went backstage, where I noticed the heavies talking to a fat man in one of the orange togas worn by the Forum ushers. Klein was telling him that there must be no uniforms near the stage while the Stones were playing. The fat man nodded in disbelief and asked, 'What happens when twenty thousand kids rush the stage?'

'We'll cross that bridge when we come to it,' Klein said.

The man in the toga said, 'Oh, I see. Great.'

When Tina Turner approached the end of her set, the police began clearing the aisles and then gathered a number of us in a gaggle behind the stage, and in Shirley Watts's opinion there was far too much fuss over what might have been worthwhile—fun, even—if kept simpler. But it was too late for that; we were in a mammoth arena with many different kinds of cops—rental cops, regular Inglenook suburban LA police, and Forum guards in orange togas.

Out front the lights were down again and the crowd was on its feet, stamping, the high metal arches ringing. In the backstage doorway Jagger was standing, dressed in black trousers with silver buttons down the legs, black scoopneck jersey, wide metal-studded black belt, long red flowing scarf, on his head an Uncle Sam hat, his eyes wide and dark, looking like a bull-fighter standing in the sun just inside the door of the arena, toreros and *banderilleros* beside and behind him. And then, the Rolling Stones.

I was born in a crossfire hurricane
And I howled at my ma in the driving rain
But it's all right now.

At the end of the first song, 'Jumpin' Jack Flash', the crowd settled back. There were more cops than ever hovering around as Jagger asked, 'Has it really been three years?'

'Nooo,' the crowd yelled, as the band started 'Carol', Mick dancing, leaping high in the air, prancing, the Black Prince, swirling flowing scarf, blue-beaded Indian moccasins quiet on the soft carpet. As the Stones began 'Sympathy for the Devil', I noticed Allen Klein standing beside the stage, lighting a briar pipe.

When the song ended, Stu, the road manager, came across the stage carrying two high stools, wearing a pale yellow swallowtail dress suit. He set the stools around one microphone, Jagger sat on one, Keith on the other, and the two of them did the Rev. Robert Wilkin's 'Prodigal Son' and Fred McDowell's 'You Got to Move',

Keith bent over his National steel-bodied guitar, stiff chords rising from it, rhinestones on his haggard shoulders sparkling in the blue lights. Charlie joined them for Robert Johnson's 'Love in Vain'.

The crowd, quiet during the slow songs, screamed for 'Midnight Rambler'. They were standing for the next song, 'Under My Thumb', and the next, 'I'm Free'—the song, written by Jagger as a declaration of sexual independence that now seemed to be about many kinds of freedom—but it didn't ring quite true. During the next two songs, the crowd surged forward, and I was pressed up against the right aisle wall with Shirley Watts, the cops and Ron Schneider—another member of the entourage of endless business managers and promoters.

'I wish I could see you,' Mick said. 'You're probably even more beautiful than I am. Could someone turn on the lights?' Mick peered out, hand over eyes, Indian fashion. The lights came up, the crowd, bright with colour, pressed forward even more, and I was about to be seriously trapped. I shoved my notebook into the front of my breeches and swung up on to the stage, Stu's piano ringing in my ears, Jagger leaping straight up, genitals visible, almost palpable. As the song ended, the lights went down for a few seconds and back up again, the crowd bobbing, a swaying mass of heads against the stage. Looking from right to left, I saw that the audience had been driven to a state of frenzy, and that Klein, beside the stage, was grabbing people in the crowd by their shoulders, throwing them down the aisle that led backstage, screaming 'Out! Out!'

'Street Fightin' Man' was the last song. '*I'll kill the king and rail at all his servants,*' Mick sang, he and Keith facing Charlie Watts, giving him the boogaloo beat, Charlie pounding it out, the whole place vibrating, Mick running around the stage throwing rose petals from a basket, while in the aisle below me, Klein now faced the crowd with a long pole, a fat little man, slamming it into people who were trying to dance.

The second show was an hour and a half late. Backstage the atmosphere was terrible. I leaned backstage against an equipment wagon, hundreds of people milling about, all of them wearing badges and stick-on credentials that hardly any of them were entitled to wear. The place was so crowded with phonies that the people who belonged there were herded into a bunch, and over my shoulder I heard that the badges would no longer signify: we would have a sign, and the sign was the Boy Scout three-finger salute. I started writing notes, hoping that I'd be left alone. A fat guard in an orange toga spied me writing, asked, 'Is he all right?' and was answered by the entire group: 'No!' I flashed the Boy Scout salute over my head and kept writing.

Ike and Tina Turner came offstage, the audience roaring. Shirley Watts, having been pushed by a cop, was standing against the back wall, furious. Ron Schneider was talking about busted heads and cracked ribs given to fans during the first show by cops—and by Klein, I wondered?

As five a.m. approached the lights went down. 'Here we go,' Mick said. As the Stones started to play a completely new crowd swelled forward. All our tiredness seemed to lift, as if we were dreaming and not subject to ordinary physical limits. I saw no uniformed police, nor Klein, but many guards, and Schneider pushing people away. The music ripped through the smoky air, and Mick said, 'Wake up a little bit, you been waiting so long, we might as well stay on a long time.'

People were climbing on to the stage and being carried off. Some people in the crowd had crossed eyes from lack of sleep, others were staring, bright-eyed. We were going through the same experience once again, and at the back of my mind was an anxious vision of being trapped, saying, 'I know the sign!' to uncomprehending guards who would smash me as I gave the Boy Scout salute.

The lights came up for the end, a giant sign in the audience, JESUS LOVE AND PEACE. Darkness again, and then the spotlights washed over the stage and over the crowd, which broke forward as if released by it. It pressed up against the stage, past the line of guards which was there to keep everyone back. Sam Cutler pushed Ron Schneider aside to save a boy who was being dragged backstage by guards.

Mick, silhouetted above squirming, screaming bodies, was dancing at the edge of the stage, pouring pink champagne into a glass, raising it high, a toast, a toast, hands waving like undersea flowers before him. A boy being manhandled by guards beside the stage closed his eyes and put his hands together in a gesture of prayer. The whole building was jumping; I thought it might collapse. '*We'll kill the king,*' Mick sang again, and when the show ended Sam Cutler told me he had been backstage rescuing kids from cops who had been beating them with clubs.

1963

By the summer of 1963, the Stones were playing nearly every day, sometimes twice a day, and when they weren't playing or recording, they were rehearsing. On 19 July they were booked to play a debutante's ball, but Brian was sick, the Stones all got drunk, and another band played. The next night the Stones, with Brian, played their first ballroom date, at the Corn Exchange in Wisbech. 'Come On', their first single release, was at number thirty in its struggle up the top fifty. Nevertheless, the Stones were averaging less than five pounds per man for each job. On 10 August they played two shows near Birmingham, and the next day, after playing the Studio 51 Club in the afternoon, the Stones played at the third National Jazz Festival in Richmond.

On 17 August the Stones played in Northwich, near Liverpool, on a bill with Lee Curtis, who according to Keith 'pulled an incredible scene to steal the show, where he'd do Conway Twitty's "Only Make Believe", and he'd faint onstage. People came and carried him off, and he'd fight them off and come back, singing "Only Make Believe". Then they'd carry him off again.' That week the Rolling Stones played six dates, not counting rehearsals and photo sessions, and each man got paid twenty-five pounds. The pace was killing, but they all managed to maintain it except Brian. On 27 August the Stones were booked to play at Windsor in a room over the Star and Garter pub. Brian, sick again, was not there, and for the first time the band that had been 'Brian's idea in the first place' played without him.

Brian was still sick the next night with an asthma attack—'He just used to collapse,' Keith said—and the Stones played their regular Wednesday night at the Eel Pie Island club with Stu on piano. At seven the following morning Brian left in the van with the others, to do a television show in Manchester. That night Bill Wyman wrote in his diary about being 'mobbed' by fans at the television studio and afterwards at a night club. 'Mobbed,' Bill said, meant that you lost some hair or part of your clothing.

The Stones played a club in Manchester on Friday and a ballroom in Prestatyn on Saturday. On Sunday, they came back to London to play first at the Studio 51 Club and then at the Crawdaddy, and by

Wednesday night Brian was sick again, 'decomposing before our eyes,' Keith said. Brian left the Eel Pie Island club in the interval, and the band again finished the show without him.

About this time, September, the Stones left their flat on Edith Grove, Mick and Keith going to live with their new manager Andrew Oldham, Brian moving into a house in Windsor with Linda Lawrence, a girl he'd met at the Ricky Tick Club, and her parents. They all lived together for years, Brian and Linda in one bedroom, Linda's parents in another.

A part of their lives was ending. One afternoon in late September, after paying the band twenty pounds each for the past week, Brian went shopping with Bill Wyman and bought fifteen blue shirts for the Stones to wear on their first national tour, coming up in less than two weeks, with the Everly Brothers and Bo Diddley.

The first week of January 1964 the Stones opened a tour of England, billed second to a trio of black American girl singers called the Ronettes, who quickly saw that to follow the Rolling Stones onstage was professional suicide. After that the Stones always played last and got top billing.

Things were going well for the Stones, except Brian, for whom things were going to hell. Linda Lawrence, to Brian's alarm, was pregnant with his third child. At this rate he could father fifty bastards: look at him, the teen idol, strolling the sidewalks of Windsor arm in arm with his pregnant girl friend, his bloody pet goat, Billy G., following like a puppy dog.

Brian was still missing performances, excusing his absences because, for example, he and his chauffeur were 'lost in a fog'. The day after that one, the Stones played Shrewsbury, and Brian complained about a sore throat. Stu turned toward a chemist's in a one-way street, and Brian jumped out of the car. Just as Stu noticed they were headed the wrong way, the traffic started coming toward them, and they had been recognized: fans were swarming. 'Leave him,' Keith said. Brian had lost hair and clothing by the time he managed to reach the Granada Theatre.

Other fans were now breaking the Stones' dressing room windows, stripping the van of its lights, mirrors, even the rubber window mounts; popularity had become hysteria. Stu said, 'It wasn't pleasant to see what the music did to people.'

But while the Stones were playing concerts almost every night and appearing on at least one national television programme every week, the three records they had released were not entirely successful. The week the tour with the Ronettes ended, the Stones' first extended-play record was number two in the popular EP charts, and 'I Wanna Be Your Man' was the number nine single. It would go no higher, but it was still a hit; a top ten record. Now they had to do it again.

Meanwhile the Beatles left England for their first performances in the United States, on the Ed Sullivan television programme and two concerts at Carnegie Hall. Fifty thousand people requested the Sullivan show's seven hundred and twenty-eight seats, and the Carnegie Hall shows sold out in a matter of hours.

The Beatles' appearance on the Sullivan show was reported to have been seen by seventy-three million people, and to have reformed the United States' teenagers for as long as it lasted: across the country not one major crime was committed by a teenager.

The Rolling Stones, on tour with some peculiar English acts, did not seem to be doing much to deter crime. Rather the opposite. 'Some of those crowds were too much,' Stu said. 'They saw that the Stones always dropped their bleedin' guitars on the last number and ran for it. So then the crowd from the first show started hanging about till the second show had finished, and they waited for us. It got to be quite a problem. Nobody liked the Stones. They were hated, and they never got any good publicity.'

On 21 February, the Stones' EP record was number one in the EP charts. 'Not Fade Away' was released and went into the top ten. They were still touring, causing riots each night. That same day, a reporter from *Melody Maker* interviewed the Stones, and his story had probably the most-quoted headline of their early career: 'Would You Let Your Daughter Go With a Rolling Stone?' It fitted the image of the Stones held by many people—leering Rolling Stone locked in savage embrace with fair young girl. True or not (and it was both), the image was too strong to be forgotten.

During this time, besides playing to berserk crowds twice and sometimes four times daily, the Stones recorded their first long-playing album, were given scripts for their first film, signed to tour the United States, and Mick and Keith became more skilled as song-writers—'though we didn't like anything we wrote,' Keith said, 'and we couldn't seem to get anybody else in the band to play it.' But Gene Pitney had a hit in England with one of their songs, 'That Girl Belongs to Yesterday', and Andrew Oldham produced a hit with another Jagger/Richards song, 'As Tears Go By', recorded by Marianne Faithfull, a girl they had recently met at a party.

The Rolling Stones, their artily untitled (Oldham's idea) first album, was released and went directly to the top of the popular music album charts, a position held by the Beatles for almost all the previous year. 'Not Fade Away', their first release in the United States, entered the *Cashbox* magazine Hot 100. It was number ninety-eight, but it was there.

And every day, the crowds kept coming. In some towns the Stones would arrive, find the hall surrounded and couldn't get inside to play. At other places, where there were low stages, the Stones would start, the little girls would run right over the bouncers in front of the stage, and the Stones would drop their guitars and run. In the places where tickets were counterfeited, or promoters sold more tickets than they had seats, things were even worse.

'The first time Chuck Berry came to England,' Stu said, 'we were supposed to be playing two shows elsewhere, at the Savoy Room in Catford. The first one was at about nine o'clock, and the next one half-past ten. Berry was at Finsbury Park, and we'd never seen Berry live. Catford is south London, Finsbury Park is north. So we say, "Well, what's it gonna be?" Of course we went to see Chuck Berry. He was a little bit late though, and it must have been well after nine o'clock before he finished.' The Stones then drove down to Catford.

'You couldn't see the bloody ballroom for ambulances,' Stu said. 'They were carrying girls out one after another. The promoter had let far more people into the hall than it would hold. And they were passing out right, left and centre. There was a vast great wide stairway on one side of the building, and when we finally left, it was covered in bodies. They carried hundreds out that night. It was awful. All fuckin' Chuck Berry's fault.'

The next night the Stones played in Bristol, and Brian, driving down alone from London, missed the first show. Retribution was immediate. Three days later the Stones played St George's Hall in Bradford, across the street from the Victoria Hotel, where they stayed. Between shows, Stu said, 'They didn't want to sit around their dressing room until the

second half. No cops about. They said, Shall we chance running across the road to the hotel? They all made it except Brian, who chickened out before he got to the hotel entrance because there were people running after him. He eventually turned round and ran the other way. All these people chased Brian through the streets in Bradford, tearing clothes off him. The police finally brought him back without a jacket, without a shirt, and he'd lost a shoe and handfuls of hair.'

Two days before, the Stones had taken smallpox vaccinations for their first trip to the United States.

The Tour: Oakland

MANIFESTO

Greetings and welcome Rolling Stones, our comrades in the desperate battle against the maniacs who hold power. The revolutionary youth of the world hears your music and is inspired to even more deadly acts. We fight in guerrilla bands against the invading imperialists in Asia and South America, we riot at rock 'n' roll concerts everywhere. We burned and pillaged in Los Angeles and the cops know our snipers will return.

They call us dropouts, delinquents, draftdodgers, punks and hopheads, and heap tons of shit on our heads. In Viet Nam they try to make us war on our own comrades but the bastards hear us playing you on our little transistor radios and know that they will not escape the blood and fire of the anarchist revolution.

We will play your music in rock 'n' roll marching bands as we tear down the jails and free the prisoners, as we tear down the State schools and free the students, as we tear down the military bases and arm the poor, as we tattoo BURN BABY BURN! on the bellies of the wardens and generals and create a new society from the ashes of our fires.

Comrades, you will one day return to this country when it is free from the tyranny of the State and you will play

HOT TOWN —
PIGS IN THE STREETS . . .
BUT THE STREETS
BELONG TO THE PEOPLE !
DIG IT ?

> your splendid music in factories run by the workers, in the domes of emptied city halls, on the rubble of police stations, under the hanging corpses of priests, under a million red flags waving over a million anarchist communities. ROLLING STONES, THE YOUTH OF CALIFORNIA HEARS YOUR MESSAGE! LONG LIVE THE REVOLUTION!!!
>
> Broadsheet distributed at
> the Rolling Stones'
> concerts in Oakland

It's Sunday. I showered, dressed, and rushed to catch a flight to Oakland with Jo Bergman, Michael Lydon, photographer Ethan Russell and a number of others. In rented cars, we drove to the Edgewater Inn, down the freeway from the airport, past the Oakland Coliseum, where the Stones would play and where, hours before the show, kids were already crowding outside.

In the motel restaurant—done in red and black, and flocked velvet—we found a fat young man who said his name was Jon Jaymes. He had been at the Forum last night. I didn't know who he was or whom he worked for. He was speaking into a white telephone, preparing the Oakland airport for the arrival of the Rolling Stones. 'I've notified the police,' he said. 'People must stay in their seats and let the Stones off'—his voice rising—'or there'll be *chaos* at the *airport.*'

Within minutes, I found myself riding back to the airport, this time with Jaymes himself, who drove insanely as he explained that he was Chairman of the President's Committee for Lowering the Voting Age to Eighteen. Before that he had been chairman of two other presidential committees. Before that an FBI narcotics agent, and he now had 'an obligation—to a company called Chrysler—to see that this tour is kept clean. This means that, through political influence if necessary, if everybody gets busted I can get everybody off.'

Jaymes said that Chrysler wanted nothing from the Stones in the way of endorsements or promotional photographs; they just wanted the Stones to use Chrysler equipment so that, at the end of the tour, Chrysler could say that they had transported the Stones and tons of

equipment around the United States. If all went well and there were no scandals, there'd be a happy tie-in with the youth market. We were careering through red lights, Jaymes blowing the horn, stepping on the accelerator and the brake at the same time, as he said of Jagger (who'd changed plans abruptly, deciding to take a later flight to Oakland than the one he'd scheduled), 'With all due respect, and I believe he's due it, I think Jagger has the idea that he's Mick Jagger, Rolling Stone, and he can do anything he wants, and he's surrounded with people who tell him he can when he can't. And someplace on the tour, that's gonna blow up on him.'

We lurched to a stop at the kerb and ran through the airport—a cop with us, holding the gun under his coat in its shoulder holster—to gate number one, where the Stones should have been but were not. Jaymes was saying, 'There should be press here, where are they?' A birdlike little old lady was looking at him as if he were something strange and wonderful. Someone ran up and said, 'Gate three', holding up four fingers.

From a window I saw the plane landing. Almost at once the Stones were walking down the ramp, not too fast, flutter flutter all around, people stopping to watch—the pace picking up till we were past the front lobby and outside, where there were four more cars, rented by Jaymes in the two or three minutes we'd been in the airport. The door of one car was open, and I slid into the driver's seat. Keith was right behind me, followed by Mick Taylor, Jagger, Wyman, and Watts. Away we zoomed. I had not been expecting the hottest act in show business suddenly to pile in the car with me, so although you could nearly see the motel from the airport, I, suddenly excited, went off the wrong way, followed by a line of cars.

It was like being gypsies, I thought, wheeling through the darkness, looking for the motel. I turned down a dark side road, pulled right, hit the brakes and threw the front end left, placing us directly athwart the highway. Cars were coming from both directions. Jagger was groaning, 'What you up to?' But we made it, turned around, went back to the main road, and in a minute we were at the motel.

We went in, some of us had drinks, and then in the Stones' suite there was a press conference—more long-haired kids with cameras and tape recorders after which we drove to the Coliseum. Inside the

Stones' dressing room, above the table covered with cheeses, meats, beers, wines, champagne, was a large poster of the show's promoter, Bill Graham, smiling broadly, holding his middle finger aloft to the camera.

Ike and Tina had already played, and the crowd were stomping for the Stones. Sam Cutler on the microphone was saying, 'We're sorry we're late, there were no cars to meet us at the airport, we'll be here in two minutes literally.'

I wandered the aisles looking at the kids, hairy and wild but at the same time healthy and fresh, smelling of aromatic herbs and incense, stomping in time-honoured fashion—a Saturday afternoon matinee when the film projector breaks before the cavalry arrives. Then—it had been no more than five minutes—the cavalry did arrive, to whistles and yells of pleasure. Just like Saturday afternoon.

Keith hit the opening chords of 'Jumpin' Jack Flash', Mick Taylor chiming in, Charlie bashing, Wyman's small, light bass creating a mountainous sound with great reverberating overtones. Jagger sashayed around the stage, waving hello with his thin elegant arms.

The joint was jumping, but in the middle of the second song, Keith's amplifiers died, and the band ground to a halt. 'It seems electricity has failed us,' Jagger said, 'so we're gonna do some acoustic numbers.' Keith was trying to coax an amplifier to work, Stu was dragging two stools on stage. Mick sat down, Keith picked up his National, and they did 'Prodigal Son'.

But when the acoustic songs ended, the equipment men were still working on the amplifiers.

'When we all get ready,' Jagger said. Then Keith hit the first chord for 'Carol', and the amplifiers blew again. In anger and frustration, Keith broke his guitar. The band kept playing, Keith picked up another guitar, the music staggered on. At the end of Chuck Berry's 'Little Queenie', with the house lights up, the Stones started 'Satisfaction'. The kids rushed forward, carrying the guards with them, surrounding the cameramen whom Bill Graham had carefully arranged, and supplied, in front of the stage. Graham rushed forward to protect the cameras as the cameramen climbed onstage, handing their equipment out of a sea of rocking flesh. Sam Cutler, watching Graham, thought he was too rough with the kids, tried to stop him, and Graham tried to throw Sam offstage. The Stones made it through 'Honky Tonk Women' and 'Street Fightin' Man' and rushed to the dressing room, Keith kicking the table as he came in. 'That *cunt,*' he said.

One thing was on everyone's mind: Bill Graham. Keith was furious. Rock Scully, manager of the Grateful Dead, who had rushed equipment to the Stones to replace the blown Ampegs, was running Graham down for being a capitalist pig. The poster of Graham above the banquet table was spattered with food.

In the press room next door, Jon Jaymes was again making arrangements: trying to line up some airplanes so we could get back to Los Angeles because we were going to be very late should the Stones get to do a second show here at all. I was drinking bourbon and offered Jaymes a drink. In the middle of a speech about how Graham's cameras cost 2,500 dollars apiece and he had every right to protect them, he stopped to say: 'Never get me drunk.'

When I returned to the Stones' dressing room, Jagger was gone. Bill, Charlie, and Keith were still talking with Rock Scully.

Scully, wearing Levis and a plaid cowboy shirt, bearded, bright eyes, was just an open-faced charming western guy. Or at least he seemed to be. He was talking about the proper way to give a free concert, how it might be done, with whose help. The Grateful Dead had done this sort of thing many times, and Scully might actually have known how to give a free concert in, say, Golden Gate Park. A Be-In, a mass gathering, had taken place in the Park with no unpleasantness. The Hell's Angels had acted as security, and it was natural using the Angels to help you do your thing, or so it seemed to Rock Scully. He said that 'the Angels are really some righteous dudes. They carry themselves with honour and dignity.' He was so blue-eyed and open about it, it seemed really convincing. Nobody was even particularly paying attention, but I noticed the way he used the words *honour* and *dignity*.

B. B. King had missed the first show and was late for the second, scrambling the show's order. It was nearly 2.30 a.m. when the Stones took over the stage.

The Stones just wanted people to dance. But after the fast early numbers and the acoustic blues interlude, when the band was playing

'Little Queenie', as Mick was saying, 'Come on, San Francisco, let's get up and *dance,* let's shake our *asses,*' Bill Graham was crouching before the stage, pointing to kids who were dancing, shouting, 'Down! Down!' Finally, as the crowd surged to the stage, he took his cameras and left. There was then no feeling of violence, only the desire to get close and boogie. 'Street Fighting Man' ended at 3.45 a.m. The Oakland Coliseum was ringing with a sound I had heard the last two nights. It was not the band, not the crowd; it was a third sound. I didn't know what it was, but I liked it.

It's Monday, and tonight it's San Diego, a big military town where they burned the dope seized at the Mexican border.

The Stones met at the Golden West charter flight service at Burbank airport. Jagger's with a girl who looked just like Jean Harlow. We arranged ourselves, about a dozen of us, among the plane's twenty seats. I was sitting behind Mick and Harlow, who had taken her hairbrush from her purse and was brushing Mick's hair, to his obvious displeasure.

It took only about half an hour to reach San Diego. The door of the plane opened and there on the tarmac were four black limousines. We all piled in and rode to the San Diego International Sports Arena, where a big sign read ROLLING STONE TONIGHT. The Arena was smaller than the last two halls, capacity about ten thousand, and it was not filled, though there would be only one show. B.B. King was playing when we arrived. The Arena seemed cold, the audience distant. The place smelled like an old pea coat.

When the Stones came on, I went out front, found a seat, and sat down.

It was a dreary night in San Diego, but it wouldn't last long, Jagger had already sung 'Under My Thumb' and was starting 'I'm Free'. In this atmosphere it seemed less true than ever, a man saying he wouldn't give you any bullshit telling people they were free. But they were kids mostly and loved it and may even have believed it. Mick sang 'Live With Me', and at the line, 'Don't you think there's a place for you—in between the sheets?' there was a rush forward, the children all dancing. 'Little Queenie' was next, then 'Satisfaction'. A girl who had fainted down front was being lifted on to the stage—but she was awake, a Mexican girl, looking around wildly, rolling her head. I realized that she was blind. She was lifted on to the stage and led away.

As 'Street Fightin' Man' started, Mick said, perhaps sensing the militarism of the town, 'Sometime we may have to get up against the wall.' Mick was making a V-sign with each hand as Keith ripped the opening chords: '*Everywhere I hear the sound of marchin', chargin' feet, boys.*' I had left my seat and was by the stage, a helmeted cop beside me putting his fingers over his ears, grimacing. In the roar, the keening, as the song ended, Mick danced along the rim of the stage just out of reach of the clutching hands, skipping along like Little Bo Peep, throwing rose petals from a wicker basket. When the petals were all gone he threw the basket, it arced high over the crowd, and we hotfooted it out of the Arena, jumped into the limos, and raced back to the plane.

Not a particularly good show, it was brief and it was over. We were headed home. A sort of camaraderie was beginning to grow among those of us who had sat around the LA houses too long with too much hype. We were starting to feel like a small band against the world of cops and promoters, and we were starting to enjoy each other's company. When we got into our seats Keith held aloft a fifth of Old Charter and said, 'Cocktails, anyone?'

As we taxied out, Ron Schneider, all lapels and crinkly sideburns, leaned over the back of the seats where Mick and Keith were sitting and asked, 'Do you want to do a second show in Detroit?'

'Yes,' Keith said without hesitation.

'How fast did they sell out?' Mick asked.

'About a week.'

'No, not if it took them a week,' Mick said.

'But it sold out with no promotion,' Schneider said. 'The guy's guaranteeing a full house.'

Mick still looked doubtful.

'If there's one empty seat we won't go on,' Keith said.

We were reaching the top of our climb to flying altitude, and Keith called, 'Is it cool to smoke?' The no smoking light went out and at once half a dozen joints were circulating in the tiny cabin, where the air space was so limited that everybody must soon have been stoned, including the pilots. Mick was talking about the blind girl who was lifted onstage. 'All those kids are so *stoned,*' he said. It was true, the

Stones were playing for the first time to kids who were under the influence of dope, almost all of them stoned every night.

1964

Returning from the United States, after their first American tour, the Stones drove from Heathrow Airport to Oxford for a booking at the University, made the previous year. Two days later they played an all-night Welcome Home show with at least fifty other performers—not much fun—and 'It's All Over Now', recorded in the United States, was released. They took two weeks off, and before the holiday was over *Melody Maker* listed the record as the best-selling single record in England, the Stones' first number one single.

When the Stones started back to work, they played the Queen's Hall in Leeds, a concert hall with a revolving stage. 'It was in the centre of the hall, and at the end of the show they had to dash for it,' Stu said. 'And again it was Brian who got left behind. Beforehand everyone had it all worked out; a gang of bouncers would surround them, and they would run. Four of them got among the bouncers. Brian's fucking about onstage, half asleep, doing something or other, as all the bouncers take the others off, and all the kids go after them. And there's Brian still on the stage with his guitar. Brian realized, Ah, they've gone, and panics: "*Do* something," and of course within seconds the kids realized he was still there, and ka-pow. Brian destroyed again.'

A little later, the Stones played Blackpool: 'July 24, 1964—which was very nearly the date on my gravestone,' Stu said. He explained: 'In Glasgow, all the factories and construction companies shut down the same fortnight of the year for the Glasgow Fair. In that fortnight, they move out of Glasgow. Glasgow shuts down, literally. And the rest of the country trembles.

'One of their pet places is Blackpool. So, unsuspecting, we get into the town, and it's absolutely full of these ravers. It's the last night, and they all—or as many as possible—crowd into this Empress Ballroom. They were all very drunk, and the feeling was getting nastier and nastier. They were really looking for bother. The Stones'd play a number, and there'd be big cheers and claps and a little bit of screaming, but also a lot of derisive cheering as well. No cops, no bouncers.

'Keith can't stand being booed, and he was saying "Aw fuck you" to them and they could hear him. So they started spitting, and eventually Keith was literally covered. Finally, there was one guy right in front—a bit taller than the rest—and, when he spat at Keith, Keith just kicked him in the head. And that's it. Good night. One of their people had been kicked, and that was the spark. The whole hall just *ee*rupted. I'm surprised they didn't get hold of Keith's leg and pull him off the stage. He wouldn't be here now, if they had. But I was next to him—the other guys had already turned to get off the stage—and I just pushed him, saying "For fuck's sake get out of here while you're still alive." Backstage we could hear cymbals going through the air, thumps as all the amps got smashed up, and then there was the most glorious fucking crash of all time—there'd been a grand piano on the stage. They didn't steal any of the instruments: they just smashed them. Of the amplifiers, there were bits of wood, and I think we got one loudspeaker chassis. Everything else was totally mangled. They took about a dozen people to hospital. Not having been able to get hold of the Stones, they started fighting among themselves.'

One week after Blackpool, the Stones went to Belfast. 'There were kids everywhere,' Stu said, and they were getting on the stage, more and more until the Stones just got surrounded. Quite a night. We should have got mangled that night. Never been nearer. Lots of kids hurt. Bloody horrifying. Show lasted twelve minutes. Cops didn't want it to go on in the first place.'

The Stones then flew to Holland for a concert in the Hague. There were police onstage, but after three songs the fans attacked and it was closing time, gentlemen.

Back in England at the Tower Ballroom in New Brighton: 'The stage was so high that they had to use a block and tackle to get the gear up it,' Stu said. 'The kids were pressing the front, getting underneath the stage so they couldn't see anything, and the trouble started.' Two hundred fainted, and about fifty were thrown out for fighting. A girl pulled a switchblade on two guards who were trying to subdue her two escorts, and four guards were required to disarm her and carry her out of the hall.

Near the end of this tour, at the Gaumont Theatre in Ipswich, Stu watched as 'the barrier in front of the stage collapsed and a girl got a broken back. I saw her go down and I heard her back break. But a lot of them you never heard about. They were in the local papers the next day and that was all.'

Charlie Watts and Shirley Ann Shepherd barely had time to get married before the Stones were off for Belgian and French television appearances and their first appearance at the Olympia Theatre in Paris. With a successful Paris concert soon behind them—a spokesman for the Olympia said that the theatre had suffered £1,400 worth of damages—the Stones then came home and had a day to pack before leaving for their second assault on the United States.

The Stones began this one by appearing, after rehearsing for two days, on the Ed Sullivan show. The Show, every Sunday night for twenty years, was the phoenix of vaudeville, bringing to US television the most varied acts imaginable: the finest ballet dancers and opera singers doing two and a half hot minutes, comedians, jugglers, animal acts—all the stars who had reached the top, because in its time and place, the Sullivan show was the top.

When the well-rehearsed Stones were on the Sullivan show, the reception from fans inside and outside the theatre was so enthusiastic that Sullivan said he'd never book the Stones again. The next day they flew to Los Angeles. They played Sacramento, then took a day off, noticing that in the five months they had been away, the men in America had grown their hair longer.

After rehearsing for two days at the Santa Monica Civic Auditorium, the Stones appeared on the Teen Awards Music International show. The Stones closed the show, following, among others, the Beach Boys, who wouldn't speak to them; Marvin Gaye; the Supremes; the Miracles; Chuck Berry, who was pleasant, talked with them and even gave Wyman a pair of cufflinks; and, ultimately, James Brown, who said he would make the Stones wish they'd never left England. The Stones had never seen James Brown. 'The kids were eating out of his hand,' Stu said. 'Mick and them were trembling, having to follow this. But they did it, they got canned and bowled on and did it.' It was one of their most spirited performances; even Wyman moved a bit.

In the next few days, the Stones did shows in southern California, recorded six songs at RCA Studios in LA and then they left for Cleveland. They were preceded by a radio announcement from the local mayor, advising the citizens that the Rolling Stones gave immoral performances and that no teenagers should be allowed to see them. In spite of this the show was poorly attended, perhaps because on this night Lyndon Johnson was elected president of the United States by the greatest percentage of the popular vote in the country's history. Next, New York City, the Astor, then to Providence and a cinema where no live act had ever performed. The management had covered the orchestra pit with thin plywood, and when the Stones started playing, girls ran down the aisles, jumped on to the plywood and disappeared into the pit.

The Stones went back to Manhattan, and two days later they flew to Chicago, where they would spend most of the next week, and Brian would spend all of it. Brian didn't make it to the shows in Milwaukee, nor to the concert the next night in Fort Wayne, Indiana, nor to the one after that, in Dayton, Ohio. Brian was in Chicago at the Pasavant Hospital with a temperature of one hundred and five degrees—delirious, the doctors said, from bronchitis and extreme exhaustion.

'He was certainly ill, all right,' Stu said, 'but he aggravated it by taking too much of something, and generally behaved very stupidly. He nearly got hoofed out there and then. He hadn't really contributed anything to the records we made then. He was either stoned or pissed or just sick.'

On January 6, 1965, the Stones flew to Ireland, did interviews, a television show and two concerts in Dublin, 'another of these occasions when Brian got lost in the crowd,' Stu said.

'He used to really dig being mobbed,' Keith said. 'He'd be dead scared of it, but he used to really dig it, too. He would demand to be surrounded by heavies, then he'd take his jacket off, and say "Now. Now. Now. Now!"' Ireland was followed by a tour of Australia and the Far East, beginning in Sydney where the Stones had the entire floor at the Chevron Hilton, with an excellent view of Sydney Harbour and the fans outside. 'That's where the staff sends the birds up to you instead of trying to keep them out,' Stu said.

'Amazing number of them there,' Keith said. 'Bill was on the phone to the hall porter the whole time: "Send me up that one in the pink." Nine in one day he had, no kidding. He just sat all day long in his bedroom looking out the window, and he's right in with the hall porter, "No, not that one, the one with the blonde hair, not that 'orror." Used to tell him off for sending up uglies.'

The Stones' first Australian shows went well, and they left for New Zealand where they stayed for ten days, in near hundred-degree weather, being refused admittance to hotels, watched in stony silence by the crowd at Dunedin, pelted with eggs in Auckland, and with Brian and Bill carrying on a competition among the sun-tanned legs.

'They were the only two who actively used to go out looking,' Stu said. 'Bill would usually be the first one to find summink, and then Brian would move in.'

'Bill had an absolute compulsion,' Keith said. 'He had to have a bird, otherwise he couldn't sleep, he'd get homesick, he'd start shaking, really, he'd collapse completely if he didn't have something in bed with him, no matter what it was.'

The Stones returned to Australia for more shows in Melbourne, Adelaide, and Perth. At a party after one of the Adelaide shows Bill picked up a girl and again Brian nicked her away. Next day, in Perth for the last shows of their first tour of Australia, Bill, whose suite adjoined Brian's, came in through the connecting doors to Brian's bedroom, where Brian was already in bed, about to be joined by a girl who was sitting on the side of the bed in her bra and panties. Bill greeted him cheerily, sat beside the girl in the dark room, whispered in her ear, and away they went together.

The Stones then returned to LA by way of Singapore and Hong Kong, where they played concerts. They took almost a week off before starting a new tour, their fifth of England, with new releases 'The Last Time' and *The Rolling Stones No. 2* high in the charts. After another short week off, the Stones started a short Scandinavian tour, flying to Copenhagen, where they had the entire nineteenth floor of the Grand Hotel. 'And I'm afraid,' Stu said, 'the Grand Hotel, which is still the best hotel in Copenhagen, will no longer let anybody who even looks as if he's got long hair inside the door. Nineteen floors up, the Stones were throwing empty bottles out the window. To the fans down below.'

The Tour: New York

The Rockefeller Centre, New York: the press conference was held on the sixty-ninth floor in the Rainbow Room, behind big windows looking out on the city. At the door a girl in a long-sleeved dress sat by a small white-clothed table, checking names against a list. Al Steckler, inside, saw us and waved us in. A long table, also white-clothed, held drinks and steak tartare canapés. The waiters wore dinner jackets, and a string quartet was playing Mozart.

Before long the place was filled with press people who ranged in appearance from dapper black men in suits to scruffy hippies in dirty jeans.

Jon Jaymes stood beside the table, hands raised toward the press, looking like a man conducting the antics of a bevy of magpies. As the crowd grew quieter, though it never stopped snarling and pushing, questions drifted across the room.

'Do you see yourselves as youth leaders?'

'What do you think of the Vietnam War?'

'What do you think of America?'

'Do you think it's getting better?'

'You look more beautiful than ever,' Jagger said. That brought a laugh.

'Mr Jagger,' a woman wearing glasses and a tailored suit read from a notebook, 'some time ago you recorded a song, "I Can't Get No Satisfaction". Are the Stones more satisfied today?'

'Sexually, d'you mean, or philosophically?'

'Both.'

'Sexually—more satisfied. Financially—dissatisfied. Philosophically—still trying.'

'Are you sadder but wiser?'

'Just a little wiser.' I didn't know it yet, but about thirty minutes before Jagger had learned that Marianne Faithfull had left him, left his house in London, and was living with a film director in Italy. 'Do you have any valium?' Mick had asked Jo, who scrounged one five-milligram tablet from a *Daily News* reporter.

'I have a question for Mick Taylor,' someone said. 'How does it feel to replace a member of the group who was loved by so many? I'm talking about Brian Jones.'

Whatever Mick Taylor said was lost in the groan that arose in the room. Even in this crowd, bad taste had its limits. As if on cue, someone asked, 'Are the Stones going to give a free concert?'

'Yes,' Jagger said. 'The free concert will be in San Francisco on December the sixth, but there is no exact location yet.'

At the first press conference in Los Angeles, the hippies had asked for a free show, and now on the other side of America the Stones had promised them one. The tone of the questions as they continued asked not for a statement of position but for a declaration of support. Once again the hippies were asking whether the Stones were on their side in the battle against repression.

'Mr Jagger, in California you were wearing an Omega button, which is a symbol of draft resistance—'

'I thought it stood for infinity. I don't know.'

'Mr Jagger, what is your opinion of the mass concerts such as Woodstock and the Isle of Wight?'

'Well, they all happened in the same year—I think next year they will be more—huge and better organized.'

'Why are you giving a free concert in San Francisco?'

'Because there's a scene there, and the climate's nice. Besides, it's unfortunate when Ralph Gleason has to pay fifty dollars to get in.'

The questions dwindled to a halt, and Sam said, 'That's all, folks.'

'Thank you New York,' Jagger said, and the Stones zipped away: the freaks, straights, beards, sideburns, cameras, and recorders rushed for the elevators.

1965–1967

On 5 December 1965, after forty-two days, the Stones ended their fourth tour of the United States at the Los Angeles Sports Arena. In a month and a half they had made two million dollars. They stayed in LA for the next week, recording a single and *Aftermath,* the first album composed entirely of Jagger/Richards songs. Then the members of the band went their own ways, all of them returning to England for Christmas except Brian, who was in the Virgin Islands with new girlfriend Anita Pallenberg and a tropical virus.

The new single, '19th Nervous Breakdown', contained what may have been the first reference in a popular song to what were called psychedelic drugs. It was released on 4 February and entered the *New Musical Express* singles chart at number two on 11 February. That day the Stones flew to New York to tape another appearance on the Ed Sullivan Show, refused to be photographed at the airport and nearly got

into a fight with the photographers. They split up for their New York stay, hoping to avoid fans and because no decent New York hotel would accommodate all of them together. Then they began touring again: Australia, Europe—in Marseilles, Mick's forehead was gashed by a chair thrown from the audience ('They do it when they get excited,' he told reporters)—and the United States again.

The Stones flew back to London to prepare for the next Sunday, when they would appear for the first time on the London Palladium Show, the British equivalent of the Ed Sullivan Show. When the show was announced, a newspaper commented that 'pop groups can no longer rely on teenaged viewers alone to get TV bookings, but must appeal to a wider audience.' To which Jagger said, 'Times are changing, and with the changing times comes a different market—one market. We think the Palladium is ready for the Stones, and the Stones are ready for the Palladium.' He was wrong.

Keith and Brian arrived for rehearsal two hours late, both of them crammed with LSD. Brian, wearing a combination of his and Anita's clothing, played piano on one song and insisted on placing a large *hookah* on top where no one could fail to see it. Not trusting the television sound engineers, the Stones brought a tape recording of their instruments, in violation of a musicians' union ban of taped music. But the main issue was the roundabout, the Palladium's revolving stage, where each week's acts gathered at the end of the show to wave and throw kisses at the audience. The roundabout was a great tradition. But Jagger had told the newspapers that, although the Stones would play the Palladium Show, they wouldn't go on the roundabout. At the end of rehearsal, Jagger and the Stones refused to revolve.

Everyone was outraged. But it was only the beginning. The week after, the newspapers revealed Jagger's 'Secret Romance' with Marianne Faithfull. 'I got Marianne's call in the middle of the night to come,' Jagger told reporters at the airport in Nice, 'and so here I am.' Marianne, twenty years old, mother of a fourteen-month-old son, had left her husband four months before. She had phoned Mick complaining of loneliness when her song, 'The One Who Hopes', failed to reach the finals of the San Remo Song Festival. ('He gets the worst women,' Keith said, 'and when it's a black one it's the whitest one he can find.') 'I'm fed up with the fuss and dancing in night clubs until dawn,' said blonde, blue-eyed Marianne. Jagger hired a small boat with three red sails and

Saturday evening found them sailing toward Cap d'Antibes 'into a red sunset'.

But by the following Sunday, Jagger was back in London and on a radio talk show defending the Stones against the Show's two other guests and against the *News of the World,* which that day had accused Mick, among others, of taking LSD. Mick said he had never taken LSD and that his lawyers would sue. Two days later, the *News of the World* was served with a writ for libel.

The next Sunday the Stones would never forget. At about eight o'clock in the evening, nineteen policemen and -women descended on Keith's country house, Redlands. Mick, Keith, Marianne, art-dealer Robert Fraser and some other people were down from London for the weekend. 'Anita and Brian were gonna come but Brian started a fight,' Keith said. 'We just left them fighting.' The police took some substances from the premises and left.

On 20 March, Keith and Mick received court summonses alleging offences against the Dangerous Drugs Act. Five days later, the Stones left for three weeks in Europe, their last tour with Brian.

When the Stones played Warsaw, taking what Mick called 'a piddle of our usual fee,' they brought full-scale rock and roll for the first time to Communist Eastern Europe. 'The only time I've seen like it was when we tried to get out of the Long Beach Auditorium in 1965 and a motorcycle cop got run over and crushed,' Keith said. 'All the cops had white helmets and the big long batons. Exactly the same equipment. Exactly the same uniforms. Deployed in the same way.'

The tour was a series of fights, featuring the Stones, customs officials, fans, and police, and involving guard dogs and fire hoses and the throwing of furniture. Back in London when it was over, Jagger said, 'I see a great deal of danger in the air.... Teenagers are not screaming over pop music any more, they're screaming for much deeper reasons. When I'm onstage, I sense that the teenagers are trying to communicate to me, as if by telepathy, a message of some urgency. Not about me or about our music, but about the world and the way they live. And I see a lot of trouble coming in the dawn.'

Trouble was certainly coming to the Stones. On 10 May, while Jagger and Richards were at a preliminary hearing in Chichester Magistrates' Court, putting up one hundred pounds bail apiece, pleading not guilty and electing to be tried by jury, Brian was leaving his Courtfield Road flat surrounded by six Scotland Yard drug detectives.

In Chichester, on 27 June, Keith and Mick appeared before Judge Leslie Block at the West Sussex Quarter Sessions, Mick in an apple-green jacket and olive trousers, Keith wearing a navy frock coat and a lace-collared shirt. Mick's case was considered first, with Malcolm Morris, Queen's Counsel, leading for the prosecution and Michael Havers, Queen's Counsel, for the defence. Chief Inspector Gordon Dinely, the first witness, testified that on 12 February, at about eight o'clock in the evening, he and eighteen other police officers, three of them women, went to Redlands and found there one woman and eight men, among them Michael Philip Jagger.

Sergeant John Challen of the police party testified that in searching the premises, 'I first went into the drawing-room and then went upstairs to a bedroom. There I found a green jacket, in the left-hand pocket of which I found a small phial containing four tablets. I took the jacket downstairs and Jagger admitted that it belonged to him and that his doctor prescribed the pills.' Challen asked Mick who his doctor was, and Mick said, 'Dr Dixon Firth, but I can't remember if it was him.' Asked what the tablets were for, Mick said, 'To stay awake and work.'

Called by the defence, Dr Firth testified that the tablets, which were amphetamine, had not been prescribed by him, but that Mick had told him he had them and asked if they were all right to use. The doctor remembered this conversation as having taken place sometime before February and his having advised Mick that they were to be taken in an emergency but not regularly.

The doctor and the prosecutor exchanged opinions as to the propriety of telling Mick he could have the drugs and whether Mick's conversation with the doctor amounted to a prescription. Judge Block said he had no hesitation in saying that it did not, and that the only legitimate defence, a written prescription, was therefore not open to Michael Jagger. 'I therefore direct you,' he told the jury, 'that there is no defence to this charge.'

Within five minutes the jury came back with a guilty verdict. Judge Block granted Mick an appeal certificate and remanded him in custody at Lewes Prison.

On the second day of the trial, Keith, in a braided black suit, met with the same judge and counsels before a new jury and pled not guilty to letting Redlands be used for smoking cannabis. The proceedings began with submissions concerning the relevance of certain evidence. Judge

SEA
A

Block ruled that, within limits set by Mr Morris, certain parties should not be named but the evidence should be submitted. Mr Morris explained to the jury that it was necessary for him to prove that Keith had wilfully and knowingly allowed cannabis to be smoked. The evidence would show, he said, that incense was being burned at Redlands to cover up the odour of cannabis. 'That there was a strong, sweet smell of incense in these premises will be clear from the evidence,' Morris said, 'and you may well come to the conclusion that that smell could not fail to have been noticed by Keith Richards. There was ash—resulting from cannabis resin and smoking Indian hemp—actually found on the table in front of the fireplace in the drawing-room where Keith Richards and his friends were. The behaviour of one of the guests may suggest that she was under the influence of smoking cannabis resin in a way which Richards could not fail to notice.'

The English newspapers ran photographs of Marianne Faithfull alongside the stories mentioning the unnamed female guest. Years later she would confirm that the green velvet jacket and the amphetamines for which Mick was jailed were hers.

Keith testified that he had driven down from London with Mick and Marianne for a weekend party attended by Michael Cooper, Christopher Gibbs, Robert Fraser, and Fraser's Moroccan servant, Mohamed. (Fraser, in possession of heroin during the raid, had been found guilty and jailed along with Mick.) George Harrison of the Beatles and his wife Patti came late and left before the police arrived. Two other guests, not friends of Mick or Keith, also came—David Schneidermann, a Canadian familiarly known as 'Acid-King David', and a person described in *The Times* as 'an exotic' from Chelsea, customarily seen in the King's Road in red silk trousers and shirt, bells around his neck, and flowers behind his ears. His only known occupation at the time of the party was 'forever blowing bubbles through one of those wire wands.' The group drove down more or less in convoy to Redlands, arriving there late Saturday night or early Sunday morning. The party finally broke up about five o'clock in the morning. The four bedrooms upstairs in the house were occupied, so Keith slept in a chair downstairs.

'It just so happened,' Keith said a number of years later, 'we all took acid and were in a completely freaked-out state when they arrived. There was a big knock at the door. Eight o'clock. Everybody was just

sort of gliding down slowly from a whole day of freaking about. Strobe lights were flickering. Marianne Faithfull had just decided that she wanted a bath and had wrapped herself up in a rug and was watching the box.

'Bang, bang, bang,' this big knock at the door which I answered. 'Oh, look, there's lots of little ladies and gentlemen outside....'

'We were just gliding off from a twelve-hour trip, and I told one of the women they brought to search the ladies, "Would you mind stepping off that Moroccan cushion. Because you're ruining the tapestries...." They tried to get us to turn the record player off and we said, "No. We won't turn it off but we'll turn it down." As they started going out the door, somebody put on "Rainy Day Women" really loud: "Everybody must get stoned." And that was it.'

The police did not know about the acid, so it wasn't mentioned at the trial. But the immoral atmosphere, the sweet smell of incense, the naked girl.... The jury pronounced Keith guilty. Mick and Robert Fraser, who had been taken between court and prison in handcuffs, were brought up to join Keith in the dock for sentence.

The judge gave Keith one year's imprisonment and ordered him to pay £500 toward prosecution costs. Fraser was sentenced to six months in jail and £200 costs. 'I sentence you to three months and £100 costs,' the judge said to Mick, who burst into tears.

Brian's drug trial took place on 30 October. He was charged with possession of cannabis, methedrine, and cocaine, smoking and allowing his flat to be used for smoking cannabis. He pleaded guilty to possessing and smoking cannabis, otherwise not guilty.

The prosecutor, Robin Simpson, said that on 10 May, at four o'clock in the afternoon, the police searched Brian's flat. Asked if he had any drugs, Brian had said, 'I suffer from asthma, the only drugs I have are for that.' Eleven objects were found in different places, in different rooms, that contained or had traces of drugs: two canisters, two wallets, two pipes, two cigarette ends, a box of cigarette papers, a jar, a chair castor used as an ashtray. The total number of grains of cannabis found was thirty-five and a quarter, enough to make from seven to ten cigarettes. The police had shown Brian a tin containing some of the material now in evidence and a phial that appeared to have traces of cocaine. 'Yes, it is hash,' Brian had said. 'We do smoke. But not cocaine, man. That's not my scene.'

The defending attorney, James Comyn, QC, said that Brian had suffered a breakdown and had been under strict medical care. He had been very ill but had at last responded to treatment. Comyn said that Brian was highly intelligent (IQ 133), a versatile musician and a composer with tremendous writing talent. The defence called Dr Leonard Henry, a psychiatrist from Northolt, Middlesex, who said that Brian had been his patient, coming to see him eight times in all. Brian had been agitated, depressed, incoherent, and had to be treated with tranquilizers and anti-depressants. He was very sick and got worse. He didn't respond to treatment and was recommended for treatment in Roehampton Priory in July. Brian was now less depressed and less anxious, but the doctor said, 'If he is put in prison, it would be disastrous to his health. He would have a complete mental collapse, a breakdown, and he couldn't stand the stigma. He might injure himself.'

Then Brian took the stand. He was wearing a navy suit with flared jacket and bell-bottom trousers, a polka dot cravat, and shoes with Cuban heels. Judge Reginald Seaton said that he'd been told Brian intended cutting out drugs completely. 'That is precisely my intention,' Brian said. He told the judge that drugs had brought him only trouble and disrupted his career: 'I hope that will be an example to others.'

'I am very moved by what I have heard,' the Judge said, 'but under the circumstances nothing less than a prison sentence would be correct. I sentence you to nine months imprisonment for allowing your premises to be used for the smoking of drugs, and three months for being in possession of cannabis resin, the sentences to run concurrently.'

The judge also ordered Brian to pay £250 costs and refused to grant him bail pending an appeal.

On 12 December, Brian appeared for his appeal, before a panel of four judges. Dr Leonard Neustatter, a court-appointed psychiatrist who had interviewed Brian four times, said that he was intelligent but 'emotionally unstable, with neurotic tendencies.... He vacillates between a passive, dependent child with a confused image of an adult on the one hand, and an idol of pop culture on the other.'

In the light of these opinions and the fact that Brian had never before been convicted of anything worse than peeing in a garage—though he had been guilty of worse things many times—the court substituted a £1,000 fine and three years probation for Brian's prison term, telling him: 'The Court has shown a degree of mercy, but you cannot go and boast, saying you've been let off. If you commit another offence of any sort, you will be brought back and punished afresh. And you know what sort of sentence you will get.'

Two days later, Brian was taken to St George's Hospital in London after being found unconscious on the floor of a flat in Chelsea, rented in the name of his chauffeur, John Coray. Doctors in the hospital's emergency department wanted Brian to stay, but he left after an hour, saying he was only exhausted and wanted to go home.

s the new year began, Jo Bergman, who had come to work for the Stones in September, made an analysis of their situation:

1. Rolling Stones personal working accounts overdrawn
2. Rolling Stones number three account overdrawn
3. Telexes sent to Klein
4. Promise of £2,000 to be sent Thursday
5. Need £7,000 to clear most pressing debts
6. Money needed for studio & offices
7. Summary
   (a) due to lack of funds in personal accounts, some bills paid out of Rolling Stones account number 3
   (b) no funds for running of office
   (c) Accountant has been forced to find an alternative

The Stones started rehearsing in February and by mid-March were recording songs for a new album. Brian, who felt he could no longer play with the Stones, was participating very little. In March he hoped to get away to Morocco, but before he could get out of London, he was again in the news: 'Stones Girl Naked in Drug Drama', *The News of the World* headline said. Linda Keith—a disc-jockey's daughter who had once been Keith's girlfriend and was now, at least part of the time, Brian's—phoned her doctor, told him where she was and that she was going to overdose on drugs. The doctor called the police, who knocked down the door of the Chesham Place flat, rented to Brian's chauffeur, where Brian stayed when in London. Linda was inside, naked and unconscious. After she had been taken to the hospital, Brian arrived at the flat. 'I had been at an all-night recording session,' he told reporters, 'and when I came back just after twelve I found the police at the flat. I was absolutely shattered when the landlord of the flat asked the police to have me removed. He said, "'It's because you are trespassing. We don't

want your kind in this place."' By the end of April, the Stones had finished a new single, 'Jumpin' Jack Flash', with an optimistic chorus:

But it's all right now
In fact it's a gas

It was time. ***The Daily Express*** **on 9 May, in a story titled 'Things Look Bad for Rolling Stones', observed that the Stones had not had a number one single since 'Paint It, Black' over two years before.**

But three days later the Stones gave a surprise performance at ***New Musical Express*** **Pollwinner's Concert at Wembley Stadium—they had been named the top rhythm and blues group. It was just like the old days, girls screaming, cops with linked arms holding back hysterical fans. The Stones did 'Jumpin' Jack Flash' and 'Satisfaction', and Mick threw his white shoes into the crowd.**

Nine days later, four days before 'Jack Flash' was released, Brian was again arrested for drugs. For the last time.

6 December 1969

We are in the trailer: Mick, in the doorway, head down in the bright movie lights, his burgundy newsboy cap hiding his face, listening to the radio interviewer. 'Mick, do you and the Stones intend to go on touring?'

'Yeah, we aim to stay on the streets. We dug doing this tour, actually, more than the others. We got into playing a bit more, we could hear ourselves occasionally.'

'What do you think of this gathering?'

'It reminds me of when we were in Marrakesh—Keith and I were in Marrakesh the last time, outside the city walls. There were a great many musicians and dancers, very medieval.'

Sam Cutler, sitting at the trailer's kitchen-table with Keith and Rock Scully, his eyes red in a grey-white bristly face, says, 'You should go on about five p.m. Sunset's at twenty to six.'

'Are you ready to split, Keith?' Mick asks.

'I'm stayin',' Keith says.

'Okay. See you soon.'

Mick asks the Maysles brothers if they'll be staying. 'There should be filming starting at dawn,' he says.

'Oh, sure,' David Maysles says. 'We'll stay.' His brother Al looks at him. They have been with us the last sleepless night in Muscle Shoals, have crossed the country and followed us in another car as we drove out from San Francisco, and now Mick on his way back to the hotel asks them if they'll be staying for a second sleepless night.

'We'll have a helicopter bring out some film stock,' David says.

'See you later, Measles,' Ronnie says, as he, Mick and I board the limo.

'They will stay, won't they?' Mick asks.

'Yeah, they'll stay,' Ronnie says. 'I'll make sure they get some film.'

Mick seems pleased and excited, and why not? This is what the Stones—all of us?—have been after all along. And here we are, thousands of strangers coming together in a strange place like some mad sect. But why this place?

'How'd we get this place?' I ask Ronnie.

We are away from the stage now, driving very slowly, gently, through the steady onward press of young people with their baskets and sleeping bags and jugs and dogs. It is so late and we have been up for so long that, even with the cocaine, Ronnie's voice comes and goes in and out of my hearing. Something about no rock in the park, so this fellow offered this place mostly for the publicity after they had first tried to get Sears Point Raceway, which was owned by Filmways, and Filmways had showed their interest by demanding hundreds of thousands in deposits and millions of dollars of insurance plus distribution rights to the film shot at the festival. So here we are at Altamont. It doesn't make a hell of a lot of sense to me, but it has been a while since much of anything has.

'So how much is it costing the Stones?'

'Nothing,' Ronnie says. 'The film rights will pay for it.'

'That's nice,' I say. 'It really is a free show.'

We have come to a stop behind some other cars lined up before the gate, and people are crowding around the limousine. 'I wanted to do all the shows free,' Mick says, 'but that was before I talked to the accountants. I'd like nothing better than to do a free show on the East Coast.'

There are kids at the window now, knocking, and Mick finds the button to slide it down. The driver is honking the horn, though the other cars are parked and empty and are not about to move by themselves.

'Are you real?' a girl is asking Mick. She has long dark hair and is bundled up in a heavy green stadium coat. 'Is it really you?'

'Yeah, I'm real, are you real?' Mick says.

She reaches in, taking his hand—'Let us in,' she says, 'it's so cold out here.'

But Mick is tired and wants to sleep, so he says, 'Are you havin' a good time?'

'Yeah, who are they?' the girl says, looking at me and Ronnie.

'Just some friends,' Mick says. 'Are you havin' a good time?' Mick asks again as the gate guard comes over, wearing a beige rent-a-cop uniform, and says to the people around the limo, 'Would you please move so this car in front here can move so this car can move so the one behind it can move so we can get this other car out? All right?' Grumbling gently, hip but tractable—as if in a 1957 movie, 'Don't Knock the Rock' or whatever—the kids fall back, and we pull away and Ron says, 'The kids are so lovely.'

'I'd like to stay but I've got to rest,' Mick says, 'I've got to sing—if I had to play the guitar tomorrow I think I'd stay, but I've got to sing.'

The cars in front have been moved and we roll out through the gate, the guard locking up behind us against the hundreds of people who are outside, hundreds or thousands of the hundreds of thousands who'll be coming.

We are slowly making progress, and now in the near-dawn hour the pilgrims are increasing, a steady stream of them on both sides of the car in their rough clothes and long hair, bleached out in the headlights' glare. I'm wondering whether I should miss a minute of this mass phenomenon that I do not even like the looks of. We have never been—none of us—alone in the desert with hundreds of thousands of other young freaks, the Rolling Dead, all kinds of dope and *no* rules! DO WHAT THOU WILT: that shall be the whole of the law. At Woodstock, a commercial event which turned into something else, a *détente* existed between people and police, because the police were outnumbered, but here you couldn't find the police even if you wanted.

But right now it is cold and uncomfortable and I have to sleep. I know we won't be at the hotel long, and I want to get my tape recorder and a little rest because I am tired. But still a lot of people are showing up, and anything might happen, just anything.

'I'd like to get some mescaline for tomorrow,' Mick says, also watching the people stream past. 'Like to take some after the show.'

'Like to take some before the show,' I say.

'No, I have to sing, I can't sing if I'm stoned, I'll be freakin' out all over the stage—'

'I've got some. We can take it whenever you want,' I say.

'Do you? Great, I haven't had any psychedelics in a couple of years. I'd like to take some and just wander around in the crowd and talk to the people.'

'All right, I'll take some with you,' I say, 'but I don't know, I'm a little surprised. You believe all this generation-revolution hype a lot more than I do.'

'No I don't. I don't. I'm just thinking about the film, that's all. It's going to be very interesting for the film. If we travel next year as well, go to the East and maybe Africa, do a world tour, I'd like to show all sorts of different music and a lot of strange and exotic, ah, erotic things. Like these chicks I saw in Bangkok. You went to this place—like a whorehouse—and there are all these chicks on a red carpet behind this sort of glass curtain. And they're all wearing white socks and blue jeans and T-shirts with numbers, very weird. They all look like—what d'you call them?—cheerleaders, and you pick the one you want: "Numbah 52, please." They take you away and do whatever—tread on you, massage you, suck your cock. You can't make it with them there, but you can make a date to take them some place else and fuck them. It was so strange, sort of weird science fiction atmosphere. There was a concert there too, native music: it was much better than most rock and roll, more exciting. I think that would entertain people. I really do. I mean, I'm entertained by that sort of thing, and you could cut in all sorts of things—us playing and then maybe some African drums—just like the Ed Sullivan show. I don't think there's anything wrong with that form, inherently—just putting one thing after another—as long as the things are interesting—'

'It would have to be done right, though,' Ronnie says, 'or it would just be Around the World with the Rolling Stones.'

'Well, that—what's wrong with that?' Mick asks.

'Seems as if you'd need something more,' I say.

'It'll develop as you do it,' Ronnie says, 'you don't have to worry about it in detail now. First you should get some bread for it. You can probably get half a million from Warner's with a treatment.'

'What could be in a treatment?' Mick asks. 'An itinerary, maybe. We don't know where we're gonna go yet.'

I open my eyes. We are on the highway now, still in the pitch-black night. We have been riding along talking with our eyes closed. Mick is quiet. It is impossible to tell whether he is sulking or just trying to sleep. Then he says, 'I think a film of the Rolling Stones around the world would be interesting. I'd go to see that film.'

We ride on in silence. After a long time, or what seems a long time, Mick says, 'I wish Charlie could have seen this. He was very upset. He thought it was all going wrong.'

I can't see what you could tell from what we saw that would be reassuring—it is too vast to be named yet—but Mick says, 'Charlie felt he was sucked into it—because he really doesn't have much money and they don't know that he really could use the money. I could have done the whole tour free because I'm big shit, y'know, and I've got money. But he hasn't. And he has a family and could use it. I wish he could have seen how nice it is out there: we'll leave a note under his door.'

In the summer of 1968, 'Jumpin' Jack Flash' had carried the Stones back to the top of the pop charts. Their new album, *Beggar's Banquet,* was released in November after a long dispute over the Stones' proposed cover photograph of the graffiti on a toilet wall in a Mexican automobile body shop in Los Angeles. Decca refused to release the album with that cover. 'The record company is not there to tell us what we can make,' Mick had said. 'If that's the way they feel about it, then they should make the records and we'll distribute them.' At last the record was released with a white cover designed as an invitation. 'We copped out,' Keith said, 'but we did it for money, so it was all right.'

Also released in November was *One plus One,* a film by Jean-Luc Godard that was in part about the recording of 'Sympathy for the

Devil'. Filming had been completed for a movie called *Performance,* starring Mick and Anita Pallenberg. In December the Stones produced a filmed entertainment called 'The Rolling Stones Rock and Roll Circus'. It presented circus acts—tigers, acrobats, clowns, a fire eater—and rock and roll from the Stones, Taj Mahal, John Lennon, Eric Clapton, Jethro Tull, and The Who. The Stones intended selling it to BBC-TV, but it was never finished.

At the end of the year, Keith and Anita, and Mick and Marianne went to Peru and Brazil. Seeing the black cowboys on the *pampas* inspired Keith to write a Jimmy Rodgers type of song called 'Honky Tonk Women'. Brian spent the holidays with new girlfriend Suki in Ceylon. John Lewis, a young English friend of Brian's, would tell me sometime later that while in Ceylon Brian consulted an astrologer—supposedly, at one time, Hitler's astrologer—who told Brian to be careful swimming in the coming year, not to go into the water without friends.

On 13 January, Brian was back in London to appear before a court that denied his appeal to set aside the guilty verdict from a drug charge. That left him with two drug convictions on his record. At the end of January Mick and Keith came back to England and started months of work on the tracks for *Let It Bleed.* In March the Stones were asked to play at the Memphis Blues Festival and considered doing it with Eric Clapton because of the problems they would have getting Brian into the country.

Brian had used the disturbance of his impending trial as an excuse for missing sessions and had even avoided England, telling the London newspapers from Morocco, 'I have the feeling my presence is not required.' 'After the trial was over and Brian didn't get it together,' Jo Bergman said, 'the handwriting was on the wall.'

On 8 June, with 'Honky Tonk Women' ready for release, Keith, Mick, and Charlie went to Cotchford Farm to talk to Brian. Years later Charlie would say, 'It was the worst thing so far that I've ever had to do.' But he also said that when they told Brian what they wanted to do, he seemed relieved. 'It was as if a whole weight had been lifted from his shoulders, and he said, "Yeah, I want to leave."'

Brian announced to the press that he had left the Stones. He called his father to say that it was only temporary, they wanted to play America, he would tour Europe with them next year.

After Altamont, when I was living in London, I talked many times with Shirley Arnold, who ran the fan club then. A few years later, when the Stones were living abroad and she never saw them any more, she stopped working for them. She told me the following:

'I went home on Tuesday evening, and I'd just had the telephone put in at home. One person knew the number, Joan Keylock, wife of the Stones' bodyguard and chauffeur. So when the phone rang at one o'clock in the morning it could only have been Joan.

'She said, "Are you awake?"

'I said, "Yeah, I'm downstairs, what's wrong?"

'She said, "I've got some bad news."

'I said, "Brian."

'She said, "He's dead."

'She rang me before she rang the others. She said, "Brian went for a swim and didn't come out." I always knew that one day one of them would die, and I used to think that it would be Brian.

'I'm sure all of us sat up all night. I left home about half-past six, got into a minicab. When we got to the West End, all the newspapers were out—"Brian Jones Dies in Swimming Pool"—and as I looked at all these headlines I thought, "He's really dead, he's front-page news again." I walked up into the office and opened it up. The first phone call was Alexis Korner. He was in a state of shock, and he said, "Is anyone there, has anyone heard the news, who am I speaking to?" I said, "You're speaking to Shirley," and he said, "Well, then, you know how I feel." He was trying to say, I'm so sorry for you, and he just broke down like a baby.

'The boys all showed it in different ways, Charlie actually cried, whereas I think Mick was too shocked. Then they started talking about Hyde Park, and the first thing Mick said was, "We'll cancel it," and then they said, "No, we'll do it, we'll do it for Brian."'

An audience of a quarter of a million had been expected for the Stones' free concert in Hyde Park, but there may have been twice that many. Sam Cutler was master of ceremonies. The English Hell's Angels, younger and much gentler than their American counterparts, acted as security.

BLACK

Stanley Booth

Altamont

We climbed into the helicopter and we were away. Long before we reached Altamont we could see long lines of cars backed up on the highway and parked cars and then great swarms of people. We descended at a crazy angle to a spot a long way up the hill behind the stage, coming down with a bump. The doors opened and we were outside in the crowd. Mick and Ronnie got out first and a boy ran up to Mick and hit him in the face, saying, 'I hate you! I hate you!' I couldn't see it, I just saw a scuffle and heard the words. I grabbed Charlie and held on to him, because I didn't want him to get lost—God knows what might happen to him.

I don't know how Mick and Ronnie and Mick Taylor moved so fast, but they disappeared, leaving me with Jo and Charlie Watts, the world's politest man. I tried to move him through the sea of sleeping bags, wine bottles, dogs, bodies, and hair. Like a mule in quicksand, he didn't want to go forward, didn't want to go back. 'Come on, Charlie,' I would say. 'Just step right on them, they don't mind, they can't feel a thing.' The ones who were conscious and moving about said, 'Hello, Charlie,' and Charlie smiled hello.

As we moved along, heading down toward the stage, we heard the Burritos playing in the distance, 'Lucille' and 'To Love Somebody'. It was chilly but the sun was shining. There were Frisbees in the air. We learned later that Jefferson Airplane, who played just before the Burritos, had been disturbed by Hell's Angels punching a black man in front of the stage. Marty Balin, the Airplane's lead singer, intervened and was knocked unconscious. We were pushing through the crowd, stumbling, trying to avoid the big dogs. People were tossing us joints and things. Looking at a yellow-green LSD tab, Charlie asked, 'D'you want it?'

'I ain't too sure about this street acid,' I said.

'Maybe Keith will want it.'

We were getting into the backstage area, trucks and trailers all around, the people there standing up, but it was still crowded. We moved quickly now, glimpsing faces painted with crescents and stars, and one big naked fat boy whose nostrils were pouring blood. The trailer we were headed for was surrounded by people with cameras and little girls and Hell's Angels. Once up the steps and inside, we were in the peaceful eye of a hurricane.

The Burritos' set had ended, Keith and I sprawled on a bed in a corner of the crowded trailer with a two-year-old girl who sat on my lap and told Keith, 'I'm gonna beat you up.'

This trailer was where we had eaten chocolate chip cookies and sniffed cocaine in the early morning hours, but now the air was so thick with marijuana smoke that Jo started hyperventilating, shaking and quaking. Some of the New York heavies were outside the trailer, and I took them drinks, beer and coffee. Tony was there, his right hand bandaged with splints. 'I punched a couple of guys out,' he said, taking a big Buck knife out of his pocket. 'I got this to compensate.'

Mick was leaning out the door, talking to people. A little while later Mick tried to walk around to see some of the show—Crosby, Stills, Nash, and Young were playing—but there was no way, it was too crowded, you couldn't move in the crush and what you could see you didn't want to be close to. Michelle Phillips of The Mamas and the Papas came into the trailer bearing tales of how the Angels were fighting with civilians, women, and each other, bouncing full cans of beer off people's heads. Augustus Owsley Stanley III, the San Francisco psychedelic manufacturer, known as Owsley, was giving away LSD, the Angels eating it by handfuls, smearing the excess on their faces. It didn't sound good but there was nothing to do about it now.

Soon we went out to a large yellow canvas tent a few yards away where the guitarists would tune. Jo was still trembling and I walked with my arm around her. The Stones had planned to go on at sunset, but the light was gone. Hell's Angels were guarding the tent. Inside, on a cardboard table, were a box of Ritz crackers and a chunk of yellow cheese. Keith and Bill and Mick Taylor started tuning. All around the tent, people were trying to peek in. A boy looked into a slit in the canvas and an Angel reached through and pushed his face back.

Jon Jaymes waddled in, giving the Angel at the tent flap a sad look, and I eased over to hear his news. 'There are four Highway Patrol cars,' he told Mick. 'Those are the only ones available to take you to the airport. We can have them right at the back of the stage, so when you come off—'

Mick was shaking his head. 'Not with the cops,' he said. 'I ain't goin' out with the cops.'

'I knew you'd say that,' Jon said.

Just as we all knew that, surrounded by Hell's Angels in the world's end of freakdom, Jagger was denying the only safe way out.

'Where's the stage?' Mick asked. We went to the back of the tent and peered out between two folds of canvas at the hastily-constructed wooden platform about thirty yards away.

'Would you mind taking this guitar out there for me?' Keith asked me.

Keith handed me his twelve-string. As I started out, an Angel, very short, maybe five-five, Mexican-looking, oily black curls, straggly whiskers, drooping greasy moustache, said, 'I'll take you there.' I appreciated his help. Night was upon us, and I wouldn't have wanted to fight my way through the dense backstage crowd. Trucks were parked behind the stage, a narrow passage between two of them. People were everywhere, exhausted, bewildered, lost, expectant. I followed close behind the Angel to the stage, where I handed the guitar to Stu, who looked worried.

He put the guitar on its wire stand in front of one of Keith's amps. I stood behind the amps, looking around. There were people all over the stage, most of them Angels and their women. The Angels were pushing off everybody who wasn't an Angel or part of the stage crew. I had seen Angels before, and *en masse* they were just as I'd expected: filthy boots and jeans or motorcycle leathers, one bearded specimen wearing a bear's head for a hat, looking as if he had two ferocious grizzly heads, one on top of the other.

Through the PA system Sam was saying, 'The reason we can't start is that the stage is loaded with people. I've done all I can do. The stage must be cleared or we can't start.' His voice sounded dead tired and flat and beyond caring.

An Angel—President Sonny Barger of the Oakland chapter, I believe—took the mike and said, in a voice not unlike Howlin' Wolf's, 'All right, everybody off the stage, including the Hell's Angels,' and people started to move. Angels were on top of the trucks, behind the stage, on the side of the stage, on the steps to the stage. I was holding my notebook, thinking, God, where to begin, when I was wheeled around—'All *right, off* the *stage.*' Looking to see what had me, I found this body to my left, dressed in greasy denim, but no head. Still, it picked me up by the biceps so quickly and brought me with such dispatch to its eye level that I couldn't complain about losing lots of time. Its eyes were hidden under the lank rat-blond hair that fell over its grime-blackened face. There they were, glints in the gloom, but they were not looking at me or at anything; it was so high it was blind.

Eyeballs rolling like porcelain marbles in their sockets, jaws grinding, teeth gnashing saliva in anger, '*Off the stage,*' he repeated in mild admonition, gentle reproof. It was that ever fresh, ever new, ever magic moment when you are about to be beaten to a pulp or to whatever your assailant can manage. I was in mid-air, still holding my notebook, thinking that I could reach up and blind him; I could put my hands behind his head and bring my knee up fast, depriving him of his teeth; or I could shove two fingers into his nostrils and rip his face off; but a little bird on the hillside was telling me that the moment I did any of these things, five hundred Angels would start stomping. I don't remember what I told him. My next clear memory is of being alone again behind the amps. I wasn't even wearing any badges. Earlier today, on the way to the helicopter, Ronnie had been talking about newspapermen calling for press passes, not believing there weren't any. It's free, he told them, just come. Free at last. Well, not exactly.

The Stones were coming up the four steps between the trucks on to the stage, a brightly-lit centre in the black fold of hills. The crowd, estimated by the news media at between two and five hundred thousand, had been tightly packed when we struggled through it about five hours ago. Now it was one solid mass jammed against the stage. There were eager-eyed boys and girls down front, Angels all around, tour guards trying to maintain positions between the Angels and the Stones. A New York City detective at Altamont was a long way off his beat. The expressions on the cops' faces said they didn't like this scene at all, but they weren't scared, just sorrowful-eyed like men who knew trouble and knew that they were in the midst of a lot of people who were asking for it. Against the stage, in the centre of the crowd, a black cop with a moustache watched, his expression mournful, his white canvas golf-hat brim pulled down as if he were in a downpour.

Sam came to the singer's mike and in an infinitely weary voice said, 'One, two, testing.' Then with a glimmer of enthusiasm, 'I'd like to introduce to everybody—from Britain—the Rolling Stones.'

There was a small cheer from the crowd—they seemed numb, not vibrant like the audiences after Tina Turner—whoops and yells and shrieks but not one great roar. Bass-thumps, guitars tuning, drum flummers, Mick: 'All right! Whoooooh!'—rising note—'Oww babe! Aw yeah! Aww, so good to see ya *all*! Whoo!' Last tuning notes, then the opening chords of 'Jumpin' Jack Flash'.

I was born in a cross-fire hurricane
And I howled at my ma in the drivin' rain
But it's all right, it's all right
In fact it's a gas

Some people were dancing, Angels dancing with their dirty bouffant women. A pall of wariness and fear seemed to be upon the people who were not too stoned to be aware, but the music was pounding on and though the drums were not properly miked and the guitars seemed to separate and disappear in places and you couldn't really hear Wyman's bass, it was hanging together.

'Ooh, yah,' Mick said as the song ended. He stopped dancing, looked into the distance, and his voice, which had been subdued, now began to sound pacific, as he glimpsed for the first time the enormity of what he had created. One surge forward and people would be crushed. Half a million people together, with neither rules nor regulations. 'There are so many of you—just be cool down front now, don't push around—just keep still.' He laughed as if he were talking to a child, looking down at the pretty stoned faces before him. 'Keep together.'

Keith tested the first three notes of 'Carol', unleashed the riff, and Mick leaned back to sing:

Oh, Carol! Don't ever steal your heart away
I'm gonna learn to dance if it takes me all night and day

The sound was better, drums and bass clearer, guitars stronger. At the end Mick hoisted a bottle of Jack Daniel's that was sitting in front of the drums. 'I'd like to drink one to you all.'

Keith set out on 'Sympathy for the Devil'. As Mick sang, '*I was around when Jesus Christ had his moment of doubt and pain,*' there was a low explosive *thump!* in the crowd to the right of the stage and an oily blue-white smoke. People were pushing, falling, a great hole opening as they moved instantly away from the centre of the trouble. I had no idea people in a crowd could move so fast. Mick stopped singing but the music chugged on, four bars, eight, then Mick shouted: 'Hey! Heeey! Hey! Keith—Keith—*Keith*!' By now only Keith was playing, but he was playing as loud and hard as ever, the way the band is supposed to play until the audience tears down the chicken wire and comes onstage with chairs and broken bottles. 'Will you cool it and I'll try and stop it,' Mick said, so Keith stopped.

'Hey—hey, peo-ple,' Mick said. 'Sisters—brothers and sisters—*brothers* and *sisters*—come *on* now. That means everybody just cool *out*—will you cool out, everybody—'

'Somebody's bike blew up, man,' Keith said.

'I know,' Mick said. 'I'm hip. Everybody be cool now, come on—all right? Can we still make it down in the front? Can we still collect ourselves, everybody? Can everybody just—I don't know what happened, I couldn't see, but I hope you all right—are you all right?' The trouble spot seemed still. Charlie was making eager drum flutters, Keith playing stray notes.

'Okay,' Mick said. 'Let's just give ourselves—we'll give ourselves another half a minute before we get our breath back, everyone just cool down and easy—is there anyone there who's hurt? Huh? Everyone all right? Okay. All right.' The music was starting again. 'Good, we can groove. Something very funny happens when we start that numbah!'

Keith and Charlie had the rhythm pattern going, tight and expert, and Mick asked again to be allowed to introduce himself, a man of wealth and taste, but not about to lay anybody's soul to waste. Keith's solo cut like a scream into the brain, as Mick chanted, 'Everybody got to cool out. Everybody has got to cool right out—yeah! Aw right!'

Sounding like one instrument, a mad whirling bagpipe, the Stones chugged to a halt. But the crowd didn't stop, we could see Hell's Angels spinning like madmen, swinging at people. To the right a tall white boy with a black cloud of electric hair was dancing, shaking, infuriating the Angels by having too good a time. He was beside an Angel when I first saw him, and I wondered how he could be so loose, nearly touching one of those monsters. He went on dancing and the

Angel pushed him and another Angel started laying into the crowd with a pool cue and then a number of Angels were grabbing people, hitting and kicking, the crowd falling back from the fury with fantastic speed, the dancer running away from the stage, the crowd parting before him like the Red Sea, the Angels catching him from behind, the heavy end of a pool cue in one long arc crashing into the side of his head, felling him like a sapling so that he lay straight and didn't move and I thought, My God, they've killed him. But they weren't through. When he went down they were all over him, pounding with fists and cues, and when he was just lying there they stood for a while kicking him like kicking the dead carcass of an animal, the meat shaking on the bones.

The song was over and Mick was saying, 'Who—who—who's fighting and what for? Hey, peo-ple—who's fighting and what for? Why are we fighting? Why are we fighting?' His voice was strong, emphasizing each word. 'We don't want to fight. Come on—who wants to fight? Hey—I—you know, I mean like—every other scene has been cool. We've gotta stop them right now. You know, we can't, there's no point.'

Sam took the microphone. 'Could I suggest a compromise, please.' He was a bit more awake now. 'Can I ask please to speak to the—.' He stopped then because the logical conclusion was—'to the Hell's Angels and ask them please to stop performing mayhem on people.'

'Either those cats cool it,' Keith said, 'or we don't play. There's not that many of 'em.'

It was a fine brave thing to say, but I had made up my mind about fighting the Hell's Angels while one of them had me in the air, and probably the rest of the people present had concluded some time ago that the first man who touched an Angel would surely die. Even as Keith spoke an Angel was ripping into someone in front of stage left. 'That guy there,' Keith said, 'if he doesn't stop it—'

There was a pause while another Angel did slowly stop him. Still another Angel yelled to ask Keith what he wanted. 'I just want him to stop pushing people around,' Keith said.

An Angel came to the mike and bellowed into it. 'Hey, if you don't cool it you ain't gonna hear no more music! Now, you wanta all go home, or what?' It was like blaming the pigs in a slaughter-house for bleeding on the floor.

Stu, in his blue windbreaker, was at the mike, saying in a cool but unhappy voice, 'We need doctors down here *now,* please. Can we have a doctor down here now to the front?'

I felt that in the next seconds or minutes we could die, and there was nothing we could do to prevent it, to improve the odds for survival. A bad dream, and we were all in it.

I looked around, checking my position, which if not the worst was not good, and saw David Maysles on top of a truck behind the stage. He and Al Maysles were up there with their cameras, and more people, including a couple of Hell's Angels, were sitting in front dangling their legs over the side like little boys fishing at a creek.

'Hey! David!' I said.

'You want to get up here?'

'Sure.' I stuck my notebook behind my belt and swung aboard, being careful not to jostle the Angels. At least now I would be behind them, instead of having it the other way round, which had given me worse chills than the wind did up here. It was cold away from the warm amps but this was, I hoped, a safer place and better to see from.

Hunkered behind the Angels, I noticed that only one wore colours; the other one in his cowboy hat and motorcycle boots was just a sympathizer. Sam was saying, 'The doctor is going through in a green jumper and he's just here—' pointing in front '—waving his hand in the air, look.' The mass, like a dumb aquatic beast, had closed up again except for a little space around the body. (The boy didn't die, to my—and probably his—surprise.) 'Can you let the doctor go through please and let him get to the person who's hurt?'

Charlie was playing soft rolls, Keith was playing a slow blues riff. 'Let's play cool-out music,' Keith said to Mick.

They played a repeating twelve-bar pattern that stopped in half a minute. 'Keep going,' Mick said, and it started again, a meditative walking-bass line, the Stones trying to orient themselves by playing an Elmore James/Jimmy Reed song they had played in damp London caverns. '*The sun is shining on both sides of the street,*' Mick sang. '*I got a smile on my face for every little girl I meet.*' The slow blues did seem to help things, a little. A huge Angel with long blond hair, brown suede vest, no shirt, blue jeans, was standing behind gentle Charlie, patting his foot, one giant hand resting on Charlie's white wool pullover. The song ended without event and Mick said, 'We all dressed up, we got no place to go,' which was all too true.

JOSE

'Stray Cat,' Keith said, but there was another flurry of fighting to the right, partly hidden from us by the PA scaffolding, a tower of speakers.

'Hey—heyheyhey, look,' Mick said. Then to Keith or to no one he said, 'Those *scenes* down there.'

I leaned forward and spoke to the cowboy hat. 'What's happening,' I asked. 'Why are they fighting?'

Over his shoulder, out of the corner of his mouth, he said, 'Some smart asshole, man, some wise guy wants to start trouble. And these guys are tired, man, they been here all night. Some wise guy starts something, they don't like it. Arhh, I can't tell you what happened.' Taking a jug of acid-apple juice from his Angel friend, he drank till his eyes looked, as Wynonie Harris used to say, like two cherries in a glass of buttermilk. Me, I lay low.

'Stray Cat' started, Mick sounding perfunctory, forgetting the words here and there, Keith playing madly.

A girl down front was shaking with the music and crying. In the backstage aisle between the trucks, the Angels and their women were doing their stiff jerking dance. Most of the women were hard-looking tattooed types with shellacked hairdos, but one of them, no more than fourteen, with a dirty, pretty-baby face, wearing a black leather jacket, was moving the seat of her greasy jeans wildly.

The Angel standing with his hand on Charlie's shoulder was being asked to step down off the stage by one of the New York heavies, a red-faced, red-haired, beefy man. You could follow what they were saying by their gestures. The cop told the Angel to step down, the Angel shook his head, the cop told him again and pushed him a little. The cop had a cigarette in his mouth and the Angel took it out, just plucked it from between the cop's lips like taking a rose from the mouth of the fair Carmen, causing the cop to regard the Angel with a sorrowful countenance. It was only when two more New York heavies turned around and faced the Angel with expressions equally dolorous that he went down the steps. He came back a minute later but stayed at the rear of the stage, dancing and twitching.

As 'Stray Cat' ended, Mick said, 'Ooh baby,' looking up as if for deliverance and finding a shapeless human mass reaching into the darkness as far as he could see. 'Baby. All along a hillside. Hey, everybody. Ah—what are we gonna do?'

'Love in Vain,' Keith said. The slow elegant Robert Johnson line began, building slowly. '*I followed her to the station with my suitcase in my hand. Oh, it's hard to tell, when all your love's in vain.*' The Stones had not forgotten how to play, but nobody seemed to be enjoying the music, at least nobody who could be seen in the lights that made the stage the glowing centre of a world of night. Too many people were still too close together and the Angels were still surly. To the right, an Angel with a skinful of acid was writhing and wringing his hands in a pantomime of twisting Mick's neck. At stage left Timothy Leary huddled with his wife and daughter, looking as if he'd taken better trips.

'Aw yeah,' Mick said as the song ended. 'Hey, I think, I think, I think, that one good idea came out of that number, which was, that the only way you're gonna keep yourselves cool is to *sit down.* If you can do it I think you'll find it's better. So are you sitting comfortably—now, boys and girls—are you sitting comfortably? When, when we get to the end and we all want to go absolutely crazy and jump on each other then we'll stand up again—d'you know what I mean? But we can't seem to keep it together, standing up—okay?'

In the background Keith was tooling up the opening chords of 'Under My Thumb.' A few people in front of the stage were sitting, going along with Mick, who for the first time in his life had asked an audience to sit down. The anarchist was telling people what to do. Then, just before he began to sing, he said, 'But it ain't a rule.'

'Under My Thumb' started. '*Hey! Hey! Under my thumb is a girl who once had me down—*' and Mick had sung only the first line of the song when there was a sudden movement in the crowd to the left. I looked away from Mick and saw, bordered with falling bodies, a black man in a black hat, black shirt, iridescent blue-green suit, arms and legs stuck out at crazy angles, a nickle-plated revolver in his hand. The gun waved in the lights for a second, two, then he was hit, so hard, by so many Angels, that I didn't see the first one, short, Mexican-looking, as he jumped into the air. But I saw him as he came down, burying a long knife in the black man's back. Angels covered the black man like flies on a carcass. The attack carried the victim behind the stack of speakers, and I never saw him again.

The black man, Meredith Hunter, nicknamed Murdock, was eighteen years old. Paul Cox was standing beside him before the violence started. 'An Angel kept looking over at me and I tried to ignore him. He kept looking, and the next thing I know he's hassling this Negro boy at my side. And I was trying not to look at him, and then he reached over and shook this boy by the side of the head—thinking it was fun, laughing. Something was going to happen so I backed off.

'The boy yanked away, and next thing I know he was flying in the air—like so many others that night. He scrambled to his feet, and, backing away, he was trying to run from the Angels, and all these Angels started chasing—a couple had jumped off the stage and another couple was running alongside. His girlfriend was screaming and he had pulled out his gun. He held it in the air—his girlfriend was climbing on him and pushing him back—and then some Angel stepped out of the crowd, leaped up and brought this knife down in his back. The Angel stabbed him again, and while he was stabbing him, the boy started running. This Negro boy was running into the crowd, and you could see him stiffen up each time he was stabbed.

'He ran toward me, and fell down on his knees. A Hell's Angel grabbed both his shoulders and kicked him in the face about five times. He let go and the boy fell on his face. He muttered some words. He said, "I wasn't going to shoot you."

'One of the Hell's Angels asked, "Why did you have a gun?" but he didn't wait for an answer. He grabbed one of those garbage cans, the ones with the metal rims, and smashed the boy over the head with it, and then started kicking his head in. Five others joined, kicking the boy's head in. Kicked him all over the place. And then the guy who started the whole thing stood on the boy's head for a minute or so and then walked off. And no one would let us touch the boy for about two or three minutes. "Don't touch him, let him die."'

The Stones had stopped playing. 'Okay, man,' Keith said, 'look, we're splitting, if those cats, if you can't—we're splitting, if those people don't stop beating everybody up in sight. I want 'em *out of the way.*'

An Angel in front of the stage was trying to tell Keith something, but Keith wouldn't listen. 'I don't want *you* to tell me'—he went on, but another Angel, onstage, stopped him.

'Look, man,' the Angel said, 'a guy's got a gun out there, and he's shooting at the stage—'

'Got a gun,' someone else yelled.

Mike Lang, one of the organizers of Woodstock, who had been helping with this concert, took the microphone. 'People. Hey, people. C'mon, let's be cool. People, please—there's no reason to hassle anybody, please don't be mad at anybody. Please relax and sit down....'

Sam, who'd been standing by with his hands jammed in his pockets, took over. 'If you move back and sit down,' he said, 'we can continue and we will continue. We need a doctor under the left-hand scaffold as soon as possible please.' He was listening to shouts from the front of the crowd. He listened to a girl for a few seconds and went on: 'There's a Red Cross building at the top of the stage and there's been lots of lost children, under the scaffold. If you've lost a child go and collect him or her there please. It's a Red Cross van.'

After another pause during which no one onstage did anything but look anxiously around, Mick said, 'It seems to be stuck down to me. Will you listen to me for a minute? First of all, everyone is going to get to the side of the stage who's on it now except for the Stones who are playing. Please, everyone. Please, can you get to the side of the stage who's not playing? Right? That's a start. Now, the thing is, I can't see what's going on, who is doing what. It's just a scuffle. All I can ask you, San Francisco, is this: this could be the most beautiful evening we've had this winter. Don't fuck it up. Let's get it together. Everyone, come *on* now. I can't see you up on the hillsides. You're probably very cool. Down here we're not so cool, we've got a lot of hassles going on.'

There were shouts from the darkness. Mick peered out blindly past the stage lights. 'You know,' he said with a sudden burst of passion, 'if we *are* all one, let's fucking well *show* we're all one. Now there's one thing we need. Sam, we need an ambulance, we need a doctor by that scaffold there. If there's a doctor, can he get to there? Okay, we're gonna, we gonna do—I don't know what the fuck we gonna do. Everyone just sit down. Keep cool. Let's just *relax,* let's get into a groove. Come on, we can get it together. Come on.'

'Under My Thumb' was starting to churn again. The band sounded amazingly sharp. The crowd was still. Without knowing exactly what, we all felt that something bad had happened. I assumed, and I was not given to flights of horrible imaginings, that the Angels had killed several people. Someone told me that he had seen Meredith Hunter lifted up, with a great spreading ketchup-coloured stain on the back of his suit. Ronnie was running to the First Aid tent, outdistancing the Hell's Angel who had been leading him, and Meredith Hunter was already there when Ronnie came up, calling for a doctor. A cop said, 'You don't have to scream for a doctor for this guy, he's dead.'

Over the last notes of 'Under My Thumb,' Mick sang, '*It's all right, I pray that it's all right, I pray that it's all right, it's all right—*'

'Let's do "Brown Sugar",' Mick Taylor said. The Stones had recorded it illegally, only two days before.

'Thank you,' Mick said to the crowd. 'Thank you. Are we all getting it together? We gonna do one for you which we just ah—' pausing, remembering that making the record was breaking the law '—we just ah—you've never heard it before because we've just written it for you. *We gonna play it for you for the very first time, it's called "Brown Sugar".*'

Scarred old slaver knows he's doin' all right
Hear him whip the women, just around midnight
Oh—Brown Sugar—how come you taste so good
Oh—Brown Sugar—just like a black girl should

It was a song of sadism, savagery, race hate and race love, a song of redemption, a song that accepted the fear of night, blackness, chaos, the unknown.

'Ahhh, one mo' time—whoo, baby. Yeah—thank you—awww.' Taking a harp from Stu, Mick played a few menacing riffs of 'Midnight Rambler'. Keith had changed guitars and was tuning again. Mick played soft harp notes that trailed off as, head bent over the mike, he began singing lullaby phrases. A few more notes on the harp, and then, as if he were coming out of a reverie, gaining strength with each word, Mick said, 'We gonna do you one which we hope you'll *dig*—which is called "The Midnight Rambler".'

Sighing down the wind so sadly—
Listen and you'll hear him moan
I'm talkin' 'bout the Midnight Rambler
And everybody got to go

The song had scared me when I first heard it, because it was true, as nobody at Altamont could deny, the dark is filled with terror, murder and evil. *'I'll stick my knife right down your throat, honey, and it hurts!'*

Things seemed to be settling down, as if the killer-lover lament had worked some psychic release on the crowd.

'Aw yah! Aw yah! Stand up if you can stand up,' Mick said. 'Stand up if you can keep it cool.' He raised the Jack Daniel's bottle. 'One more drink to you all.' He drank and spoke again in his lullaby tone, 'Awww, babies.... It's so—sssweet! It's really sssweet! Would you like to live with each other? I mean, you're really close to each other.' He stared into the crowd and seemed to drift away again. 'Wow,' he said.

'You ready?' Keith asked.

'Yah, I'm ready,' Mick said.

'One, two, three, faw,' Keith snarled, and they started 'Live with Me.'

Around the stage people were dancing, but in front of the stage, staring at Mick, one curly-haired boy in a sailor's cap was saying, 'Mick, Mick, no'—I could read his lips. Behind the boy a fat black-haired girl, naked to the waist, was dancing, squeezing her enormous breasts, mouth open, eyes focused on a point somewhere north of her forehead. As the song ended, the girl, her skin rose-florid, tried to take the stage. Completely naked now, she climbed over the crowd to get a foot onstage, but five Angels were at once between her and the Stones. They kicked and punched her back, her weight falling on the people behind her.

'Hold it,' Mick said.

'Stop that one,' Keith said.

'Hey—heyheyheyheyheyheyhey*hey*! One cat can control that chick, y'know what I mean. Hey fellows, hey fellows. One of you can control her, man,' Mick said, speaking the last sentence to the Angel nearest him onstage.

'Yeah, we're gonna do it,' the Angel said, in a world of his own, as were all the Angels who were trying to reach the girl with fists or boots, wanting to get down there to grab her, smash her face, stomp her, thumb her crazy eyes out, kick her till she bled to death.

'Hey, come on, fellows,' Mick was saying, getting a bit frantic. 'One of you can control one little girl. Come on now. Like—like—like—just sit down, honey,' he said to the girl, who was in fact on her back.

'Fellows,' Mick said, trying to move the Angels gently away, 'can you clear out. Let—let—let them deal with her. They can deal with her.' The people in front were managing to reach the girl, the Angels wanting to stay and get their hands on her. 'Fellows, come on, fellows,' Mick said, 'they're all right.'

Keith started playing and Wyman and Charlie and Mick Taylor joined in, as the Angels slunk bloodlusty to the side. Mick was singing:

Yeah, I see the storm is threatening
My very life today
If I don't get some shelter
I'm gonna fade away
War, children, it's just a shot away

How are we gonna get out of here? I wondered. *Will* we get out, or will we die here? Is it going to snap and the Angels kill themselves and all of us in a savage rage of nihilism, the plain to be found in the morning a bloody soup littered with teeth and bones, one last mad Angel, blinded by a comrade's boots and brass knuckles, gut sliced asunder by his partner's frogsticker, growling, tearing at the yawning slit under his filthy T-shirt, chomping on his own bloody blue-white entrails.

'*Rape, murder, it's just a shot away,*' Mick sang over and over. In the crowd to the left, where the trouble with the black boy had taken place, an Angel was punching someone, but the victim went down fast and it was over.

'Yuhh,' Mick said, very low, then 'Yuhhh,' again, lower, like a man making a terrible discovery. 'Okay… are we okay, I know we are.' He was looking into the crowd. As if he had woken up once again, he shouted, 'Are you having a good ti-i-ime? OOH-yeah!'

'Little Queenie' was starting; it was the moment in the show when the lights went on to reveal rapt fresh faces. But not tonight. Even the people who were dancing in spite of the danger looked unhappy. At times Mick's voice sounded light, as if he had lost the bottom part of it, but Keith was playing like a man ready to dance on his own grave.

The song ended to cheers from the crowd. 'I—I—I thank you very much,' Mick said. 'Thank you very much.' The opening notes of 'Satisfaction' turned on like a current of electricity. It would probably never be played better. Charlie kept a straight boogaloo like the Otis Redding version and it went on and on, Mick chanting, '*We got to find it, got to find it, got to find it... early in the mornin', late in the evenin'*—' He shouted the song to an end, gave three Indian-style war whoops, and as his voice died to a whisper, looked out at the multitude, hundreds of thousands of people who had come because he had asked them, and he could give them nothing better than this, mayhem and terror.

'Justliketosaaaayyy,' Mick said, then paused and seemed to lose himself once more, wondering what it was he'd like to say. After a moment he went on briskly: 'Well, there's been a few hangups you know, but I mean generally, I mean, you've been beau-ti-ful— All the loose women may stand and put their hands up. All the loose women put their hands up!' But the loose women were tired like everybody else. A few girls stood up, a few hands were raised into the murk. On this night no one would think of playing 'I'm Free', though that had been the whole idea of the concert, to give some sense of genuine freedom to Ralph Gleason's rock-and-roll-starved proletariat and to get away from the violence of the system, the cops' clubs, Klein's mop-handle. The biggest group of playmates in history was having recess, with no teachers to protect them from the bad boys, the bullies, who may have been mistreated children and worthy of understanding but would nevertheless kill you. The Stones' music was strong but it could not stop the terror. There was a look of disbelief on the people's faces, wondering how the Stones could go on playing and singing in the face of this madness and violent death. Not many hands were in the air, and Mick said, 'That's not enough, we haven't got many loose women, what're you gonna do?'

The band started 'Honky Tonk Women,' playing as well as if they were in a studio, Keith's lovely horrible harmonies sailing out into the cool night air. Nobody, not even the guardians of public morality at *Rolling Stone* who pronounced that 'Altamont was the product of diabolical egotism, hype, ineptitude, money manipulation, and, at base, a fundamental lack of concern for humanity,' could say that the Rolling Stones couldn't play like the devil when the chips were down.

The last song, 'Street Fighting Man', started. '*The time is right for fighting in the street,*' Mick sang, a leader with an international constituency, unable to save anyone.

Ah, but what can a poor boy do
But to sing with a rock 'n' roll band
'Cause in sleepy London town
There's just no place for a street fighting man.

The music pounded hard. '*Bye, bye bye bye,*' Mick sang. '*Bye bye bye bye.*' Stu handed me Keith's twelve-string guitar and told me that the station wagons to take us to the helicopters would be at the top of the hill, straight back and up to the left. I slipped off the truck, taking the guitar by the neck, and struck out into the night, trying to get the people in the passageway between the backstage trucks to move and let me out. '*Please let me through,*' I shouted.

Behind me Mick was saying, '*Bye—by-y-y-y-e—bye,*' as I plunged on among shouts from unknown voices, trying not to run into people. I heard the Stones coming, all of us stumbling through the fucking blackness. At last, with our lives, we were off the stage, struggling through the dark, trying not to lose anyone. 'Regroup!' Ronnie's voice rasped, and then we had reached the hillside, a steep slope that we were scrambling up through dusty clay and dead grass, me on one hand, elbow, and knees, holding the guitar. At the top of the hill was a cyclone fence, but we passed through a hole in it, still running, to a car and an ambulance. I got into the back of the ambulance, followed by half a dozen or so New York heavies. Blowing the horns, we drove through the crowd, moving as fast as we could. When we stopped near a helicopter and got out, I gave the guitar to Sam. The Stones and so many others—Astrid, Jo, Ronnie, Sam, Tony, David Horowitz, Jon Jaymes, Ethan Russell, and more—boarded the small aircraft. I stood just outside the spinning blades wondering what would happen if I was left, lost in the blackness in this crowd, but Sam called, 'Come on!' Michelle got on and then I got on. A little bulbous capsule, packed with heads and knees. The helicopter was shaking and lifting like an ostrich waking up, its hums and rattles drowning out everything except shouts.

In a few minutes the over-loaded helicopter descended at a small airport, dropping too fast, the ground rushing up at us. We hit sharply but kept upright and bounced flat. We climbed out as Keith,

walking under the blades headed for the airport terminal, was complaining about the Angels: 'They're sick, man. They're worse than the cops. They're just not ready.'

Mick sat on a wooden bench in the little airport. He was bewildered and scared, unable to comprehend what had happened—who the Hell's Angels were or why they were killing people at his free peace-and-love show. 'How could anybody think those people are good, think they're people you should have around' he said. 'I'd rather have had cops,' Mick said.

Keith was walking around. 'If Rock Scully doesn't know any more about things than that, man: to think the Angels are—what did he say?—honour and dignity? They're homicidal maniacs. They should be thrown in jail.'

Mick had said he'd rather have cops, and now Keith wanted to throw the bastards in jail.

Following the tour that ended with Altamont, I went to live in England and stayed until, after a certain weekend at Redlands, I decided that if Keith and I kept dipping into the same bag, we would both be dead.

I spent a great deal of time with the Stones on later tours, and they were always good, but there never seemed to be so much at stake. For one thing, we were never again in the desert, beyond all laws. At later Stones' concerts I gave my seat to people like Sir John Gielgud and once to a candidate for vice-president of the United States. Guitar players, producers and women—except for Shirley Watts and Astrid, who finally began calling herself Astrid Wyman—came and went. Terrible and wonderful things happened—in concert halls, outdoor arenas, nightclubs, jail-houses, courtrooms, bedrooms—and we persisted in our folly.

from Harvill Press

GRANTA

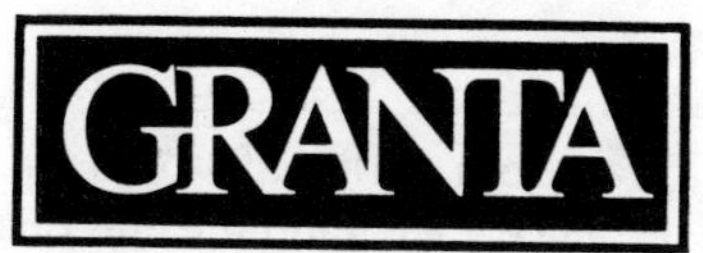

RAYMOND CARVER
THE CABIN

Mr Harrold came out of the café to find it'd stopped snowing. The sky was clearing behind the hills on the other side of the river. He stopped beside the car for a minute and stretched, holding the car door open while he drew a big mouthful of cold air. He'd swear he could almost taste this air. He eased in behind the steering wheel and got back on the highway. It was only an hour's drive to the lodge. He could get in a couple of hours of fishing this afternoon. Then there was tomorrow. All day tomorrow.

At Parke Junction he took the bridge over the river and turned off on to the road that would take him to the lodge. Pine trees whose branches were heavy with snow stood on either side of the road. Clouds mantled the white hills so that it was hard to tell where the hills ended and the sky began. It reminded him of those Chinese landscapes they'd looked at that time in the museum in Portland. He liked them. He'd said as much to Frances, but she didn't say anything back. She'd spent a few minutes with him in that wing of the gallery and then moved on to the next exhibit.

It was going on noon when he reached the lodge. He saw the cabins up on the hill and then, as the road straightened out, the lodge itself. He slowed, bumped off the road on to the dirty, sand-covered parking lot, and stopped the car close up to the front door. He rolled down the window and rested for a minute, working his shoulders back and forth into the seat. He closed and then opened his eyes. A flickering neon sign said *Castlerock* and below that, on a neat, hand-painted sign, DELUXE CABINS—OFFICE. The last time he'd been here—Frances had been with him that time—they'd stayed for four days, and he'd landed five nice fish down river. That had been three years ago. They used to come here often, two or three times a year. He opened the door and got out of the car slowly, feeling the stiffness in his back and neck. He walked heavily across the frozen snow and stuck his hands in his coat pockets as he started up the planked steps. At the top he scraped the snow and grit off his shoes and nodded to a young couple coming out. He noticed the way the man held the woman's arm as they went down the steps.

Inside the lodge there was the smell of wood smoke and fried ham. He heard the clatter of dishes. He looked at the big Brown trout mounted over the fireplace in the dining-room, and he felt glad to be back. Near the cash register, where he stood, was a display case with leather purses, wallets, and pairs of moccasins arranged behind the glass. Scattered around on top of the case were Indian bead necklaces and bracelets and pieces of petrified wood. He moved over to the horseshoe-shaped counter and took a stool. Two men sitting a few stools down stopped talking and turned their heads to look at him. They were hunters, and their red hats and coats lay on an empty table behind them. Mr Harrold waited and pulled at his fingers.

'How long you been here?' the girl asked, frowning. She'd come on him soundlessly, from the kitchen. She put down a glass of water in front of him.

'Not long,' Mr Harrold said.

'You should've rung the bell,' she said. Her braces glittered as she opened and closed her mouth.

'I'm supposed to have a cabin,' he said. 'I wrote you a card and made a reservation a week or so ago.'

'I'll have to get Mrs Maye,' the girl said. 'She's cooking. She's the one who looks after the cabins. She didn't say anything to me about it. We don't usually keep them open in the winter, you know.'

'I wrote you a card,' he said. 'You check with Mrs Maye. You ask her about it.' The two men had turned on their stools to look at him again.

'I'll get Mrs Maye,' the girl said.

Flushed, he closed his hands together on the counter in front of him. A big Frederic Remington reproduction hung on the wall at the far end of the room. He watched the lurching, frightened buffalo, and the Indians with the drawn bows fixed at their shoulders.

'Mr Harrold!' the old woman called, hobbling towards him. She was a small grey-haired woman with heavy breasts and a fat throat. The straps of her underwear showed through her white uniform. She undid her apron and held out her hand.

'Glad to see you, Mrs Maye,' he said, as he got up off the stool.

'I hardly recognized you,' the old woman said. 'I don't know what's the matter with the girl sometimes...Edith...she's my granddaughter. My daughter and her husband are looking after the place now.' She took her glasses off and began wiping away the steam from the lenses.

He looked down at the polished counter. He smoothed his fingers over the grainy wood.

'Where's the Missus?' she asked.

'She didn't feel too well this week,' Mr Harrold said. He started to say something else, but there was nothing else to say.

'I'm sorry to hear that! I had the cabin fixed up nice for the two of you,' Mrs Maye said. She took off the apron and put it behind the cash register. 'Edith! I'm taking Mr Harrold to his cabin! I'll have to get my coat, Mr Harrold.' The girl didn't answer. But she came to the kitchen door with a coffee pot in her hand and stared at them.

Outside, the sun had come out and the glare hurt his eyes. He held on to the banister and went slowly down the stairs, following Mrs Maye, who limped.

'Sun's bad, isn't it?' she said, moving carefully over the packed snow. He felt she ought to be using a cane. 'The first time it's been out all week,' she said. She waved at some people going by in a car.

They went past a gasoline pump, locked and covered with snow, and past a little shed with a TYRES sign hung over the door. He looked through the broken windows at the heaps of burlap sacks inside, the old tyres, and the barrels. The room was damp and cold-looking. Snow had drifted inside and lay sprinkled on the sill around the broken glass.

'Kids have done that,' Mrs Maye said, stopping for a minute and putting her hand up to the broken window. 'They don't miss a chance to do us dirt. A whole pack of them are all the time running wild from down at the construction camp.' She shook her head. 'Poor little devils. Sorry home life for kids, anyway, always on the move like that. Their daddies are building that dam.' She unlocked the cabin door and pushed on it. 'I laid a little fire this morning so it would be nice for you,' she said.

'I appreciate that, Mrs Maye,' he said.

There was a big double bed covered with a plain bedspread, a bureau, and a desk in the front room, which was divided from the kitchen by a little plywood partition. There was also a sink, wood stove, woodbox, an old ice-box, an oilcloth-covered table and two wooden chairs. A door opened to a bathroom. He saw a little porch to one side where he could hang his clothes.

'Looks fine,' he said.

'I tried to make it as nice as I could,' she said. 'Do you need anything now, Mr Harrold?'

'Not now anyway, thanks,' he said.

'I'll let you rest then. You're probably tired, driving all that way,' she said.

'I should bring in my things,' Mr Harrold said, following her out. He shut the door behind them and they stood on the porch looking down the hill.

'I'm just sorry your wife couldn't come,' the old woman said.

He didn't answer.

From where they stood they were almost on a level with the huge rock protruding from the hillside behind the road. Some people said it looked like a petrified castle.

'How's the fishing?' he said.

'Some of them are getting fish, but most of the men are out hunting,' she said. 'Deer season, you know.'

He drove the car as close as he could to the cabin and started to unload. The last thing he took out of the car was a pint of Scotch from the glove compartment. He set the bottle on the table. Later, as he spread out the boxes of weights and hooks and thick-bodied red and white flies, he moved the bottle to the draining-board. Sitting there at the table smoking a cigarette with his tackle box open and everything in its place, his flies and the weights spread out, testing leader strength between his hands and tying up outfits for that afternoon, he was glad he'd come after all. And he'd still be able to get in a couple of hours fishing this afternoon. Then there was tomorrow. He'd already decided he would save some of the bottle for when he came back from fishing that afternoon and have the rest for tomorrow.

As he sat at the table tying up outfits, he thought he heard something digging out on the porch. He got up from the table and opened the door. But there was nothing there. There were only the white hills and the dead-looking pines under the overcast sky and, down below, the few buildings and some cars drawn up beside the highway. He was all at once very tired and thought he would lie down on the bed for a few minutes. He didn't want to sleep. He'd just lie down and rest, and then he'd get up, dress, take his things, and walk down to the river. He cleaned off the table, undressed, and then got in between the cold sheets. For a while he lay on his side, eyes closed, knees drawn up for warmth, then he turned on to his back and wiggled his toes against the sheet. He wished Frances were here. He wished there were somebody to talk to.

He opened his eyes. The room was dark. The stove gave off little crackling noises, and there was a red glow on the wall behind the stove. He lay in bed and stared at the window, not able to believe it was really dark outside. He shut his eyes again and then opened them. He'd only wanted to rest. He hadn't intended to fall asleep. He opened his eyes and sat up heavily on the side of the bed. He got on his shirt and reached for his trousers. He went into the bathroom and threw water on his face.

'God-damn it!' he said, banging things around in the kitchen cupboard, taking down some cans and putting them back again. He made a pot of coffee and drank two cups before deciding to go down to the café for something to eat. He put on wool slippers and a coat and hunted around until he found his flashlight. Then he went outside.

The cold air stung his cheeks and pinched his nostrils together. But the air felt good to him. It cleared his head. The lights from the lodge showed him where he was walking, and he was careful. Inside the café, he nodded to the girl, Edith, and sat down in a booth near the end of the counter. He could hear a radio playing back in the kitchen. The girl made no effort to wait on him.

'Are you closed?' Mr Harrold said.

'Kind of. I'm cleaning up for the morning,' she said.

'Too late for something to eat then,' he said.

'I guess I can get you something,' she said. She came over with a menu.

'Mrs Maye around, Edith?'

'She's up in her room. Did you need her for something?'

'I need more wood. For in the morning.'

'It's out back,' she said. 'Right here behind the kitchen.'

He pointed to something simple on the menu—a ham sandwich with potato salad. 'I'll have this,' he said.

As he waited, he began moving the salt and pepper shakers around in a little circle in front of him. After she brought his plate to him, she hung around, filling sugar bowls and napkin holders, looking up at him from time to time. Pretty soon, before he'd finished, she came over with a wet rag and began wiping off his table.

He left some money, considerably more than the bill, and went out through a door at the side of the lodge. He went around the back where he picked up an armload of wood. Then the snail's-pace climb up to the cabin. He looked back once and saw the girl watching him from the kitchen window. By the time he had got to this door and dropped the wood, he hated her.

He lay on the bed for a long time and read old *Life* magazines that he'd found on the porch. When the heat from the fire finally made him sleepy, he got up and cleared off his bed, then arranged his things for the next morning. He looked through the pile of stuff again to make sure he had everything. He liked things in order and didn't want to get up the next morning and have to look for something. He picked up the Scotch and held the bottle up to the light. Then he poured some into a cup. He carried the cup over to the bed and set it on the bedside table. He turned off the light and stood looking out of the window for a minute before getting into bed.

He got up so early it was still almost dark in the cabin. The fire had burned down to the coal during the night. He could see his breath in the cabin. He adjusted the grate and pushed in some wood. He couldn't remember the last time he'd got up so early. He fixed peanut-butter sandwiches and wrapped them in waxed paper. He put the sandwiches and some oatmeal cookies into a coat pocket. At the door he pulled on his waders.

The light outside was vague and grey. Clouds filled the long valleys and hung in patches over the trees and mountains. The lodge was dark. He moved out slowly down the packed, slippery trail towards the river. It pleased him to be up this early and to be going fishing. Somewhere in one of the valleys off behind the river he heard the *pop-pop* of shots and counted them. Seven. Eight. The hunters were awake. And the deer. He wondered if the shots came from the two hunters he'd seen in the lodge yesterday. Deer didn't have much of a chance in snow like this. He kept his eyes down, watching the trail. It kept dropping downhill and soon he was in heavy timber with snow up to his ankles.

Snow lay in drifts under the trees, but it wasn't too deep where he walked. It was a good trail, packed solid, thick with pine needles that crunched into the snow under his boots. He could see his breath streaming out in front of him. He held the fishing rod straight ahead of him when he had to push through the bushes or go under trees with low limbs. He held the rod by its big reel, tucked up under his arm like a lance. Sometimes, back when he was a kid and had gone into a remote area to fish for two or three days at a time, hiking in by himself, he'd carried his rod like this, even when there was no brush or trees, maybe just a big green meadow. Those times he would imagine himself waiting for his opponent to ride out of the trees on a horse. The jays at the crowded edge of the woods would scream. Then he'd sing something as loud as he could. Yell defiance until his chest hurt, at the hawks that circled and circled over the meadow. The sun and the sky came back to him now, and the lake with the lean-to. The water so clear and green you could see fifteen or twenty feet down to where it shelved off into deeper water. He could hear the river. But the trail was gone now and just before he started down the bank to the river, he stepped into a snowdrift up over his knees and panicked, clawing up handfuls of snow and vines to get out.

The river looked impossibly cold. It was silver-green in colour and there was ice on the little pools in the rocks along the edge. Before, in the summer, he'd caught his fish further down river. But he couldn't go down river this morning. This morning he was simply glad to be where he was. A hundred feet away, on the other side of the river, lay a beach with a nice riffle running just in front of the beach. But of course there was no way of getting over there. He decided he was just fine where he was. He lifted himself up on to a log, positioned himself there, and looked around. He saw tall trees and snow-covered mountains. He thought it was pretty as a picture, the way the steam lay over the river. He sat there on the log swinging his legs back and forth while he threaded the line through the guides of his rod. He tied on one of the outfits he'd made up last night. When everything was ready he slipped down off the log, pulled the rubber boots up over his legs as high as they'd go, and fastened the buckle tops of the waders to his belt. He waded slowly into the river, holding his breath for the cold water shock. The water hit and, swirling, braced against him up to his knees. He stopped, then he moved out a little further. He took the brake off his reel and made a nice cast upstream.

As he fished, he began to feel some of the old excitement coming back. He kept on fishing. After a time he waded out and sat down on a rock with his back against a log. He took out the cookies. He wasn't going to hurry anything. Not today. A flock of small birds flew from across the river and perched on some rocks close to where he was sitting. They rose when he scattered a handful of crumbs towards them. The tops of the trees creaked and the wind was drawing the clouds up out of the valley and over the hills. Then he heard a spatter of shots from somewhere in the forest across the river.

He'd just changed flies and made his cast when he saw the deer. It stumbled out of the brush up river and ran on to the little beach, shaking and twisting its head, ropes of white mucous hanging from its nostrils. Its left hind leg was broken and dragged behind as, for an instant, the deer stopped, and turned her head back to look at it. Then she went into the river and out into the current until only her back and head were visible. She reached the shallow water on his side and came out clumsily, moving her head from side to side. He stood very still and watched her plunge into the trees.

'Dirty bastards,' he said.

He made another cast. Then he reeled in and made his way back to the shore. He sat down in the same place on the log and ate his sandwich. It was dry and it didn't have any taste to it, but he ate it anyway and tried not to think about the deer. Frances would be up now, doing things around the house. He didn't want to think about Frances, either. But he remembered that morning when he'd caught the three steelhead. It was all he could do to carry them up the hill to their cabin. But he had, and when she came to the door, he'd emptied them out of the sack on to the steps in front of her. She'd whistled and bent down to touch the black spots that ran along their backs. And he'd gone back that afternoon and caught two more.

It had turned colder. The wind was blowing down the river. He got up stiffly and hobbled over the rocks trying to loosen up. He thought about building a fire, but then decided he wouldn't stay much longer. Some crows flapped by overhead coming from across the river. When they were over him he yelled, but they didn't even look down.

He changed flies again, added more weight and cast upstream. He let the current draw the line through his fingers until he saw it go slack. Then he set the brake on his reel. The pencil-lead weight bounced against the rocks under the water. He held the butt of the rod against his stomach and wondered how the fly might look to a fish.

Several boys came out of the trees up river and walked on to the beach. Some of them were wearing red hats and down vests. They moved around on the beach, looking at Mr Harrold and then looking up and down the river. When they began moving down the beach in his direction, Mr Harrold looked up at the hills, then down river to where the best water was. He began to reel in. He caught his fly and set the hook into the cork above the reel. Then he started easing his way back towards the shore, thinking only of the shore and that each careful step brought him one step closer.

'Hey!'

He stopped and turned slowly around in the water, wishing this thing had happened when he was on the shore and not out here with the water pushing against his legs and him off balance on the slippery rocks. His feet wedged themselves down between rocks while he kept his eyes on them until he'd picked out the leader. All of them wore what looked like holsters or knife sheaths on their belts. But only one boy had a rifle. It was, he knew, the boy who'd called to him.

Gaunt and thin-faced, wearing a brown duck-billed cap, the boy said: 'You see a deer come out up there?' The boy held the gun in his right hand, as if it were a pistol, and pointed the barrel up the beach.

One of the boys said, 'Sure he did, Earl, it ain't been very long,' and looked around at the four others. They nodded. They passed round a cigarette and kept their eyes on him.

'I said—hey, you deaf? I said did you see him?'

'It wasn't a him, it was a her,' Mr Harrold said. 'And her back leg was almost shot off, for Christ's sake.'

'What's that to you?' the one with the gun said.

'He's pretty smart, ain't he, Earl? Tell us where it went, you old son of a bitch!' one of the boys said.

'Where'd he go?' the boy asked, and raised the gun to his hip, half pointing it across at Mr Harrold.

'Who wants to know?' He held the rod straight ahead, tight up under his arm and with his other hand he pulled down his hat. 'You little bastards are from that trailer camp up the river, aren't you?'

'You think you know a lot, don't you?' the boy said, looking around him at the others, nodding at them. He raised up one foot and set it down slowly, then the other. In a moment, he raised the rifle to his shoulder and pulled back the hammer.

The barrel was pointed at Mr Harrold's stomach, or else a little lower down. The water swirled and foamed around his boots. He opened and closed his mouth. But he was not able to move his tongue. He looked down into the clear water at the rocks and the little spaces of sand. He wondered what it would be like if his boots tipped into the water and he went down, rolling like a chunk.

'What's the matter with you?' he asked the boy. The icy water came up through his legs then and poured into his chest.

The boy didn't say anything. He just stood there. All of them just stood there, looking at him.

'Don't shoot,' Mr Harrold said.

The boy held the gun on him for another minute, then he lowered it. 'Scared, wasn't you?'

Mr Harrold nodded his head dreamily. He felt as if he wanted to yawn. He kept opening and closing his mouth.

One of the boys prised loose a rock from the edge of the water and threw it. Mr Harrold turned his back and the rock hit the water two feet away from him. The others began throwing. He stood there looking at the shore, hearing the rocks splash around him.

'You didn't want to fish here, anyway, did you?' the boy said. 'I could've got you, but I didn't. You see that deer, you remember how lucky you was.'

Mr Harrold stood there a minute longer. Then he looked over his shoulder. One of the boys gave him the finger, and the rest of them grinned. Then they moved together back into the trees. He watched them go. He turned and worked his way back to the shore and dropped down against the log. After a few minutes he got up and started the walk back to the cabin.

The snow had held back all morning and now, just as he was in sight of the clearing, light flakes began falling. His rod was back there somewhere. Maybe he'd left it when he stopped that one time after he turned his ankle. He could remember laying the rod on the snow as he tried to undo his boot, but he didn't recall picking it up. Anyway, it didn't matter to him now. It was a good rod and one that he'd paid over ninety dollars for one summer five or six years ago. But even if it were nice tomorrow, he wouldn't go back for it. Tomorrow? He had to be back home and at work tomorrow. A jay cried from a nearby tree, and another answered from across the clearing by his cabin. He was tired and walking slowly by now, trying to keep weight off his foot.

He came out of the trees and stopped. Lights were on down at the lodge. Even the lights in the parking area were on. There were still many hours of daylight left, but they had turned on all the lights down there. This seemed mysterious and impenetrable to him. Had something happened? He shook his head. Then he went up the steps to his cabin. He stopped on the porch. He didn't want to go inside. But he understood he had to open the door and enter the room. He didn't know if he could do that. He thought for a minute of just getting into his car and driving away. He looked once more down the hill at the lights. Then he grasped the door knob and opened the door to his cabin.

Someone, Mrs Maye, he supposed, had built a little fire in the stove. Still, he looked around cautiously. It was quiet, except for the sizzling of the fire. He sat down on the bed and began to work off his boots. Then he sat there in his stocking feet, thinking of the river and of the large fish that must even now be moving up river in that heart-stopping cold water. He shook his head, got up, and held his hands a few inches from the stove, opening and closing his fingers until they tingled. He let the warmth gradually come back into his body. He began to think of home, of getting back there before dark.

Richard Ford

Winterkill

I had not been back in town long. Maybe a month was all. The work had finally given out for me down at Silver Bow, and I had quit staying around down there when the weather turned cold, and come back to my mother's, on the Bitterroot, to lay up and set aside my benefits for when things got worse.

My mother had her boyfriend, then, an old wildcatter named Harley Reeves. And Harley and I did not get along, though I don't blame him for that. He had laid off himself down near Gillette, Wyoming, where the boom was finished. And he was just doing what I was doing and had arrived there first. Everyone was laid off then. It was not a good time in that part of Montana, nor was it going to be. The two of them were just giving it a final try, both of them in their sixties, strangers together in the little house my father had left her.

So in a week I moved up to town, into a little misery flat across from the Burlington Northern yards, and began to wait. There was nothing to do. Watch TV. Stop at a bar. Walk down to the Clark Fork River and fish where they had built a little park. Just find a way to spend the time. You think you'd like to have all the time be your own, but that is a fantasy. I was feeling my back to the wall then, and I didn't know what would happen to me in a week's time, which is a feeling to stay with you and make being cheerful hard. And no one can like that.

I was at The Top Hat having a drink with Little Troy Burnham, talking about the deer season, when a woman who had been sitting at the front of the bar got up and came over to us. I had seen this woman other times in other bars in town. She would be there in the afternoons around three, and then sometimes late at night when I would be cruising back. She danced with some men from the airbase, then sat drinking and talking late. I suppose she left with someone finally. She wasn't a bad-looking woman at all. Blonde, with wide, dark eyes set out, wide hips and dark eyebrows. She could've been thirty-four years old, although she could've been forty-four or twenty-four, because she was drinking steady, and steady drink can do both to you, especially to women. But I had thought the first time I saw her: Here's one on the way down. A miner's wife drifted up from Butte, or a rancher's woman just suddenly run off, which can happen. Or worse. And I hadn't been tempted. Trouble comes cheap and leaves expensive is a way of thinking about that.

'Do you suppose you could give me a light?' the woman said to us. She was standing at our table. Nola was her name. Nola Foster. I had heard that around. She wasn't drunk. It was four o'clock in the afternoon, and no one was there but Troy Burnham and me.

'If you'll tell me a love story, I'll do anything in the world for you,' Troy said.

It was what he always said to women. He'd do anything in the world for something. Troy sits in a wheelchair due to a smoke jumper's injury, and can't do very much. We had been friends since high school and before. He was always short, and I was tall. But Troy had been an excellent wrestler and won awards in Montana, and I had done little of that—some boxing once was all. We had been living in the same little apartments on Ryman Street, though Troy lived there permanently and drove a Checker cab to earn a living, and I was hoping to pass on to something better.

'I *would* like a little love story,' Troy said, and called for whatever Nola Foster was drinking.

'Nola, Troy. Troy, Nola,' I said, and lit her cigarette.

'Have we met?' Nola said, taking a seat and glancing at me.

'Yes. At The East Gate. Some time ago,' I said.

'That's a very nice bar,' she said in a cool way. 'But I hear it's changed hands.'

'I'm glad to make an acquaintance,' Troy said, grinning and adjusting his glasses. 'Now let's hear that love story.'

He pulled up close to the table so that his head and big shoulders were above the table top. Troy's injury had caused him not to have any hips left. There is something there, but not hips. He needs bars and a special seat in his cab. He is both frail and strong at once, though in most ways he gets on like everybody else.

'I *was* in love,' Nola said quietly, as the bartender set her drink down and she took a sip. 'And now I'm not.'

'That's a short love story,' I said.

'There's more to it,' Troy said, grinning. 'Am I right about that? Here's cheers to you,' he said, and raised his glass.

Nola glanced at me again. 'All right. Cheers,' she said and sipped her drink.

Two men had started playing a pool game at the far end of the room. They had turned on the table light and I could hear the balls click and someone say, 'Bust 'em up, Craft.' And then the smack.

'You don't want to hear about that,' Nola said. 'You're drunk men, that's all.'

'We do *too*,' Troy said. Troy always has enthusiasm. He could very easily complain, but I have never heard it come up. And I believe he has a good heart.

'What about you? What's your name?' Nola said.

'Les,' I said.

'Les, then,' she said. 'You don't want to hear this, Les.'

'Yes he does,' Troy said, putting his elbows on the table and raising himself. Troy was a little drunk. Maybe we all were a little.

'Why not,' I said.

'See? Sure. Les wants more. He's like me.'

Nola was a pretty woman, with a kind of dignity to her that wasn't at once so noticeable, and Troy was thrilled by her.

'All right,' Nola said, taking another drink.

'What'd I tell you?' Troy said.

'I had really thought he was dying,' Nola said.

'Who?' I said.

'My husband. Harry Lyons. I don't use that name now. Someone's told you this story before, haven't they?'

'Not me. God-damn,' Troy said. 'I *want* to hear this story.'

I said I hadn't heard it either, though I had heard there was a story.

She took a puff on her cigarette and gave us both a look that said she didn't believe us. But she went on anyway. Maybe she had thought about another drink by then.

'He had this death look. Ca–shit–ic, they call it. He was pale, and his mouth turned down like he could see death. His heart had already gone out once in June, and I had the feeling I'd come in to the kitchen some morning, and he'd be slumped on his toast.'

'How old was this Harry?' Troy said.

'Fifty-three years old. Older than me by a lot.'

'That's cardiac alley there,' Troy said and nodded at me. Troy has trouble with his own organs now and then. I think they all moved lower when he hit the ground.

'A man gets strange when he's going to die,' Nola said in a quiet voice. 'Like they're watching it come, though Harry was still going to work out at Champion's every day. He was an estimator out there. Plus he watched *me* all the time. Watched me to see if I was getting ready, I guess. Checking the insurance, balancing the chequebook, locating the safe-deposit key. All that. Though I would, too. Who wouldn't?'

'Bet your ass,' Troy said, and nodded again. Troy was taking this all in, I could see that.

'And I *was* doing it, too, I admit to it,' Nola said. 'I loved Harry. But if he died, where was I going? Was I supposed to die, too? I had to make some plans for myself. I had to think Harry was expendable at some point. To *my* life, anyway.'

'Probably that's why he was watching you,' I said. 'He probably didn't feel expendable in *his* life.'

'I know,' Nola said and looked at me seriously and smoked her cigarette. ' But I had a friend whose husband killed himself. Went in the garage and left the motor running. And his wife was *not* ready. Not in her mind. She thought he was out putting on brake shoes. And there he was when she went out there. She ended up having to move to Washington, D.C. Lost her balance completely over it. Lost her house.'

'All bad things,' Troy agreed.

'That wasn't going to be me, I thought,' Nola said. 'If Harry had to get wind of it, I thought, well, so be it. Some days I'd wake up and look at him in bed and I'd think, "Die, Harry. Quit worrying about it." '

'I thought this was a love story,' I said. I looked down at where the two men were playing an eight-ball rack. One man was chalking a cue while the other man was leaning over to shoot.

'It's coming. Just be patient, Les,' Troy said.

Nola drained her drink. 'I'll guarantee it is,' she said.

'Then let's hear it,' I said. 'Let's get on to the love part.'

Nola looked at me strangely then, as if I really *did* know what she was going to tell, and thought maybe I might tell it first myself. She raised her chin at me.

'Harry came home one evening from work, right?' she said. 'Just death as usual. Only he said to me, "Nola, I've invited some friends over, sweetheart. Why don't you go out and get a flank steak at Albertson's?" "When are they coming?" I said. "In an hour," he said.

And I thought, An hour! Because he never brought people home. We went to bars, you know. We didn't entertain. But I said, "All right. I'll go get a flank steak." And I got in the car and went out and bought a flank steak. I thought Harry ought to have what he wants. If he wants to have friends and steak he ought to be able to. Men, before they die, will want strange things.'

'And it's a fact, too,' Troy said seriously. 'I was full dead all of four minutes when I hit. And I dreamed about nothing but lobster the whole time. And I'd never even seen a lobster, though I have now. Maybe that's what they serve in heaven.' Troy grinned at both of us.

'Well this wasn't heaven,' Nola said, and signalled for another drink. 'Because when I got back, here was Harry with three Crow Indians, in my house, sitting in the living room drinking Mai Tais. A man and two women. His *friends,* he said. From the plant. He wanted to have his friends over, he said. And Harry was raised a strict Mormon. Not that it matters.'

'I guess he had a change of heart,' I said.

'That'll happen,' Troy said gravely. 'LDS's aren't like they used to be. They used to be bad, but that's all changed. Though I guess Coloureds still can't get inside the temple all the way.'

'These were inside my house, though. I'll just say that. And I'm not prejudiced about it. Leopards with spots, leopards without. They're all the same to me. But I was nice. I went right in the kitchen and put the flank steak in the oven, put some potatoes in water, got out some frozen peas. And went back in to have a drink. And we sat around and talked for half an hour. Talked about the plant. Talked about Marlon Brando. The man and one of the women were married. He worked with Harry. And the other woman was her sister. Winona. There's a town in Mississippi with the same name. I looked it up. So after a while of all nice and friends, I went in to peel my potatoes. And this other woman, Bernie, came in with me to help, I guess.
And I was standing there cooking over a little range, and this Bernie said to me, "I don't know how you do it, Nola." "Do what, Bernie?" I said. "Let Harry go on with my sister like he does and you stay so happy about it. I couldn't ever stand it with Claude." And I just turned around and looked at her. *Winona,* I thought. That name seemed so unusual for an Indian. And I just started yelling it—"Winona, Winona"—at the top of my lungs right at the stove. I

just went crazy a minute, I guess. Screaming, holding a potato in my hand, hot. The man came running into the kitchen. Claude Smart Enemy. Claude was awfully nice. He kept me from harming myself. But when I started yelling, Harry, I guess, figured everything was up. And he and his Winona woman went right out the door. And he didn't get even to the car when his heart quit. He had a myocardial infarction right out on the sidewalk at this Winona's feet. I guess he thought everything was going to be just great. We'd all have dinner together. And I'd never know what was what. Except he didn't count on Bernie saying something.'

'Maybe he was just trying to make you appreciate him more,' I said. 'Maybe he didn't like being expendable and was sending you a message.'

Nola looked at me seriously. 'I thought of that,' she said. 'I thought about that more than once. But that would've been hurtful. And Harry Lyons wasn't a man to hurt you. He was more of a sneak. I just think he wanted us all to be friends.'

'That makes sense,' Troy said, nodding and looking at me.

'What happened to Winona?' I said.

'What happened to Winona?' Nola took a drink and gave me a hard look. 'Winona moved herself to Spokane. What happened to *me* is a better question.'

'Why, you're here with us,' Troy said enthusiastically. 'You're doing great. Les and me ought to do as well as you do. Les is out of work. And I'm out of luck. You're doing the best of the three of us, I'd say.'

'I wouldn't,' Nola said frankly, and turned and stared down at the men playing pool.

'What'd he leave you?' I said. 'Harry.'

'Two thousand,' Nola said coldly.

'That's a small amount,' I said.

'And that's a sad love story, too,' Troy said, shaking his head. 'You loved him and it ended rotten. It's like Shakespeare.'

'I loved him enough,' Nola said.

'How about sports. Do you like sports?' Troy said.

Nola looked at Troy oddly then. In his chair, Troy doesn't look exactly like a whole man, and sometimes simple things he'll say will seem surprising. And what he said, then, surprised Nola. I have got used to it, myself, after all these years.

'Did you want to try skiing?' Nola said, and glanced at me.

'Fishing,' Troy said, up on his elbows again. 'Let's all of us go fishing. Put an end to old gloomy.' Troy seemed like he wanted to pound the table.

I wondered when was the last time he had slept with a woman. Fifteen years ago, maybe. And now that was all over for him. But he was excited just to be here and get to talk to Nola Foster, and I wasn't going to be in his way.

'No one'll be there now,' he said. 'We'll catch a fish and cheer ourselves up. Ask Les. He caught a fish.'

I had been going mornings in those days, when the 'Today Show' got over. Just kill an hour. The river runs through the middle of town, and I could walk over in five minutes and fish down-stream below the motels that are there, and could look up at the blue and white mountains down the Bitterroot, towards my mother's house, and sometimes see the geese coming back up their flyway. It was a strange winter. January was like a spring day, and the Chinook blew down over us a warm wind from the eastern slopes. Some days were cool or cold, but many days were warm, and the only ice you'd see was in the lows where the sun didn't reach. You could walk right out to the river and make a long cast to where the fish were deep down in the cold pools. And you could even think things might turn out better.

Nola looked at me, then. The thought of fishing was seeming like a joke to her, I know. Though maybe she didn't have money for a meal and believed we might buy her one. Or maybe she'd never even been fishing. Or maybe she knew as well as I did she was on her way to the bottom, where everything is the same, and here was this something different being offered, and it was worth a try if nothing else.

'Did you catch a big fish, Les?' Nola said.

'Yes,' I said.

'See?' Troy said. 'Am I a liar? Or am I not?'

'You might be,' Nola said. She looked at me oddly then, but, I thought, sweetly too. 'What kind of fish was it?'

'A Brown trout. Caught deep. On a hare's ear,' I said.

'I don't know what that is,' Nola said, and smiled. I could see that she wasn't minding this because her face was flushed, and she looked pretty then.

'Which?' I said. 'A Brown trout? Or a hare's ear?'

'That's it,' she said.

'A hare's ear is a kind of fly,' I said.

'I see,' Nola said.

'Let's get out of the bar for once,' Troy said loudly, running his chair backwards and forwards. 'We'll go fish, then we'll eat chicken-in-the-ruff. Troy's paying.'

'What'll I lose?' Nola said and shook her head. She looked at both of us smiling, as though she could think of something that might be lost.

'You got it all to win,' Troy said. 'Let's go.'

'Sure,' Nola said. 'Whatever.'

And we went out of The Top Hat with Nola pushing Troy in his chair, and me coming on behind.

On Front Street the evening was as warm as any in May, though the sun had gone behind the peaks already, and it was nearly dark. The sky was deep beryl blue in the east behind the Sapphires, where the darkness was, but salmon pink above the sun. And we were in the middle of it. Half drunk, trying to be imaginative in how we killed our time.

Troy's Checker was parked in front, and Troy rolled over to it and spun around.

'Let me show you this great trick,' he said, and grinned. 'Get in and drive, Les. Stay there, sweetheart, and watch me.'

Nola had kept her drink in her hand, and she stood by the door of The Top Hat. Troy lifted himself off his chair on to the concrete. I got in beside Troy's bars and raised seat and started the cab with my left hand.

'Ready,' Troy shouted. 'Ease forward. Ease up.'

And I eased the car up.

'Oh my God,' I heard Nola say, and saw her put her palm to her forehead and look away.

'Yaah. Yaah,' Troy yelled.

'Your poor foot,' Nola said.

'It doesn't even hurt me,' Troy yelled. 'It's just like a pressure.' I couldn't see him from where I was.

'I know I've seen it all now,' Nola said, and she was smiling.

'Back up, Les. Just ease it back again,' Troy yelled.

'Don't do it again,' Nola said.

'One time's enough, Troy,' I said. No one else was in the street. I thought how odd it would be for anyone to see that, without knowing something in advance. A man running over another man's foot for fun. Just some drunks, you'd think, I guess. And be right.

'Sure. OK,' Troy said. I still couldn't see him. But I put the cab in the park and waited. 'Help me, sweetheart, now.' I could hear Troy say this to Nola. 'It's easy getting down, but old Troy can't get up again by himself. You have to help him.'

And Nola looked at me in the cab, the glass still in her hand. And it was an odd look she gave me, a look that seemed to ask something of me, but I did not know what it was and couldn't answer. And then she put her glass on the pavement and went to get Troy back in his chair.

When we got to the river it was as good as dark, and the river was only a big space you could hear, with the south-of-town lights up behind it, and the three bridges and Champion's Paper, down-stream a mile. And it was cold now with the sun gone, and I thought there would be fog in before morning.

Troy had insisted on driving with us in the back, as if we'd hired his cab to take us fishing. On the way down he sang a smoke jumper's song, and Nola sat close to me and let her leg be beside mine. And by the time we stopped by the river, below The Lion's Head motel, I had kissed her twice, and smelled a sweet smell on her, and knew all that I could do.

'I think I'll go fishing,' Troy said, from his little raised-up seat in front. 'I'm going night fishing. And I'm going to get my own chair out and my rod and all I need and I'll have a time.'

'How do you ever change a tyre?' Nola said. She was not moving. It was just a question she had. People say all kinds of things to cripples.

Troy whipped around suddenly, though, and looked back at us where we were on the wide cab seat. I had put my arm around Nola, and we sat there looking at his big head and big shoulders below which there was only half a body any good to anyone. 'Trust Mr Wheels,' Troy said. 'Mr Wheels can do anything a whole man can.' And he smiled at us a crazy man's smile.

'I think I'll just stay in the car,' Nola said. 'I'll wait for chicken-in-the-ruff. That'll be my fishing.'

'It's too cold for ladies anyway,' Troy said gruffly. 'Only men. Only men in wheelchairs is the new rule.'

I got out of the cab with Troy then and set up his chair and put him in it. I got his fishing gear out of the trunk and strung it up right. Troy was not a man to fish flies, and so I put a silver dace on his spin-line and told him he should hurl it far out and let it flow for a time with the current until it was deep, and then work it, and work it all the way in. I said he would catch a fish with that strategy in five minutes or ten.

'Les,' Troy said in the cold dark behind his cab.

'What?' I said.

'Do you ever think of just doing a criminal thing? Just do something terrible. Change everything.'

'Yes,' I said. 'I think about that.'

Troy had his fishing rod across his chair now, and he was gripping it and looking down the sandy bank towards the dark and sparkling water.

'Why don't you do it?' he said.

'I don't know what I'd choose to do,' I said.

'Mayhem,' Troy said. 'Commit mayhem.'

'And go to Deer Lodge for ever,' I said. 'Or maybe they'd hang me and let me dangle. That'd be worse than this I think.'

'That's right,' Troy said, still staring. 'But *I* should do it, shouldn't I? I should do the worst thing there is.'

'No you shouldn't,' I said.

And then he laughed. 'Hah. Right. Never do that,' he said. And he wheeled himself down towards the river into the darkness, laughing all the way, 'Hah, hah, hah.'

In the cold cab after that I held Nola Foster for a long time. Just held her with my arms around her, breathing and waiting. From the back window I could see The Lion's Head motel, and see the restaurant there that faces the river and that is lighted with candles where people were eating. I could see the WELCOME out front, though not who was welcomed. I could see cars on the bridge going home for the night, and it made me think of Harley Reeves, in my father's little house on the Bitterroot. I thought about him in bed with my mother.

Warm. I thought about the faded old tattoo on Harley's shoulder. *Victory,* that said. And I could not connect it easily with what I knew about Harley Reeves, though I thought possibly that he had won a victory of kinds over me just by being where he was.

Nola Foster said, 'A man who isn't trusted is the worst thing, you know that, don't you?' I suppose her mind was wandering. She was cold, I could tell by the way she held me. Troy was gone out in the dark now. We were alone, and her skirt had come up a good ways.

'Yes, that's bad,' I said, though I could not think at that moment of what trust could mean to me. It was not an issue in my life, and I hoped it never would be. 'You're right,' I said to make her happy. I felt like I could do that.

'What was your name again?' she said.

'Les,' I said. 'Lester Snow. Call me Les.'

'Les Snow,' Nola said. 'Do you like less snow?'

'Usually I do,' I said, and I put my hand then where I wanted it most.

'How old are you, Les?' she said.

'Thirty-seven,' I said.

'You're an old man.'

'How old are you?' I said.

'It's my business, isn't it?'

'I guess it is,' I said.

'I'll do this, you know,' Nola said, 'and not even care about it. Just do a thing. It means nothing more than how I feel at this time. You know? Do you know what I mean, Les?'

'I know it,' I said.

'But *you* need to be trusted. Or you aren't anything. Do you know that, too?'

We were close to each other. I couldn't see the lights of town or the motel or anything. Nothing moved.

'I know that, I guess,' I said. It was just whisky talking.

'Warm me up then, Les,' Nola said. 'Warm. Warm.'

'You'll get warm,' I said.

'I'll think about Florida,' she said.

'I'll make you warm,' I said.

What I thought I heard at first was a train. So many things can sound like a train when you live near trains. This was a *woo* sound, you would say. Like a train. And I lay and listened for a long time, thinking about a train and its light shining through the darkness along the side of some mountain pass north of there and about something else I don't even remember now. And then Troy came around to my thinking, and I knew then that the *woo* sound had been Troy.

Nola Foster said, 'It's Mr Wheels. He's caught a fish, maybe. Or else drowned.'

'Yes,' I said.

And I sat up and looked out the window but could see nothing. It had become foggy in just that little time, and tomorrow, I thought, it would be warm again, though it was cold now. Nola and I had not even taken off our clothes to do what we had done.

'Let me see,' I said.

I got out and walked into the fog and I could only see fog and hear the river running. Troy had not made a wooing sound again, and I thought to myself, There is no trouble here. Nothing's wrong.

Though when I walked a ways up the sandy bank I saw Troy's chair come visible in the fog. And he was not in it, and I couldn't see him. And my heart went then. I heard it go click in my chest. And then I thought, This is the worst. What's happened here will be the worst. And I called out, 'Troy. Where *are* you? Call out, now.'

And Troy called out, 'Here I am, here.'

I went for the sound, then, ahead of me, which was not out in the river but on the bank. And when I had gone farther, I saw him, out of his chair, of course, on his belly, holding on to his fishing rod with both hands, the line out into the river as though it meant to drag him to the water.

'Help me!' he yelled. 'I've got a huge fish. Do something to help me.'

'I will,' I said. Though I did not see what I could do. I would not dare to take the rod, and it would only have been a mistake to take the line. Never give a straight pull to the fish, is an old rule. So that my only choice was to grab Troy and hold him until the fish was either in or lost, just as if Troy was a part of a rod that *I* was fishing with.

I squatted in the cold sand behind him, put my heels down and took up his legs, which felt to me like match sticks, and began to hold him there away from the water.

But Troy suddenly twisted towards me fiercely. 'Turn me loose, Les. Don't be there. Go out. It's snagged. You've got to go out.'

'That's crazy,' I said. 'It's too deep there.'

'It's not too deep,' Troy yelled. 'I've got it in close now.'

'You're crazy,' I said.

'Oh Christ, Les, go get it. I don't want to lose it.'

I looked a moment at Troy's scared face then, in the dark. His glasses were gone off of him. His face was wet. And he had the look of a desperate man, a man who has nothing to hope for but, in some strange way, everything in the world to lose.

'Stupid. This is stupid,' I said, because it seemed to me to be. But I got up, walked to the edge and stepped out into the cold water.

It was at least a month before the run-off would begin back in the mountains, and the water I stepped in then was cold and painful as broken glass, though the wet parts of me numbed at once, and my feet just felt like bricks bumping the bottom.

Troy had been wrong all the way about the depth. Because when I stepped out ten yards, keeping touch of his line with the back of my hand, I had already gone above my knees, and on the bottom I felt large rocks, and there was a loud rushing sound around me that suddenly made me afraid.

Though when I had gone five more yards, and the water was on my thighs and hurting, I hit the snag Troy's fish was hooked to, and I realized I had no way at all to hold a fish or catch it with my numbed hands. And that all I could really hope for was to break the snag and let the fish slip down into the current and hope Troy could bring it in, or that I could get back and beach it.

'Can you see it, Les?' Troy yelled out of the dark. 'God-damn it.'

'It isn't easy,' I said, and I had to hold the snag then to keep my balance. My legs had gone numb. And I thought: This might be the time and the place I die. And what an odd place it is. And what an odd reason for it to happen.

'Hurry up,' Troy yelled.

And I wanted to hurry. Except when I ran the line as far as where the snag was, I felt something there that was not a fish and not the snag, but something else entirely, something I thought I recognized, though I am not sure why. A man, I thought. This is a man.

Though when I had reached farther into the snag branches and woods scruff, deeper into the water, what I felt was an animal. With my fingers I touched its cold, hard rib-side, its legs, its short slick coat. I felt to its neck and head and touched its nose and teeth, and it was a deer, though not a big deer, not even a yearling. And I knew when I found where Troy's silver dace had gone up in the neck flesh, that he had hooked the deer already snagged here, and that he had pulled himself out of his chair trying to work it free.

'What is it? I know it's a big Brown. Don't tell me, Les, don't even tell me.'

'I've got it,' I said. 'I'll bring it in.'

'Sure, hell yes,' Troy said out of the fog.

And it was not so hard to work the deer off the snag brush and float it up free. Though once I did it was dangerous to get turned around in the current with numb legs, and hard to keep from going down, and I had to hold on to the deer itself to keep my balance enough to heave myself towards the slow water and the bank. And I thought, as I did, that in the Clark Fork many people drown doing less dangerous things than I was doing now.

'Throw it way far up,' Troy shouted, when he could see me. He had righted himself on the sand and was sitting up like a little doll. 'Get it way up safe,' he said to me.

'It's safe,' I said. I had the deer beside me, floating, but I knew Troy couldn't see it.

'What did I catch?' Troy yelled.

'Something unusual,' I said, and with effort I hauled the little deer up on the sand a foot and dropped it and put my cold hands up under my arms. I heard a car door close then, back where I had come from up the river bank.

'What is that?' Troy said, and put his hand out to touch the deer's dark side. He looked up at me. 'I can't see without my glasses.'

'It's a deer,' I said.

Troy moved his hand around on the deer, then looked at me again in a painful and bewildered way.

'What's it?' he said.

'A deer,' I said. 'You caught a dead deer.'

Troy looked back at the little deer then for a moment and stared at it as if he did not know what to say about it. And sitting on the wet sand, in the foggy night, he all at once looked scary to me, as though it was him who had washed up there and was finished. 'I don't see it,' he said, and sat there. And I said nothing.

'It's what you caught,' I said finally. 'I thought you'd want to see it.'

'It's crazy, Les,' he said. 'Isn't it?' And he smiled at me in a wild, blind-eyed way.

'It's unusual,' I said.

'I never shot a deer before.'

'I don't believe you shot this one,' I said.

And he smiled again, but then suddenly he gasped back a sob, something I had never seen before. 'God-damn it,' he said. 'Just God-damn it.'

'It's an odd thing to catch,' I said, standing above him in the cold, grimy fog.

'I can't change a fucking tyre,' he said and sobbed again. 'But I'll catch a fucking deer with my fucking fishing rod.'

'Not everyone can say that,' I said.

'Why would they want to?' He looked up at me crazy again, and broke his spinning rod into two pieces with only his hands. And I knew he must've been drunk still, because I was still drunk a little, and that by itself made me want to cry. And we were there for a time just silent.

'Who killed a deer?' Nola said. She had come behind me in the cold night and was looking. I had not known, when I heard the car door, if she wasn't walking back up to town alone. But it was too cold for that, and I put my arm around her because she was shivering. 'Did Mr Wheels kill it?' she said.

'It drowned,' Troy said.

'And why is that?' Nola said, and pushed closer to me to be warm, though that was all.

'They get weak, and they fall over,' I said. 'It happens in the mountains. This one fell in the water and couldn't get up.'

'So a gimp man catches it on a fishing rod in a shitty town,' Troy said and gasped with bitterness again. Real bitterness. The worst I have ever heard from any man, and I have heard bitterness voiced, though it was a union matter then.

'Maybe it isn't so bad,' Nola said.

'Hah!' Troy said loudly, from the wet ground. 'Hah, hah, hah.'

And I wished that I had never shown him the deer, wished I had spared him that, though the river's rushing came up then and snuffed his sound right out of hearing, and drew it away from us into the foggy night beyond all accounting.

Nola and I pushed the deer back into the river while Troy watched, and then we all three drove up into town and ate chicken-in-the-ruff at The Two-Fronts, where the lights were bright and they cooked the chicken fresh for you. I bought a jug of wine and we drank that while we ate, though no one talked much. Each of us had done something that night. Something different. That was plain enough. And there was nothing to talk about to make any difference.

When we were finished, we walked outside and I asked Nola where she would like to go. It was only eight o'clock, and there was no place to go but to my little room. She said she wanted to go back to The Top Hat, that she had someone to meet there later, and there was something about the band that night that she liked. She said she wanted to dance.

I told her I was not much for dancing, and she said fine. And when Troy came out from paying, we said goodbye, and she shook my hand, and said that she would see me again. Then she and Troy got in the Checker and drove away together down the foggy street, leaving me alone, where I didn't mind being at all.

For a long time I just walked, then. My clothes were wet, but it wasn't so cold if you kept moving, though it stayed foggy. I walked to the river again and across on the bridge and then a long way down into the south part of town, on a wide avenue where there were houses with little porches and little yards, all the way, until it became commercial, and bright lights lit the drive-ins and car lots. I could've walked then, I thought, clear to my mother's house twenty miles away.

But I turned back, and walked the same way, only on the other side of the street. Though when I got near the bridge again, I came past the senior citizens' recreation place where there were soft lights on inside a big room, and I could see through a window in the pinkish glow, old people dancing across the floor to a record player that played in a corner. It was a rumba or something like a rumba that was being played, and the old people were dancing the box step, smooth and graceful and courteous, moving across the linoleum like real dancers, their arms on each other's shoulders like husbands and wives. It pleased me to see that, and I thought that it was too bad my mother and father could not be here now, too bad they couldn't come up and dance and go home happy, and me to watch them. Or even for my mother and Harley Reeves, the wildcatter, to do that. It didn't seem like too much to wish for. Just a normal life other people had.

I stood and watched them a while and then I walked back home across the river. Though for some reason I could not sleep that night, and simply lay in bed with the radio turned on to Denver, and smoked cigarettes until it was light. Of course I thought about Nola Foster, that I didn't know where she lived, though for some reason I thought she might live in Frenchtown, out Route 20 west, near the pulp plant. Not far. Never-never land, they called that. And I thought about my father, who had once gone to Deer Lodge prison for stealing hay from a friend, and had never recovered from it, though that meant little to me now.

And I thought about the matter of trust. That I would always lie if it would save someone an unhappiness. That was easy. And that I would rather a person mistrusted me than disliked me. Though, still, I thought, you could always trust me to act a certain way, to be a place, or to say a thing if it ever were to matter. You could predict within human reason what I'd do, that I would not, for example, commit a vicious crime, trust that I would risk my own life for you if I knew it meant enough. And as I lay in the grey light, smoking, while the refrigerator clicked and the switcher in the Burlington Northern yard shunted cars and made their couplings, I thought that though my life at that moment seemed to have taken a bad turn and paused, it still meant something to me as a life, and that before long it would start again in some promising way.

I know I must've dozed a little, because I woke suddenly and there was the light. Earl Nightengale was on the radio, and I heard a door close. It was that that woke me.

I knew it would be Troy, and I thought I would step out and meet him, fix coffee for us before he went to bed and slept all day, the way he always did. But when I stood up I heard Nola Foster's voice. I could not mistake that. She was drunk. And she was laughing about something. 'Mr Wheels,' she said. Mr Wheels this, Mr Wheels that. Troy was laughing. And I heard them come in the little entry, heard Troy's chair bump the sill. And I waited to see if they would knock on my door. And when they didn't, and I heard Troy's door shut and the chain go up, I thought that we had all had a good night finally. Nothing had happened that hadn't turned out all right. And none of us had been harmed. And I put on my pants, then my shirt and shoes, turned off my radio, went to the kitchen where I kept my fishing rod, and with it went out into the warm, foggy morning, using just this once the back door, the quiet way, so as not to see or be seen by anyone.

GRANTA

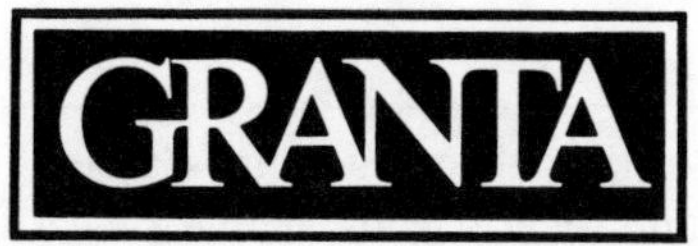

Carolyn Osborn
Cowboy Movie

All the cowboys are cheering John Wayne. They have their hats on, and I can't see too well. I lean forward to pat a large shoulder, 'Could you remove your hat, please?'

'Certainly, ma'am.'

The domino theory works. All down the row in front of me cowboys remove their hats. A hand touches my back.

'Ma'am, would you mind?' Now that I have asked, he can.

'Of course not.' The dominoes fall behind me. Mine is a big straw hat with blue and orange silk flowers on the nod all over the brim. I bought it at a garage sale for two dollars. Somebody asked me, 'Elise, what do you want that hat for?'

'To wear to the movies.'

'Umm.' Somebody else smiled. They knew about the cowboys. Saturday afternoons kiddie shows play at the Rex; Saturday nights westerns are on except for the last Saturday night in the month when you can see a musical. By that time the cowboys have either gambled or drunk up their pay. They don't fancy musicals much. Lots of people in town don't fancy westerns. They have the cowboys. They have the West. They used to have the Regal and the Ritz also. Since the Regal burned down, rats have moved into the Ritz. Nobody fancies the rats, so the Rex has to take care of us all.

If you want to see a western, you have to put up with the cowboys. You have to learn to be a fast draw with a hat.

John Wayne shoots a Mexican, who's wearing a large felt sombrero, out of the saddle. Our Mexicans don't wear hats like that. None of them are here. They're back at the Bar S, the Double Z, etcetera, looking at borrowed TVs because they're all wet—every last one of them—and might get picked up by the border patrol if they came to town.

'Why did he do that?' Since they like to explain things, I ask questions. Sometimes you can't hear the dialogue for the comments.

'He wants the land,' says Rafe, the cowboy on my left.

'Yeah,' Howard, on my right says. 'And the Meskin wants to keep it for his boss. Texas owns everything from the Rio Grande to the Red. But we'd made this treaty saying we was going to honour all the old Meskin claims. I guess John Wayne didn't know that.' Howard, like everyone else in the state, had to study Texas history for a whole year in the eighth grade.

'Aww,' Rafe drawls wonderfully, 'He shot him 'cause he drawed on him.'

The cowboy sitting behind me paws my shoulder again, 'Please, ma'am, shut them boys up.'

We all hush. The repercussions from such exchanges can be dangerous. Nobody totes a gun, but they do have bad fist fights in the lobby which upsets the manager. The cowboys don't mind. They bet on the fights. I stayed for one once. It was about how many chickens were on the picnic table in *The Virginian.* The manager only shows what he believes are the best westerns: *Stagecoach, Red River, High Noon,* things like that. *Red River* is my favourite. This is the second time I've seen it. The only part I don't like is the stampede. Nine thousand head is a lot of steers to stare at.

Sometimes while I'm watching them collect I think about why I'm here. The cowboys, the ones who know me, call me 'The Spy.' They grin when they say it just to let me know they're joking, but it's a half-joke. I was in London working at a bookstore near the British Museum. Looking at a book of photographs of the American West—much too expensive, much too large—I conceived a great hunger for space. The layers of history I walked through every day seemed too heavy. I wanted to go home, not to Kentucky, to the West.

Howard, seeing John Wayne hire cowboys for the Chisholm Trail drive, whispers, 'Ten dollars a day. Wasn't much pay, was it?'

'For then it was more.' I'm the book-keeper for the JO, a ranch belonging to an old friend. I hadn't seen Charlie since I was a child, still I wrote to him from London.

'Come on,' he replied, 'I'll find something for you to do.'

An airplane was my stagecoach. I landed in San Angelo. Charlie met me in his pick-up and drove home, about two hundred miles south-west straight into nowhere as far as I could tell. Finally there was this excuse for a town and twenty miles from it, the ranch.

The first thing I decided was; I will not fall in love with a cowboy and stay out here. I'm lighting in this part of the world just for a while. Charlie, a fine weathered old man, reminds me of Walter Brennan, just in looks, not in role; he's nobody's sidekick. A landowner can't be.

Now we're into the long drive up the Chisholm Trail to the Abilene stockyards. Every time a cloud of dust rises the cowboys cough. It's their way of applauding verisimilitude. Rafe has pulled his bandanna over his nose. Howard says, 'Thank God we don't do it that way no more.' Stampede time. Everybody's whistling and shouting, 'Head 'em! Head 'em!'

I go out to the lobby to buy popcorn. Despite being in a small town, the Rex has an ample refreshment stand: fifteen kinds of candy bars, three different soda waters, coffee, some revolting-looking hotdogs—I've never seen anybody eating one—and an elaborate popcorn machine. The boy who fills my order looks like a weak version of Dustin Hoffman. I start to ask him what he's doing here now. *Little Big Man* comes on weeks later. Instead I munch popcorn. Everybody has begun to look like a western actor. I'm afraid almost to look in a mirror for fear I might see Joanne Dru, or Vera Miles, or Faye Dunaway.

When I go back I offer popcorn right and left.

'No thank you, ma'am.'

Most of them make thirty dollars a day minus social security, and they are proud.

I go home with Howard and Rafe. Howard's been saving his money and has bought a new truck. Although he's had it for seven months now, I still keep the window down a bit when I smoke. He insists that I go ahead and use the ashtray which is, I fear, tantamount to a declaration of love. That's why I never go anywhere alone with Howard. Actually I prefer Rafe. Howard is sensible and steady; he could be anybody's foreman. Rafe...well, Rafe looks like The Gambler in a western. Howard is the kind that takes you to eat ice cream after movies. Rafe, out of deference to me, asks for a glass of water, empties most of the water out, and fills the glass up with whisky. Then he winks and passes it to me while Howard eats his ice-cream cone and pretends not to notice. I think wistfully of how I used to drink gin and tonic in London pubs from stemmed glasses with frosted sides while I sip Rafe's raw whisky and pass it back to him. We are loitering outside a drive-in, a building as garish as a child's new toy, painted red, white, blue and yellow—primary colours to appeal to primary appetites. Cups and plastic spoons litter the asphalt.

Something, some unrecognizable sound, bawls out of the loudspeaker.

'It's a song,' Howard says.

'About un-re-qui-ted love,' Rafe adds.

He's the most dangerous sort of cowboy, a drifter. Howard looks over at him. 'What kind?'

''Bout when you love her, and she don't love you.'

'Or she loves you, and you don't love her.' I poke Rafe in the ribs. If he doesn't hush he's going to be walking twenty miles back to the ranch. I won't be able to come to his rescue either. Charlie has gone to San Angelo in the only other pick-up I can drive. I really can't get involved in one of their crazy quarrels. Right now it's spring, round-up time. I have a lot of cow and calf counting to do. It's considered impolite to ask a man how many head of cattle he's got. Out here that's like asking somebody how much money he has in the bank. Because I'm the book-keeper I know; Charlie has plenty. I only hope they're all there.

Rafe passes the glass back. I shake my head and suggest we drive on home. That won't keep him from drinking all the way, but it will get me out of the sandwich-filling position between the two of them.

'You going to keep that hat?' Howard asks.

'Why not?'

He grins. Howard has a wholesome grin. If you can imagine John Ireland with blond hair and without a sliver of meanness, you can imagine Howard.

'You think it's funny looking?'

This time he laughs. Certainly it's funny looking. A lot of raggedy-looking flowers frazzling all over a big brim. It was someone's Sunday hat once. I'm sure it looks peculiar on me with my jeans, boots, and green silk western shirt, also bought at the garage sale. It has real mother-of-pearl buttons. I look, as the English would say, 'tatty,' which is OK with me. You can't wear a dress when you go to movies with two cowboys. It excites them. They start treating you like a lady. If you just want to be friends, you have to dress like one of them or a variation of one of them.

The moon shines on us all the way back to the ranch. When we get to the big house where my rooms are, Rafe opens the door and falls out. Naturally I slide out on the passenger side, but I don't expect him to be standing there with arms wide open. Before Howard can get around the truck, Rafe, laughing at every footstep, carries me to the front porch.

I kick as hard as I can.

'Put her down!' Howard hollers.

'Looks like a bride,' Rafe leers. 'I'm taking her to the threshold, Howard. Just taking her to——'

I keep kicking. Howard pulls on Rafe's shoulder. He stumbles on the steps, and we both fall across the porch.

'Sorry. I'm——'

'You sure are sorry.' Howard raises a fist.

'Aww...' Rafe lurches to his feet.

'Howard, he's drunk.'

Rafe slumps back down on the steps and shuts his eyes.

'I know that. I'm going to——'

'No, you're not. He can sleep it off right there. Now go on to the bunkhouse. I'm going in.' A woman gets bossy in a hurry out here because she can depend on a number of rules. Cowboys don't hit women; they don't hit men when they're down. Drunk counts as down. The minute Howard drives out of the yard I walk over to Rafe and nudge him with the toe of my four-hundred-dollar handmade boots. Yep, light brown suede with Texas stars twinkling in dark brown, eight-row stitching on the tops. Except for movies, jeans, a few shirts, a felt hat for winter and a straw for summer, there's nothing else to spend money on.

'Rafe?' I nudge him again. 'Come on. I know you're not really drunk.'

A hand clamps my ankle, so I stand there quietly like a hobbled horse.

'All I care is Howard thinks I am. I went to a lot of trouble. Now you tell me I'm a bad actor.'

I shift my weight to my hobbled foot. 'Let go, Rafe.'

'If I do, will you sit down?'

'If you don't I'm going to kick you in the head with my free boot.'

'I notice you don't go anywhere with anybody alone except Charlie. You sleeping with him?'

'Charlie is an old friend of my father's. If I tell him you even asked such a question, I'll be giving you severance pay tomorrow, and you only signed on last week.' I lunge toward the door, but Rafe is cat quick. He tackles me and carries me back with him whooping all the time like a bar-room villain.

'Why haven't you shouted for Emmaline yet?'

'I'm trying to take care of myself, you lout.' Emmaline is Charlie's housekeeper, a lady about seventy who puts up with no nonsense. She takes care of rattlesnakes with rocks, is a dead shot with a varmint rifle, and can throw a frying pan more accurately than most men can throw a football.

'I want to talk to you.' He holds on with one hand, bends over, and picks up my hat. 'Here.' He slaps it on my head. 'You're not from here are you, Elise?'

'No. Everybody knows that.'

'Well, I'm not either.'

He sits down on the top step, and I sit down beside him. Rafe, somewhere between thirty and forty, is dark-haired, dark-eyed. No matter how sloppily he's dressed, he looks like he has on a frilled white shirt and black silk tie.

'Where did you think I was from?'

'Anywhere.' Some cowboys drift in and out. Others stay around here all their lives. Some are on the run. We don't ask. Generally they don't tell.

'I'm from LA. I'm a scout.'

'For what?' I look at the moon and stars, hear the coyotes barking, and think of Apache ghosts listening to Rafe and laughing.

'I scout locations. I'm also the director of this movie...the one we're going to make here.'

I look at the moon again. Is it the moon or is it a huge spotlight? The coyotes yelp, or do they? Could that noise come from a sound-track? Are those stars clever glitter fakes?

'We don't need any movies made here. Everybody is starring in his own part already.'

'But I need you. I want you to play the lead.' He leans back against a porch post looking as if he's just laid four aces on the top step.

I rest my chin on my knees and stare into the dark. 'Charlie won't like it.'

'Yes he will. He'll like seeing the ranch and everybody he knows——'

'Is he going to be in it?'

'No. He looks too much like Walter Brennan.'

'I'm not going to be in it either.'

'Why not?'

'I've got my own reasons.'

'You don't have to make up your mind right away. I will ask you one favour though. Please don't talk to anybody but Charlie about the movie. It spooks people if they know one's going to be made. They get self-conscious, and the script isn't even finished yet.'

'Would you mind telling me what it's about?'

'You mainly.'

I walk across the porch and slam the door so hard I can hear the porch swing jiggling on its chains. Charlie keeps the booze in the kitchen in a cabinet next to the sink. Ordinarily I don't drink anything more than a few sips of whisky. Emmaline watches me from a doorway while I pour myself a nice stiff Scotch.

'It's that Rafe, ain't it?' Emmaline's long grey hair flows over the back of her long red robe. In the daytime she screws her hair up in a fat knot and wears frowzy print dresses. Her night clothes are entirely different. Stately or voluptuous depending on her mood, they're made of silk, satin, velour, velvet. A cook in the daytime, a queen at night. At first I thought these gowns were for Charlie's enjoyment; then I discovered he sees a woman in San Angelo every weekend. Emmaline's grandeur is entirely for her own satisfaction.

'He's after you?'

'In a way.'

'There's something about him…I don't know. Something foreign.'

That's the worst thing to be in this part of the country. Foreigners are different, therefore unpredictable, therefore untrustworthy. Don't turn your back on a stranger. Maybe he doesn't know the rules.

'We were all foreigners once.'

'Not me, honey. I was raised in West Texas.' Emmaline turns her back on me and clacks off to bed in her red satin high heels.

I sit on my bedside wondering. What if you once expected someone to come along and tell you they wanted you to be in a movie, and when that finally happened you felt it was too late? Those fantasies you never act on hide out like old booby traps—wishes to catch the unwary, dubious destinies for the daydreamer. I wanted to see the West. I came West. I wanted to live with cowboys; I'm living with them. I forgot about wanting to be in a movie. I forgot that when I was fourteen. There's no time now to fly to Mexico for a face-lift, no time to straighten my teeth and pigeon toes, to take elocution or acting lessons. I might have time to go to the My Delite Beauty Salon in town. But they would only do for me what they do for everyone else, turn me out looking like a haystack-head, back-combed, blown, and sprayed until I'd seem to be suspended from the sky by a cloud of hair. Bouffant is still a favourite word in West Texas beauty parlours. It's the only thing about the sixties anyone liked in this part of the world.

If Rafe wants me for anything, it'll have to be *cinéma vérité*. My hat lands on a bedpost, my boots fall in a corner, and I fall in bed, a good place to stay most of Sunday. Monday I have real work to do.

Counting cows is a simple matter to anyone who never had to sit on the top rail of a corral and do it. Charlie's are number branded which is supposed to make everything easier. But number 803's brand has partially disappeared under hide and hair, so Howard has to find 808 before I can mark the tally sheet.

'You mean that brockle-faced one, Elise?'

Howard only knows animals by their markings, and I don't know his language. He drives a splotchy-faced cow past me. All the calves are in another pen bawling, the new steer calves with good reason. 'Mountain oysters' is a term I'm not supposed to know, so I play dumb and suppress a desire to shout 'Balls!' How would my English friends understand a bunch of cowboys acting like nice nellies about castration?

Number 803 is now in the chute trying to kick out. Charlie crawls up on the fence beside me. He's in good spirits as usual on Monday mornings.

'Heard you were wrestling on the front porch Saturday night.'

'I run out of things to do sometimes. Charlie, who has been keeping these records for you?'

'Whoever I can get. Why?'

'Sometimes there's a note. See. Here's number 101, and it says "snakebit". Is she dead?'

'Depends on where she was bit. If it was near the head she probably is. I think we lost that one. We'll need some replacements, need 'em every year. Cows step in holes, get stuck in ponds, break out of the fence and get run over, poison themselves eating green loco weed in the spring. Any kind of stupid thing that can happen will. At least I know what's most likely to happen, and if we have a rare accident now and then it gives us something new to talk about.'

'If Rafe makes a movie out here you'll have something——'

'I been thinking on that.'

Howard and another cowboy named Spades line up a new bunch in the chute. Every cow gets rebranded if needed, and each is given a shot for anaplasmosis, a disease drifting over from south Texas that can eventually kill a herd. Then they're let out to rejoin a group which will be sprayed. It's dirty, repetitious work, the kind never shown in movies. Hereford cows, a western landscape painter's favourite breed, originated in England. Docile in any pasture, they grow confused and silly when hemmed in small spaces. Those lovely rust and white bucolic blobs—painted hoof-deep in bluebonnets on Emmaline's kitchen calendar—turn contrary, wheel every way but the right one, cluster in corners, barge into each other, roll their eyes, thrash their tails, and in general act demented. No one ropes anything all day though a lot of whips are popped on the ground, a lot of dust raised. Not a bit of what Charlie calls 'bad language' is spoken, not even when a cow steps on somebody's boot. I've heard stronger curses on a grade-school playground than I hear in the corral. Cursing is an oral art almost like story-telling; here it's reserved for leisure moments.

At sundown we quit. I haven't talked to Rafe all day. He's been one of the drivers bringing cattle to and from the corral, bossing the wetbacks, hovering around the edges. After supper he appears at the door.

'Come on in,' says Charlie. He winks at me and adds, 'Elise, did this boy tell you he was raised out here?'

I know immediately Rafe is going to get his way. He can shoot all the movies he wants. He can use Charlie's ranch, his corrals, cows, horse, pick-up, house, cowboys, cook, and accountant. He'll be allowed to wreck the windmills, cut holes in the barn roof, set fires in haylofts, shoot the antelope, stage drownings in water troughs, turn pastures into landing strips. With Charlie's permission he will mess up the rhythm of ranch life, one dependent on the needs of beasts and traditions of men. And when he and his crew leave, nothing will be the same for a long time. They'll be replaying the movie for months. Since he was raised out here, Rafe can meddle with whatever is here, and he'll take his version of here with him in film cans to LA, cut it, edit it, send it back. Charlie, Emmaline, the cowboys, and everybody in town will go to see Rafe's movie. I foresee a lot of fist fights in the lobby about how things really were. The manager will be miserable.

Rafe moves to the chair across from Charlie's by the fire place. I nod and exit.

'Hey Elise, wait. Charlie and I are going to sign a contract and——'

'Sorry, I've got to be going.'

'Where?'

'None of your business.' Since I've learned who the real spy is, it has become important to me to keep my moves secret. More than that, I really don't want to witness a contract signing.

When I run out I almost run into Howard leaning against the porch post. So many people have slouched against it I don't know why that post hasn't fallen down.

'Thought I might knock on the door after a while.' Howard takes off his hat, a sign he's going to be serious. 'What's Rafe doing in there with Charlie?'

'I don't know. Some kind of business.'

'I come to ask you to the dance next Saturday.'

Rafe lets the screen door slam behind him; even if he hadn't I would have felt his presence. There's a sort of aura surrounding him, one compounded of shrewdness, power, and sex appeal.

Howard, innocent, hard-working, and good, doesn't stand a chance beside him.

'I'll let you know tomorrow, Howard.'

'All right. It's just a country dance. There's one after round-up every year. Thought you might like to go.' He shoves his hat back on, studies Rafe a minute, and walks off towards the bunkhouse.

The moon is rising, doing its tricks, casting cloud shadows on the prairie, casting rays on us. The slats on the swing repeat themselves on the porch floor. In the living room an open newspaper screens Charlie. He falls asleep in a paper cave every night. If Emmaline doesn't wake him and help him pull his boots off, he'll sleep like that till dawn.

'Now what?' I quit tracing a star in the dust with my boot toe and face Rafe.

'You going to that dance with him?'

'Why do you care?'

'Just wondering...thinking about the script.'

'Rafe, I'm not your lead. Find yourself a real actress. I suggest Emmaline. She can play the gutsy western woman with a golden heart. Have you ever seen her dressed for bed? She's a combination Barbara Stanwyck—Mae West.'

'I'd rather see you.'

'Led myself right into that one.'

'Look, all I want to do is make this movie.'

'Who's the male lead?'

'There're two...me and Howard, although he doesn't know it yet.'

'Don't you have any kind of script?'

'The writers get here tomorrow. I'll tell them part of the story and they'll finish it. Then I'll probably have to change that. A lot is improvised. We isolate ourselves, live together, and see what happens.'

'So...instead of *Grand Hotel*, we get *Raunchy Rancho*.'

'Something like that. I guess you've never seen my work, but it isn't porno if that's what worrying you.' Rafe sits down on the swing. The slats' pattern flickers back and forth on the floor like the loose end of a reel unwinding and rewinding.

'I hadn't thought of the pornographic angle. And you're right, I haven't seen your movies. Plenty of American films come to London. Somehow I missed most of them. Generally the French films interest me more.'

Rafe smiled. 'I thought they might.' His boots scrape across the floor; the dizzying slat shadows stand still. 'Please sit down. I miss having someone I can talk to.'

I sit in the far corner of the swing with my knees under my chin while Rafe tells me about growing up in West Texas. I begin to see him as a child staring at a sunset in a sky so dusty the clouds are magenta-coloured. I imagine him leaving a small frame house before dawn to ride out after a herd of cattle with his father, then coming home to eat a huge egg-bacon-biscuit breakfast his mother has prepared. My images were all wrong. His father was a bootmaker. They lived in San Angelo, and his mother died when he was three. An aunt helped raise him. She was the one who gave him books, showed him sunsets, and took him to hear the symphony. (Yes, he said, there was one.) His father, who had been raised on a ranch, taught him how to rope, to ride, and to fight. He'd detested dust storms, loved rain, and without anyone telling him, had always known a greener world was available. 'You've always lived in it.'

'Any place can feel cramped no matter what the geography,' I say laconically, for I find it necessary to keep my past to myself. I was beginning to know Rafe. If he knew me, what would he do with my little history? Distort it probably, magnify my wanderings into a relentless quest, change my whims to the neurotic outbursts of an unmarried woman, turn my loves and losses into grim ironic despairs when some were merely interludes, romanticize my southern family by making them into a collection of half-crazy eccentrics instead of understanding them as individuals with peculiarities.

'I have to get to bed, Rafe. Tomorrow they're bringing the goats in for shearing.' I unfold my knees, slide off the swing.

'Wait.' He catches my hand. 'You haven't told me anything.'

'I know.' There's nothing else I want to do more, so I bend down and kiss him.

Dissolve to my bedroom. My hat still hangs on one bedpost. Rafe sees it, smiles, hangs his on the other. We help each other pull boots off. Rafe admires mine. 'My father could have made those.'

'Let's just say he did.'

'Where are you going?'

'To the bathroom to perform an act never shown in the movies——' I pause at the door. 'Have you ever seen anybody using contraceptives on the silver screen? Even furtively?'

'You don't take the pill?'

I shut the door. 'I can't. It gives me terrible headaches.'

'Are you going to undress in there, too?'

'Which had you rather? Do you want me to walk out of here a bare-assed, bold-faced brazen woman, or do you want to seduce me while slowly popping open all these pearly buttons?' I stick my head out of the door. 'Please make up your mind. I'm nervous.'

'I don't know who's seducing who.' Rafe is lying across the bed, his shirt already unbuttoned. Did I do that or did he?

'In that case I'll leave my clothes on.'

They aren't on long. Neither are Rafe's. Our vulnerable naked bodies are soon covering each other's. Rafe shares my bed until around 5 a.m. when he gives me a kiss, dresses, and returns to the bunkhouse. Just before closing my door he says, 'See you tonight. We'll talk about the script.' Even at this hour, he manages a wink that's both loving and lewd.

I won't talk to him though. I don't want my life reshaped by someone else's fictions. It's mine to make up as I go along.

Late in the morning while everybody is still busy at the corral Emmaline drives me to town where I will catch a bus to San Angelo; from there I'll take several flights to Bowling Green. I've left three notes behind. One to Charlie said, 'Sorry to run. The West overwhelmed me.' To Howard I wrote, 'You really are a good guy. I wish I could have stayed for the dance.' To Rafe I explained, 'You're the most likeable villain I've ever met, but I have to write my own scripts.'

The pick-up window frames Emmaline's blue-flowered dress and worn face. Last night after supper I caught sight of her in a black peignoir with ostrich feathers furling bravely round her neck. She didn't ask a question all the way in. Now she rolls the window down, frowns at me standing by my suitcase, and says, 'You sure you know what you're doing?'

'No. I'm never sure, but things were getting too complicated at the ranch.'

'Looked kind of interesting to me—you, Howard, and Rafe. Charlie signing mysterious papers. I hope he ain't selling out.'

'I don't believe he is. He's...he's expanding in a certain way.'

She sticks one arm out the window and shakes my hand.

'You come back and visit us sometime.'

'All right, Emmaline. Take care. I'll be seeing you.'

And, of course, I did. I saw them all.

They appeared in the only western I've ever seen in London, something called *The Working Cowboy*, which showed everything men do at the JO in documentary style. Before it was over I was nearly exhausted from branding, corralling, castrating, counting, dipping, dehorning, driving, doctoring, fencing, feeding, goat shearing (done by a team of six wetbacks), vaccinating. About the last five minutes they turned from work to play. There was Howard dancing glumly but vigorously with a pretty girl who might have been imported from San Angelo.

Rafe's film, made too close to home I suspect, was so zealously true to life it appeared *The Working Cowboy* nearly worked himself to an early death out of boredom or lack of choice. You would never have known that any of those men gambled, got drunk, had fist fights, ate ice cream, bought new pick-ups, went to movies, or fell in love. Relieved that nobody kissed his horse, I was furious to see too much verisimilitude turned the characters I knew into unreal automatons. At first I was sad, ready to sit here on a foreign shore and weep for the West I'd lost. Eventually I got out of the humour. It was only Rafe's earnest movie that changed them for an hour or so. You can't really lose cowboys.

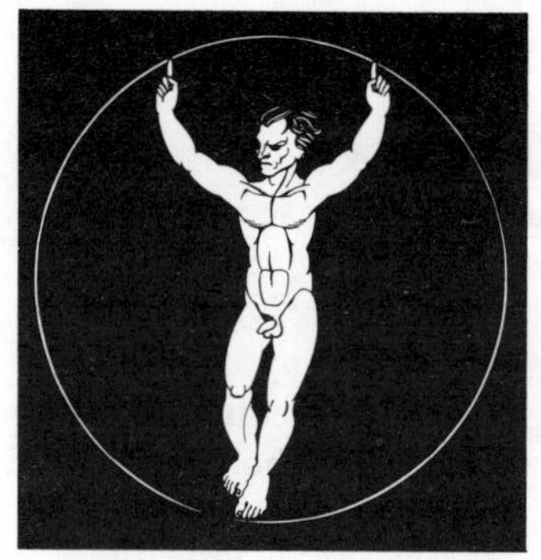

'Alasdair Gray is a visual artist as well as a writer, and the first thing to be said about his novel *1982, Janine* is that it looks good. Remove the dust-jacket and you find that the book is uncommonly handsome, with the picture from that jacket inlaid on its covers. Flick through the pages and you find yourself lured in to study the text by a vigorously graphic use of typeface, with concrete poems, marginal commentaries, explosions of capital letters, and other devices which would have delighted the heart of Laurence Sterne. All this is agreeable, and becomes impressive when you realise that it is not something extra but an integral part of the author's passion for detail. As it happens, that passion also runs to a convincing narrative. . . Here is an original and talented writer, plainly in his prime.'

Robert Nye *Guardian*

1 9 8 2 JANINE

ALASDAIR GRAY

Jayne Anne Phillips

Danner, 1965

Her father took her to work in the big white Chevrolet. Danner had a job that summer as a banquet waitress at the local Methodist college, carrying eight heaped plates to conference tables of ministers. The girls piled the plates on oval trays in the kitchen, squatted, balanced the weight on one shoulder, and held it with both hands as they stood. The manager kept the swinging door open as the waitresses, all fifteen and sixteen years old, walked to their assigned places and squatted again, straight-backed, sliding the trays on to stands. Amazed at their own feats of strength, they smoothed their dark skirts and delivered roast beef. Danner hated their uniforms: white blouses, black straight skirts, nylons, and dark shoes. August was so hot that if Jean took her to work, the black '59 Ford having baked in the sun until the seats smelled of hot rubber, Danner's legs were clammy with sweat by the time they arrived. Mitch's car had an air conditioner and if he was in a good mood he'd turn the engine on and cool the car before Danner got in. She sat in the encapsulated coolness and watched the landscape while they drove to town; fields by the Brush Fork road seemed to steam with heat and the edge of the sign that marked the city limits shone sharp and brilliant.

Mitch smoked a cigarette, leaving his window open a sliver to take the smoke. 'What time do you want me to pick you up?'

'You don't have to pick me up, it's Friday.' Riley always picked her up on Fridays after he got off work at the A & P. Without looking at Mitch, Danner knew her father was shaking his head and frowning. 'I won't be late tonight. Eleven was just too early—the drive-in doesn't even start until eight or nine. Mom said I could come in at midnight until school starts.'

'I've told Jean what I think of that, but she doesn't give a damn what I say.' He glanced over at Danner, then scowled at the road. 'I know Riley's father and I like Riley, but he's eighteen and he's a little too old for you.'

'I'm almost sixteen,' Danner said, and fell silent. After work she and Riley would go to Nedelson's Parkette to eat, then to the drive-in, where Danner would fall asleep, exhausted, midway through the first feature. The sound of the movie close to her face filled her mind with pictures. Usually she woke in an hour or so, happy, with Riley drinking a beer beside her.

'I know how old you are,' Mitch said. 'You know that's not what I'm talking about.'

Danner knew, but what difference did the time of night make? Riley had taken her parking since last winter, when her curfew was earlier. Now their rituals were established. What moved her most was the moment when he said her name involuntarily; then she was sliding down on the seat under him and it was like the sound track at the drive-in—a surface closed over her. What was near and solid drifted far off and sounds came indescribably close; his breathing was all she heard. They lay down fully clothed and he moved against her until he came, so hard in his pants that she could move her legs slightly apart and feel the shape of him. Danner had still never touched a man. Riley stroked her thighs, moving his hands higher in subtle circles until she clasped his fingers. He would major in business at Lynchburg State, forty miles away; already, Danner knew she couldn't stay with him. She didn't confide in him, not really.

'What do you think about this moving idea of your mother's?' The cigarette smoked in the ashtray. Mitch drove with one hand and kept the other on the back of his neck, as though to cushion some blow.

'Well, the house she's picked out is nice.'

'There's nothing wrong with our own house. It was good enough for her when I built it. I don't know what your mother is doing. She needs a good slap.'

Danner turned to look at him. He'd combed his grey hair back with water; under the band of his cap it had dried in the teeth marks of the comb. The cap was a summer baseball cap with a green bill. In the shadow of the bill his face was profiled. 'Don't you ever hit her,' Danner said evenly.

Mitch tilted the cap back on his head and raised his voice. 'I said, a slap. I didn't mean I was going to break her jaw.'

'It doesn't matter what you break. A man shouldn't hit a woman.' Danner smoothed her skirt nervously, then asked, less assured, 'Don't you think I'm right?'

'Hell,' Mitch said quietly.

'Think how you'd feel if Riley hit me.'

Mitch stubbed the cigarette out. The smell of ash mingled with the odour of mechanical air. 'Riley shouldn't be having anything to hit you about. If he could get that mad at you, you're way too involved.'

'We aren't too involved.' Danner drew a deep breath, and she could taste a tinge of tobacco. 'Why don't you ever say these things to Billy? He goes out on dates.'

'Your brother is just a kid, and that girl is his age. Riley is going off to college. I wasn't born yesterday. If you're going to go out, you should go out with someone in your own class.'

Danner sat back in the seat and said nothing. Now he'd have words with Jean, a cold tense scene. Danner knew the look on her mother's face exactly: she would keep her expression impassive, her lips set hard. Danner felt the expression stealing over her own face, and she focused only on the road. The concrete glistened in the noon heat, a bright white band bending away towards Bellington.

There was silence between them.

Finally, she said to her father, 'You don't have to worry about Riley, and that's the truth.'

He didn't reply, but as they drove along the atmosphere gradually lightened. Danner dreaded working another ministers' banquet and the voyage to work became an interlude of privacy. Her father's cars were always big and luxurious, not quite new, impeccably clean and cared for. The motor of the Chevrolet hummed evenly; they rode so smoothly that Danner felt lulled, almost sleepy. She leaned her head back on the seat. 'Dad,' she said, 'do you remember your dreams?'

'Well, yes, don't you?'

'What do you dream about?'

He looked out of the window to his left, considering, then said slowly, 'Haven't remembered any in a long time.'

Danner touched the air-conditioning vent and turned it towards her knees, then left her hand in the stream of cold. The heat outside was thick and fluid like clear paint. Bellington's wooden-frame houses flowed by, their big porches shaded and still with heat. 'What's the last dream you remember?' Danner asked.

He tipped his cap back and ran his fingers along the curve of the bill. 'Dreamed I was in a snowstorm,' he said.

'Alone?'

He was hesitant, or maybe responding to the pull of silence that punctuated most of his remarks in conversation. He looked over at

Danner, half frowning, half smiling, as though she should have already known the answer. 'I was driving in a snowstorm along a road,' he said, 'and snow was flying at the windscreen so fast you couldn't see where you was going.'

'Were you in this car?'

'I don't know, I was only watching the road.' He laughed. 'Couldn't see a damn thing.'

'What happened next?'

'Nothing, hon. That's all there was to it.'

They had turned down Sedgwick Street to the back campus of the college. Now Mitch pulled over on the quiet street while Danner gazed at the dining-hall. Red brick, with a concrete porch and white columns, the hall matched all the other buildings on the densely green lawns. The small campus ended here; behind the dining-hall stretched the railroad tracks and the athletic field.

'You should see the ministers running,' Danner said. 'It's so hot, you'd think they'd drop dead. Afternoons while we're cleaning, we see them running circles around the field.'

Mitch chuckled. 'Damn right. Ministers should run, that's about all they're good for.'

The banquet-hall was full of smooth clatter and murmuring talk while the ministers ate. They didn't raise their voices and weren't boisterous, but their combined noises were like those of a flock of serious, famished birds. They were all in their forties or older; Danner imagined them to be veterans of some sort —veterans of no less than six Southern churches, for instance, or of thirty years' service with merit. They ate with studious attention and talked intently. Immediately, they made the room hotter. The air conditioning in the hall didn't work well and the ministers sat moistly at long tables in their dark suits, eating roasted meat and mashed potatoes. The noon meal was the large one; for supper, the ministers ate hamburgers and French fries with ketchup. Danner thought them a sad lot and could almost be sad herself as she stood by the silverware trolley watching them chew. Automatically, she read the placard again.

Each day there was a placard with the title of the afternoon colloquium, and the titles were always questions about current events. The big card was displayed on a music stand at the back of the room. Today it said: RIOT IN WATTS, IS GOD THERE? The TV news had run pictures of Watts all week. Danner made remarks about the placards to the other waitresses. Today in particular, the question struck her as horrible and pathetic and funny, and she had to walk past the hand-lettered words every time she went into the kitchen. Now she stole a glance at the clock above the entrance doors, then gazed around the hall.

Waitresses stood at various points in the room, camouflaged in their uniforms. Most of them were pretty and they signalled each other flirtatiously. Everyone was bored at the prospect of cleaning stainless-steel counters and milk machines and floors all afternoon while the ministers talked about Watts. Finally, the men would arrive for their hamburgers or grilled sandwiches. Later, the waitresses would clear again, replenish condiments, and do an abridged version of the cleaning they'd just finished. Danner looked at the windows behind the ministers; sunlight assaulted the glass. She wanted to be at Rafferty's Public Pool where girls with no summer jobs tanned themselves all day. Lee Ann Casto, Danner's best friend, worked beside her in the banquet-hall. She'd given Danner a gift certificate admission to Rafferty's Pool. The certificate was worth one dollar, it admitted them both for one afternoon, and it was dated several years in the future.

Lee Ann caught Danner's eye now and gave her characteristic half-shrug. During meals she often stared at one minister after another, directing Danner's gaze to especially strange specimens. Danner had cracked her up in the kitchen by explaining exactly where God was during the Watts riot: gleaming, black and taut as a panther, he glided along carrying a huge silver radio. Price tags still flew from the radio and God was all in gold, blasting James Brown amidst sirens and fire. Danner sighed. The ministers ate for a full hour. To pass the time, she dropped ice cubes from the Styrofoam bucket into her water pitcher, one by one, with tongs. She wondered how many of the ministers had even been to California. None of the waitresses had; Danner had asked.

Riley wasn't interested in California. This summer he'd gone to Florida with the guys. For honeymoons, he said, it was a toss-up between Florida and Acapulco. Jean had heard him joking and told him he shouldn't be thinking about honeymoons until he got himself through college. Riley had saluted, and winked at Danner. He wasn't very excited about college; mostly, he wanted to have a good time, avoid the draft, and stay close to Bellington. He wanted to pick her up from school on Fridays this fall, take her to school on Monday mornings, then drive back to Lynchburg and participate in panty raids all week. Riley spoke of Lynchburg as a draft dodger's last resort. Then, seriously, he'd say he wouldn't mind serving his country and planned to enrol in the officers' training corps at Lynchburg. He would have gone to school in Bellington if his grades had been good enough. Danner wasn't sure he'd stick to it.

She touched the sides of the globular metal pitcher. The metal was ice cold and sweating; Danner concentrated on the feel of it. Sometimes she sat on the back patio of her house alone and looked at the fields, wondering how far she'd travel from this exact place. She didn't talk about such feelings to Riley. His mind just wasn't like hers. He acted so sure of himself, yet he was capable of crying in front of a girl, and begging. Once he'd gone out with someone else and Danner had refused to see him again. Riley had talked her into going for a drive, then he pulled off the road in a deserted spot and wept as though beside himself with grief. The scene went on nearly an hour. She should forgive him, he said, no one would ever love her again as much as he did. Thinking of the episode always made Danner uneasy. If she ever told Riley she wanted to stop seeing him, he wouldn't accept it. He'd say she was wrong, he didn't believe her, that they belonged together. More and more, Danner felt protective towards him, and guilty. Just a year ago, he'd seemed so powerful. Dressed well, in soft V-neck sweaters and Madras shirts that smelled of clean cotton, he was a smooth dancer. A basketball player, popular with girls. With his friends he was cocky, a good-natured braggart. But he wasn't like that with Danner. Sometimes he was considerate in the extreme, as though she were special or different from other people. Twice they'd gone to formal dances. Riley had actually covered a path through the garage, and the floor of his shining Mustang, with white sheets, so Danner wouldn't dirty the hem of her gown. Mitch had watched, shaking his head in pleased amusement. Danner blinked, remembering her father's expression in the car. *Nothing, hon.* When Danner was a little kid, Mitch had called her 'Princess'.

'Excuse me miss?' The head minister beckoned to Danner. She walked close up to him and bent over to hear. He smelled strongly of Old Spice, the same scent her father and brother wore.

'Right after the dishes are cleared,' he said, 'before desert, we're going to present a little performance.'

'A performance?'

'Yes, just take a few minutes. You might tell the other girls.' He smiled into her eyes and touched the edge of his plate. 'It's an entertainment, a sort of farewell.'

'Oh.' A farewell to whom? Danner nodded as though she understood, and took his plate. He smiled again, as if he'd confided a secret. Behind his slightly spotty glasses, his eyes were light blue and long-lashed. He was energetic and broad-shouldered, probably one of the men Danner had watched running, but she could never distinguish one minister from another if they weren't dressed in their suits.

The other girls, seeing Danner clear the head table, began to gather plates. Some of the ministers weren't finished eating; they lowered their heads discreetly and ate faster as the waitresses worked their way closer. Danner looked around for the manager; luckily, he was in the kitchen. She tried to signal Lee Ann to go slower but it was no use; well, best to keep going. When the manager came out the tables would already be cleared and the ministers waiting quietly for dessert. A good thing about ministers was that they seldom complained.

Danner had taken all the plates and was stacking them when the head minister stood, tapping his glass with his spoon.

'Attention, troops,' he said, and glanced in Danner's direction. 'Since this is our last big meal together and the conference ends tomorrow, we'd like to take this opportunity to thank the kitchen crew and the waitresses for their excellent service.'

Danner looked down, embarrassed, and hurried to finish loading the tray. It had to be loaded carefully or the dishes would topple when she tried to stand. The other girls kept working as well, and the minister held up both hands. 'Stay where you are, girls, please. Since we're told financial compensation isn't in order, we'd like to thank you for your work by offering a bit of entertainment.'

The four men nearest him stood. There was a hush in the room and the waitresses looked at each other confusedly. One of the men sounded a note on a pitch pipe. Then, in the silence, they began to sing. Their voices were strong and perfect. Behind them the air conditioner whirred, its steady labouring their only accompaniment.

The men stood in a semi-circle behind their table, their bodies attentive, watching each other's lips.

Amazing Grace, they sang slowly, *how sweet the sound.*

The waitresses stood still, surprised. The song filled the hall and was somehow reminiscent of childhood; the same plaintive melody was sung at countless day camps and night sings, at reunions and revivals, at funerals and YWCA and Rainbow Girls. But the ministers didn't sound plaintive, their voices were stalwart and definite. They were breaking bad news and offering comfort, and the words seemed ancient, confessional, unarguable. *I once was lost but now I'm found.* Their powerful voices made Danner a little afraid. Were they really found, and what did it mean? Lost. She imagined her father sealed into his dream like a figure in a fluid-filled paperweight, the ones in which snow flew when the globe was shaken. *Snow was flying at the windscreen so fast you couldn't see where you was going.* Men sat listening. Row after row, the long, nearly empty tables were covered with white cloths. The old fabrics were worn to a pearly sheen. Suppose they were cold, inches deep. Every winter, the old picnic table her father had built of thick birch sat out the back, covered with even snow that froze unbroken like a thick, cold cloth. *I was blind but now I see.* Danner had a sudden wintry vision of the house from above, the roof a snowy butterfly shape, the yard and fences and surrounding fields all white, deep, silent with snow. Her father had built that house. How could someone else ever live there?

She heard applause. The other girls were smiling and clapping; belatedly, Danner joined in. The ministers held their places a moment as though spellbound by their last clear note, then took their seats. The men all began applauding their colleagues as the waitresses stooped to shoulder trays. Danner stood under the heavy weight, glad the day was half over. She turned towards the kitchen. As she steadied her tray, she saw the minister who had spoken to her. He was sitting, he hands folded, watching her. Quickly, she averted her eyes. He must have seen her face during the singing; always, her face betrayed her.

They stood at the metal counter with trays of ketchup bottles while the other girls filled salt and pepper shakers or wrapped silverware.

'I thought for sure they'd sing again at supper,' Lee Ann said.

'Not over hamburgers, not sombre enough.' Danner wiped her forehead with a napkin. 'Jesus, wasn't it hot this afternoon? And from now on we have to keep the air conditioner on "low" unless there are guests eating.'

Ketchups were the worst to clean up; the emptiest bottles had to be poured into fuller ones and the empties replaced. The refilled bottles were greasy and their streaked labels had to be wiped clean with a hot rag.

'Let's do this fast,' Lee Ann whispered.

'Throw the caps in here.' Danner pushed forward a bowl of hot water. 'It's easier than wiping the gunk off.'

'Riley picking you up tonight?'

'At eight. I guess we're going to the drive-in.'

'I saw Rhonda Thompson at the intramural basketball games last night. She's dating some guy from the university, and he drives a Corvette.' Lee Ann smirked for emphasis.

'You're kidding.' Lee Ann had to report any fact about Rhonda. Rhonda and Riley had been a hot item their first two years of high school; everyone knew they'd slept together. Riley had practically lived with her; her parents had let him stay overnight several times in Rhonda's bed. 'I don't want to hear about Rhonda.' Danner paused. 'Was Riley around?'

'You sure you want me to tell you?' Lee Ann looked up from the ketchups, smiling. 'He was there with some senior boys. He spoke to her, but in a snide way. He's probably still telling them stories about her.'

Danner untwisted bottle caps, throwing them one by one into cloudy red water. 'He shouldn't tell those stories. I've told him that myself.'

'Oh, come on. Everyone tells stories about Rhonda. Rhonda is ahead of her time.'

'Well, Riley shouldn't. Here, this is clean.' She wrung out a hot dish rag and handed it to Lee Ann, who began wiping the wet bottle caps. Danner watched her. 'Riley will never tell stories about me, I'll tell you that.'

'Why not, Danner? Riley could make you famous too.' She laughed. 'Can I finish these while you start pouring? Your aim is better. Listen, suppose he tells stories on you anyway, for things you never even got to do.'

'He won't,' Danner said. 'He wouldn't dare.'

'I think you're right,' Lee Ann said seriously. 'He's really crazy about you. You don't know how crazy.' Lee Ann was well informed. Riley phoned her regularly to talk about Danner.

'He was probably crazy about Rhonda as well.'

'Yeah, but it's not the same.'

Danner poured ketchup and said nothing. Watching ketchup drip was the most pointless activity in the world. Last week they'd rushed through the clean-up and cracked the lip of a bottle; the manager had insisted they strain the entire contents for glass shards. As disciplinary action, Danner and Lee Ann had to do ketchups for the next two weeks of conferences. 'Who's coming next week?'

'Methodist Women's Clubs from North Carolina.'

'They ought to stay in North Carolina,' Danner said. She watched Lee Ann's face. Lee Ann was sweating in the warm kitchen and her glasses had slid halfway down her nose. They'd been friends since elementary school. Lee Ann had dated an older boy last year, a friend of Riley's, but now she was going steady with someone her age. He was a quiet boy who hadn't been one of their crowd; he'd moved to Bellington from out of state and didn't play sports because he had a regular after-school job. 'How are you and Mike doing?' Danner asked.

'Oh, just fine,' Lee Ann said.

Danner kept her eyes on the ketchups. It hurt her that Lee Ann didn't tell her things much any more. Last spring they'd shared a desk in typing class. Lee Ann was reading a note from Mike one day; Danner had turned casually on the swivel seat of her chair and her gaze fell on a line over Lee Ann's shoulder: *There's nothing wrong with what we did. Don't feel bad.* Danner had looked away, painfully conscious of Lee Ann's grave expression.

It had to be a total secret. You couldn't even tell your best friend.

Lee Ann glanced up suddenly as though aware of Danner's thoughts. 'Billy was at the intramurals.'

'I know. He rode his bike in to meet Kato.'

'Why weren't you there?'

'New rule. My parents won't let me see Riley more than four nights a week.' Danner twisted clean caps on to the bottles she'd filled.

'Brother,' Lee Ann said. 'I'll hear all about this from Riley, I'm sure. He must be going nuts.'

Danner loaded clean bottles on to one big tray. The tray would be so heavy that she and Lee Ann would have to carry it into the dining-room as a team. 'I don't know why Riley has to call you so often. What does he ask you?'

'He asks me how much you care about him,' Lee Ann said patiently. 'He says sometimes he wonders, can't get past first base, etcetera.' Lee Ann raised her eyebrows, smiling. Again, the understood half-shrug.

Danner returned the shrug like a co-conspirator, surprised at her own relief. Good, then Riley hadn't told anyone what they did, not even Lee Ann. Afterwards, he always pulled his shirt tail out to cover the wetness on his jeans and they drove around the dark country roads, holding hands like a married couple and telling jokes while the radio played. Thinking about him, she felt a flash of longing.

'Billy is really getting good-looking,' Lee Ann went on. 'The older girls all notice him now. You know, Kato is supposed to be pretty wild.'

'Oh, Kato is fourteen,' Danner said dismissively.

'That never stopped Rhonda, when she and Riley were going together. Actually, it was Riley that told me about Kato. He said the high school boys already call her Rhonda Two.' Lee Ann stopped talking abruptly, aware she'd said too much. 'Look, Riley didn't tell me as a joke. He was kind of concerned, but he didn't want you to hear about it and worry.'

'I don't believe stories about Kato. People only talk about her because she's pretty and comes from a poor family.'

Lee Ann nodded. Shinner Black, Kato's father, was a sometime drunk.

Together, both girls stepped back and surveyed the big tray of ketchup bottles.

Lee Ann held up her hands, displaying red-smeared fingernails. 'Watts,' she deadpanned, 'is God there?'

'Don't be silly,' Danner laughed. 'These ketchups are beautiful. Ketchups are always a great career, even in Watts.'

When she rode through Bellington with Riley, Danner felt beautiful. She was relaxed and tired when she left work; she'd taken a shower and put on make-up in the employees' bathroom and thrown away her nylons, cheap ones inevitably ruined by the end of the day. The college Banquet Service had a reputation for hiring 'personable' girls and there was a kind of status about the anonymous-looking uniform; girls sometimes wore them on dates with steady boyfriends when there wasn't much time to change. Riley's car, a canary yellow Mustang with a black top and oversized tyres, was well known around town. He was always early, waiting for her, lounging against the Mustang. By the time they met the heat had broken and Danner walked towards the bright car, the campus shade trees around her rippling a little with wind. He stood with his arms crossed in a sports shirt and clean white levis, smelling of men's cologne and smoking a cigarette. They drove down Main Street on the way to the Parkette, with the evening cooling and all the windows down. Danner sat close beside Riley, trying to see the street as though she'd never been there before. The brick and clapboard buildings were twilit, the colours deep. Main Street looked too pretty to be real.

Riley steered with one hand. 'Baby, what are you thinking about?'

'Nothing really.' She didn't like to be asked what she was thinking.

The courthouse sat back on its big lawn across from the fire station, the gold spire bright against the dark blue dusk. The huge evergreen, used every winter as a town Christmas tree, stood like a backdrop behind the highschool football scoreboard. Names of scheduled opponents and game dates were in blue, *won* or *lost* would be painted on each white line in red. The street was nearly empty. Parking meters along the sidewalk looked decorative. All the small businesses, Liberty Lunch, the Casualaire, HP Hardware, were closed, their windows lit.

Tomorrow morning Main Street would be different, crowded and hot. Saturdays, miners cashed cheques in their hard hats and rumpled clothes; country families stood in a queue at the welfare office before shopping at Woolworth's. They choked the three blocks that were Bellington's downtown. Their children were numerous and pale, dressed in ill-fitting clothes. They wore muddy shoes with no socks, or they were barefoot. Their ankles looked battered, scratched and mosquito-bitten. The women were very thin or very fat, their faces middle-aged and set as though frozen. Their hair was never styled but hung past their shoulders, occasionally restrained with a child's cheap barrette too small to have much effect. They were dirty and smelled of dirt, despite the cakes of harsh yellow soap dispensed by the County. The children were usually clean except for their feet; their once-a-week cleanliness made them look even paler. Grade schools and the junior high were full of country kids but many dropped out by high school. Danner remembered looking at them intently on the school bus from Brush Fork when she was a child. She would stare at them in profile, afraid but fascinated. Their eyelashes were flaky with the dust of sleep or neglect.

Riley pulled up at a stop light and put his arm around her shoulders. 'Mr Losch asked me if you were going to enter the Miss Jaycees contest.'

Danner gave him a surprised look. Losch ran the A & P where Riley worked. He was a member of Jaycees, merchants and professional men who sponsored the contest every fall for high-school girls.

'Why not?' Riley asked. 'You'll be sixteen by September. You could win a scholarship for college, a thousand dollars.'

Danner shifted a little away from him. Last year, Rhonda Thompson had been runner-up as a senior entrant. Danner supposed Riley wanted her to do better.

'Danner, you're one of the prettiest girls they'd have, and you're smarter than anybody who'd enter.'

'Thanks a lot. Anyway, they don't care if you're smart.'

'Losch thinks you'd have a good chance. I didn't ask him – he mentioned it to me.' Riley looked at her pointedly, still impressed. 'Doc Reb Jonas is one of the judges. Isn't he an old friend of your father's?'

Danner shrugged, looking straight ahead. 'They don't see each other much now.' Mitch certainly wasn't a member of Jaycees. He still belonged to the Elks, who kept a dim lunchroom down by the tracks. 'Riley, you know I wouldn't enter that contest.'

He made the turn on to the Winfield road, easing past the Mobil station and picking up speed. 'Boys win money for sports. Why shouldn't girls win money for looking good?'

'I don't know, but I don't want to. Think about standing on a stage in a bathing suit while Mr Losch asks you what your goals are.'

Riley smiled. 'You could talk for half an hour about your goals, and you only need to come up with three minutes.'

'How do you know anything about my goals?'

'I know,' he said, entertained. He slowed as they neared Nedelson's, checking out the parking lot for friends. The parking spaces were defined by metal posts fitted with intercoms and bright yellow menus fastened behind plastic. Riley parked on the far side of the lot and leaned out to press the intercom button. A warble of static came through the speaker.

'Hello?' Riley yelled.

'Yeah, yeah, go ahead.'

'Two double burgers with tomato, one plain cheeseburger, one large fries, two vanilla shakes.' He leaned back and lit a cigarette. 'What if Lee Ann was in the contest. Would you enter then?'

Danner frowned. 'No. Forget it, will you?'

He smiled. His eyes were extremely blue.

Food came quickly at the Parkette. Within five minutes, a girl brought the car tray, hooked it on to the half-open window, and collected money. Riley passed Danner her shake and cheeseburger. From across the lot they could hear someone's loud radio. They shared the French fries and ate comfortably, without talking. Danner loved just sitting there with him; he felt so familiar, like family.

The horseshoe circle between the rows of cars was constantly filled with slowly moving automobiles. Boys with girls simply wheeled into a spot but the ones who were alone drove around and around, yelling to each other and whooping before turning on to the highway again. Danner watched them. In a year or so Billy would have a car. He'd get his learner's licence in the fall; he had a job with State Road this summer cutting brush, already saving money. Danner couldn't imagine seeing him in his own car, like Riley. She remembered Kato then.

'Riley, what is all this about Kato?'

For a moment he didn't answer. 'Oh, hell. Lee Ann can't keep her mouth shut. It's a good thing I don't tell her anything important.'

'I call it important,' Danner said, 'and telling people only spreads the story.'

Riley regarded her, irritated. 'I didn't even tell the story.'

Danner gazed out of the windscreen of the Mustang, the straw of her milk shake in her mouth. The frothy liquid was so cold and sweet it stung her teeth. She swallowed. 'What is the story?'

'There isn't any.' He picked up his second foil-wrapped burger, pretending the subject was closed.

'You might as well tell me.'

He ate the sandwich as though considering. 'A few months ago, a couple of guys went over to Kato's house. She was home alone and they had a few beers and played around a little. Nothing really happened, nothing serious.' He paused. 'It's just that it was two guys.'

Danner said nothing, waiting.

'I guess she was tipsy. Must have been.' He crumpled the foil and put the paper and empty cups on the Parkette tray. 'It was before Billy was going out with her. Besides, he can probably handle himself.' Riley sat looking at the steering wheel. 'I'll talk to him if you want me to.'

'No, don't say a word.' She wrapped her sandwich back up in the foil and handed it to him. 'I don't want this. Let's go.'

'OK.' He moved closer, then kissed her. 'You have to understand that not everyone is as virtuous as you.'

'I'm not virtuous.'

Riley grinned, trying to coax a smile from her. 'You're not? You mean it's all an act?'

She did smile. 'What do you want? Am I supposed to act like I'm twenty-five when I'm sixteen?'

'You're not sixteen yet. And by the time you're twenty-five, we'll have three kids.' He took the tray off the window and propped it on the intercom box, then turned the ignition key of the Mustang. 'Since Mitch is so nervous lately, I'm taking you home early. But first let's skip the drive-in and visit his namesake.'

Mitch Concrete was an ideal place to park and they'd discovered it by accident. Danner hadn't been to the plant her father once owned since she was a child, but one night last winter she and Riley had driven past the entrance. Curious, Danner asked Riley to drive up the steep dirt lane to the yard. They sat looking, then stayed for an hour. The plant wasn't so far from Nedelson's Parkette, on the highway to Winfield; it was off a side road called the Graveyard Road, and up a hill. There was an office building and two prefab garages, and the tipple structure where materials were poured from above into the rolling barrels of the trucks. What materials? Sand? Gravel? Danner wasn't sure, but she had a vague memory of seeing it happen. Now the mixers sat haphazardly around the lot as though their drivers had left them abruptly. They were big rugged trucks, worn and battered. A few could be the same trucks her father had owned. Since last year, he'd sold cars at the Chevrolet garage in Bellington, and little mention was made of his work at home.

Last winter, the snowy plant had looked ghostly and beautiful by night. The piles of dirt were white mounds, the trucks dusted, the tipple a square snow-hung tower with a sheer white mountain of gravel above and behind it. Riley and Danner could see the lights of the town from the plant, and the Winfield road snaking past the parkette. Cars had moved on the road, long beams of their headlights played out across falling snow. Always, the plant was deserted. The graveyard road led only to the cemetery; no police patrolled it, no one drove by.

Danner and Riley were so sure of their privacy that sometimes, in summer, Riley spread a cloth and they lay down so they could see the stars. The plant was a kind of moonscape by August—not a scrap of green. The dirt of the yard was blond and dry and puffed like smoke when Riley skipped stones across it. Still, after dusk and into the night, there was the same private quiet as in winter. Tonight they stayed in the car, and the crickets made a staccato chiming in the brush. Danner thought of Mitch Concrete as a distant planet still revolving in the past. Hymns should sound in the background of the emptiness, very low, wisps of hymns. Riley kissed her forehead, her temples, her throat; she remembered the ministers, their bodies so attentive, singing to each other.

'Well,' Riley said. He had pulled away and was watching her when she opened her eyes. He touched the bridge of her nose, and the lines of her lips. 'I bet your parents did a little spooning here. Maybe they still do, on the sly.'

Danner shook her head. 'They were already married when he started the plant. Anyway, my parents haven't slept together in years.'

'You don't know what your parents have done.' He put one arm along the back of the seat and bunched her straight hair in his hand. 'Jean and Mitch are all right. Parents always make it seem they don't have a sex life.'

'They're all right to you—they like you. That doesn't mean they're all right to each other.'

'You're wrong,' Riley said.

She wasn't, but there was no point explaining. Danner supposed she knew more than most daughters; her mother had no one else to talk to. It was curious—Riley never wanted to admit that her parents didn't get along, as though they were his parents.

He was looking at her quizzically. 'Listen,' he said, 'I have a present for you. I'm not going to give it to you until your birthday, but I have to show it to you now so you won't be too surprised.'

Danner smiled. 'Riley, if it's for my birthday, don't show it to me now.'

'I have to,' he said. He took a small white box out of his pocket. 'Put out your hand.'

She did. He put the box on the flat of her palm, then opened it. Inside was a gold ring cushioned in white velvet; the centre of the ring was a small gold heart set with a diamond chip. 'Oh,' she said, 'It's beautiful.'

He circled her wrist with his fingers. 'Danner, I want us to be engaged.'

'I can't,' she said, nearly whispering, 'you know I can't.'

He put his finger gently against her mouth. 'I don't mean we should tell your parents. As far as they know, it's just a present. That's why it's a small diamond—when we tell them, I'll give you a different ring.'

She looked at the ring in confusion. The chip of diamond glittered. Riley kept talking. How could he see her face and just keep talking?

'. . . you've got two more years of high school. When you graduate I'll give you a real diamond, and we'll tell them together. I'll be halfway through college by then.' He looked searchingly at her, trying to pinpoint her reservations. 'I know you want to go to school. You can go to Lynchburg with me, or we can go here in town when I get my grades up, or to the university —'

'It's not that,' she said slowly, 'I can't say I'll get married.'

'What are you talking about?'

'I can't say so, I can't.' She shook her head.

He held her wrist tightly. 'You don't really love me, do you. Why don't you tell me?'

'I do love you, I do so.' She turned her hand to grasp his arm, pleading. 'Let's not say it's an engagement. What if my parents find out?'

'How would they find out?' he asked, sarcastic. 'I suppose you'd tell them, so they'd keep me from seeing you.' He took the box from her angrily and put it on the dashboard in front of them. 'OK. To you it's not an engagement ring. But to me it is. You just remember, when I'm at school. I'll be away, but I'll be thinking you're mine.'

Miserably, she put her face in her hands.

He shook her gently, pulling her towards him. 'You are,' he said, 'you are mine. Don't you know that yet?' He unbuttoned her blouse and put his hands inside, pushing the blouse apart and slipping her straps down over her shoulders. She arched up to move away and he put his arm around her waist, holding her tight against him.

She felt the hard buckle of his belt on her pubic bone and then he moved so it was just against her. He slipped his arm down under her hips. She put her hands at his shoulders, pushing him away, but she'd lost her balance and his weight forced them down on the seat. They were both wordless, tense with exertion; he held her legs, flinging his thigh over them, and leaned across her upper chest, his entire weight on his arm. Danner heard herself panting. 'You're stronger than me,' she said bitingly, 'is that what you're trying to prove?'

'You think I'm trying to rape you, Danner? Jesus, you can be stupid and tight-assed.' He tried to quiet his breathing. 'Look, I'm not trying to fuck you. I'm not going to lose control and ram it into you—like I don't know you, like I don't care about you.'

Danner, so angry she was trembling, didn't answer.

'Now you're not going to talk to me.' Her skirt had worked up high around her hips. He pushed it gently higher. 'Fine, don't talk.'

'Don't hold me down, Riley.' She had started to feel sick and weak inside, and her heart was pounding. 'If you do, I won't feel anything, I swear.'

'No?' He touched her very lightly, with the tips of his fingers, through the thin cotton of her underpants. She stopped struggling. He stroked her and there was silence, as though they'd both begun holding their breath in the same instant. He was watching her face. 'Let me,' he whispered, 'just with my hand. Let me show you.'

She couldn't speak. Her eyes had filled with tears.

He shifted his body and pulled her skirt back down to cover her legs, then he lay on top of her as she embraced him. He moved against her and made no sound; tonight it took a long time but he kept pushing and pushing. It seemed to Danner they'd gone on like this for hours. Under him, she was sore from his hardness and she hated herself; she held him and wondered what would ever happen in her life: nothing could be worse than this, than what was happening to him and to her. He stiffened, still silently. When he moved away from her they looked at each other, defeated, then at his pants. He had chafed himself until he bled; the wetness on his white jeans was tinged with pink.

'It doesn't matter,' he said, and hugged her.

David Caute
The *Guardian* and Sarah Tisdall

1

Heinrich Böll's novel, *The Lost Honour of Katharina Blum,* tells of a quite ordinary, decent young woman whose reputation was suddenly stripped from her by a tabloid newspaper. She, utterly incensed, shot the journalist who had defamed her.

Ten years later Sarah Tisdall set out from her office in Whitehall at the end of a working day, indignant but also innocent, clutching two classified documents in an envelope. In time she, too, would surrender herself at New Scotland Yard with a confession imposed upon her—in both cases the women went to prison courtesy of a single journalist.

The *Guardian,* of course, isn't a gutter tabloid but, according to its own letterheaded notepaper, 'one of the world's great newspapers'. Nevertheless, its editor capitulated last December on a vital point of principle—the protection of a source against ignominy and punishment—with the result that another ordinary, decent young woman lost both her career and her liberty.

Searching for the *Guardian,* Sarah Tisdall got lost, confusing Farringdon Road with its southerly extension, Farringdon Street—a bleak, noisy, stretch of the City where container trucks hurtle past West Smithfield and the pile of dirty thirties brick called Atlantic House. Can this tall young woman have imagined, on that light autumn evening two days before the end of summertime, how on another Friday exactly eight weeks later a man would make the same journey in reverse, holding one of her two leaked documents, his purpose being to hand it over to the Government's solicitor in an office in Holborn Viaduct? This man was the editor of the *Guardian,* Mr Peter Preston.

She had chosen the *Guardian* because, as she later said, this was the only 'left of centre, middle of the road' daily newspaper with 'national coverage'. In one respect her expectations were correct: the *Guardian* did indeed turn her two documents to immediate front-page advantage. But whatever assumptions she may have entertained concerning her own security and anonymity were to be betrayed: indeed Sarah Tisdall would have been less likely to end up in Holloway gaol had she entrusted her documents to any of the Fleet Street tabloid editors knighted by Mrs Thatcher.

Sarah Tisdall belongs to a generation which has inherited from us (who are of Mr Preston's age) a world sewn thick with 50,000 nuclear warheads. Clearly she is one of those who, by acts of defiance and gestures of witness, refuse to shut their eyes to the danger of nuclear holocaust. 'Indecent,' she said about one document in particular, 'sort of doing it by the back door and I couldn't stomach it. I felt the public had a right to know what was being done to them.' The *Guardian,* too, has its eye on this dissident constituency—the paper lost no time on the evening of 21 October in splashing the contents of the Tisdall documents across the front page of its final edition, which went on sale to the 250,000 demonstrators gathering for the big CND rally in London the following day.

Those who write in the relatively liberal climate of Western Europe must sometimes wonder how each of us would fare under fire in Poland, Czechoslovakia or South Africa. Would we be one of those who promise well in the early episodes of a play by Vaclav Havel, yet fail the final test that hurts? Or might we become one of those journalists whose principles are trimmed to stay out of trouble, even if it involves laundering newsprint, distorting the record, and picking up telephones to persuade colleagues on other newspapers to play ball?

2

Sarah Tisdall, the daughter of two Devon doctors, was a twenty-three-year-old clerk working in the private office of the Foreign Secretary, Sir Geoffrey Howe. She had been a civil servant for three years and her service record was impeccable. The two documents she was asked to photocopy on 21 October had been written the previous day by the Defence Secretary, Michael Heseltine, and were addressed to the Prime Minister, with copies distributed to six senior members of the Government, including the Foreign Secretary. Reading the documents during a quiet moment in the office, Sarah Tisdall became indignant, made an additional copy of each, and put both of them in her handbag. At the end of the day she set out from Whitehall, stopped at Ryman's in the Strand to buy an envelope and a felt-tipped pen, heavily scored out the official markings on the documents, and addressed the brown envelope to the 'Political Editor' of the *Guardian.*

17 June 1980: Defence Secretary Francis Pym announces that the US will deliver one hundred and sixty cruise missiles to Britain.

15 May 1983: Geneva Arms-Limitation Talks begin.

20 October: Defence Secretary Michael Heseltine writes two memos to Margaret Thatcher: the first concerns the delivery of cruise and how to gain the best coverage from the media and secure the best reception from the House of Commons; the second concerns security arrangements at the RAF airbase at Greenham Common. Copies of the memos are sent to six senior ministers, including the Foreign Secretary.

21 October: Sarah Tisdall makes photocopies of both memos and delivers them to *Guardian*. *Guardian* publishes front page exclusive with headline 'Whitehall Sets November 1 Cruise Arrival' in last edition.

22 October: Exclusive appears, with same headline, in Saturday morning edition of *Guardian*. CND march.

24 October: Whitehall inquiry established to discover source of leak.

29 October: Protesters cut through fence protecting Greenham RAF base; one hundred arrested.

31 October: *Guardian* publishes Heseltine's first memo, relating to the delivery of cruise. Debate on cruise takes place in the House of Commons. Thatcher acknowledges and regrets publication of document, and publicly orders urgent inquiry into leak.

1 November: Paul Brown writes article in *Guardian* based on Michael Heseltine's second memo, relating to security arrangements at Greenham Common. During Prime Minister's Question Time, Roland Boyes, Labour MP, asks for assurance that protesters will not be shot; Heseltine's reply: 'I categorically will give no such assurance.'

11 November: Treasury Solicitor asks *Guardian* for return of *the* memo.

12 November: US State Department confirms 'custodial unit' at Greenham airbase with orders to shoot if necessary.

15 November: First cruise missile arrives.

17 November: *Guardian* replies to Treasury Solicitor, noting that handwriting and markings on the photocopy of the document might reveal the source of the leak; *Guardian* claims, by virtue of section 10 of the Contempt of Court Act 1981 (that protects a publication from disclosing its sources of information, except in certain circumstances), that it cannot return document.

21–22 November: German *Bundestag* debate about the delivery of cruise and Pershing II.

22 November: Treasury Solicitor issues writ, in the names of the Defence Secretary and the Attorney General, demanding the return of the document unmutilated in any way. *Guardian* appeals against writ.

23 November: Soviet Union walks out of Geneva talks.

15 December: Master of the Rolls and Court of Appeal rule against *Guardian*; order return of document but give leave to appeal to the Lords.

16 December: Court of Appeal orders immediate return of document. *Guardian*'s editorial meeting convened to discuss destroying or returning document; document is returned. Treasury Solicitor asks about second document and is told that it has been destroyed.

17 December: *Times*'s leader supports *Guardian*'s actions.

18 December: *Observer* publishes article based on information in second document.

20–22 December: Detective Chief Superintendent Ronald Hardy, Scotland Yard's Serious Crime Squad Officer in charge of the leaked document, questions *Observer* and later *Guardian* about the source of *Observer*'s article on 18 December.

6 January: Detective Chief Superintendent Ronald Hardy questions Sarah Tisdall about the possibility that she leaked document.

9 January: Sarah Tisdall confesses to leaking document and is arrested, charged under Section 2 of the Official Secrets Act.

3 February: National Executive Committee of the NUJ censures *Guardian* for returning document and betraying its source.

23 March: Sarah Tisdall is sentenced to six months' imprisonment by Mr Justice Cantley.

24 March: *Guardian*'s 'Official' history of its involvement in the Sarah Tisdall case is published, which mentions, for the first time, the existence of the second document.

9 April: Tisdall's appeal is rejected.

Soon after she handed in the documents to the *Guardian*'s reception desk at 119 Farringdon Road, they were in the editor's possession. Some considerable time after withdrawing into his office adjoining the News Room to study them, he telephoned his Defence Correspondent, David Fairhall, who in turn checked out the accuracy of the information contained in the documents by speaking to his contacts in the Ministry of Defence.

Fairhall's eight-hundred-word story appeared on the front page of the final edition on sale to the demonstrators gathering in London for the CND rally. Without mentioning the *Guardian*'s knowledge of either document, Fairhall clearly drew heavily on them both.

The following Monday, 24 October, the paper eagerly followed up its weekend 'scoop': 'The Prime Minister was warned by officials about the *Guardian*'s disclosure before Saturday's edition went on sale and Downing Street indicated last night that an immediate investigation to find the source of the leak was expected.' The leak was so serious—boasted the paper—that it would be 'more than a "routine" investigation.' Indeed Fairhall's article had celebrated the predictable impact of such a leak on the Government's security plans: 'If the missiles are coming on November 1,' he wrote, 'and in the light *of this report* the timetable is almost certain to be called into question again in Whitehall, security at the Berkshire base will be massively strengthened' (my emphasis). He also expected the British and Americans 'hastily to review their delivery timetable' for cruise missiles.

Preston hesitated to publish either document. The fears and vacillations which characterized his conduct throughout the case were already apparent during the last week of October. Not until 31 October was one document published verbatim on page two of the *Guardian.* Henceforward referred to as 'the published document', it outlined the cruise missile timetable and Heseltine's proposed strategies for outwitting the Labour opposition and the peace movement. Its publication resulted in an intensification of the police inquiry in Whitehall. Preston shrank from publishing the second document, which described security precautions at Greenham Common air base: indeed the first explicit reference to it in the *Guardian* did not occur for five months, until 24 March 1984. Yet the second document was freely used as a source, both in Fairhall's initial story of 22 October and in a report written by Paul Brown which appeared in the edition of 1 November. It was this story that precipitated a noisy exchange in the Commons when Heseltine and the Prime Minister were challenged to deny that infiltrators at Greenham Common might, in the last resort, be shot by RAF Regiment personnel, with armed American guards stationed behind them. No such denial was forthcoming.

According to the *Guardian,* the second document was later destroyed: we do not know when, where or by whom. Anticipating a Government response to the publication of the first document, Preston telephoned his solicitors, Lovell, White & King, to ask what to do: 'Suppose the police should suddenly arrive?' They did not arrive. What did, eventually, arrive was a letter dated 11 November from the Treasury Solicitor, demanding on behalf of Heseltine and the Attorney General the return of the published document. It was Government property. Squandering the moment to destroy the sheets of paper, Preston again telephoned Lovell, White & King to ask for advice. According to the *Guardian*'s News Editor, Peter Cole, Preston was advised that it would be an 'offence' to destroy the document. So he didn't.

Here one must distinguish between Peter Preston's actions and those of his legal advisers. If it was an 'offence' to destroy the classified document, it was much more an offence to have published it; a letter of request carries no legal force and until a writ was issued there could be no question of contempt of court. Thus the editor risked little or nothing by destroying the document.

It is not the duty of solicitors to recommend even the most minor infringements of the law: if you want to park on a yellow line for ten minutes you must resolve to be Bold and Bad all on your own. Instead of destroying the document, Preston naively informed the Government through his solicitors that it contained markings which 'might disclose or assist in the identification of the source'. Therefore Preston begged to be allowed to erase the markings before returning the document. The Treasury Solicitor, no doubt astounded by the vulnerability of the other party, declined to make any such concession and backed up the demand for the return of the unmutilated document with a writ issued on 27 November.

The *Guardian*'s naivety was compounded by its assumption that the excision of the blacked-out markings on the document would secure the source of the leak against forensic detection. It is the sheet of paper which under examination reveals the specific photo-copier used; and so it turned out in the case of Sarah Tisdall. Even if Preston or Cole had dared to put the document through their own office photo-copier it would possibly have been enough to prevent detection of the source. But none of this was done. Cole attempts to explain why in his official history of the affair published in the *Guardian* on 24 March: the impression is that of a belated search by a knitting circle for a ball of wool stolen by a cat three months dead.

On legal advice the *Guardian* decided to invoke Section 10 of the 1981 Contempt of Court Act in support of the paper's insistence that the markings should be erased before the document was returned. Section 10 is designed to protect the media from the obligation to disclose their sources of information, but this protection is heavily qualified and does not apply where, for example, a national security factor is held to be involved.

For this reason the *Guardian*'s defence strategy was probably doomed from the outset; many of the paper's staff later tended to lay the blame on poor legal advice. But Section 10 was the only defence available once Preston had (repeatedly) failed to grasp the obvious solution and destroy the document in the office shredder. Ultimately the *Guardian*'s lawyers ended up quibbling in court about copyright over markings and whether a piece of paper enjoys the same immunity under Section 10 as the name of a known source.

> **No court may require a person to disclose, nor is any person guilty of contempt of court for refusing to disclose, the source of information contained in a publication for which he is responsible, unless it be established to the satisfaction of the court that disclosure is necessary in the interests of justice or national security or for the prevention of disorder or crime.**
>
> **Section Ten, 'Sources of Information', 1981 Contempt of Court Act**

The only viable defence in a case such as this is a political defence: on behalf of the Fourth Estate the *Guardian* should have committed itself to the protection of its source whatever the cost, arguing not only that it owed a debt of honour to the individual, but also an obligation to resist those strategies of the state—like Heseltine's—which are designed to deceive the electorate or keep it in ignorance.

To embark on such a political defence, however, requires the choice of sympathetic lawyers: the *Guardian* chose to retain as counsel a pillar of the Tory establishment, Lord Rawlinson,[1] who, one may assume, believes in the right to leak classified documents on a point of conscience as ardently as the Ayatollah believes in a woman's right to remove her veil whenever she chooses. Indeed Rawlinson lost little time, once in court, in condemning the 'betrayal' of trust by the civil servant who had passed the published document to the *Guardian.* A fine start! That Preston was determined to present himself as a highly responsible patriot is apparent from his affidavit

[1]When Conservative Attorney General in 1972, Rawlinson had obtained a High Court injunction restraining the *Sunday Times* from publishing an investigation of the thalidomide tragedy largely based on documents obtained from a 'mole' within the Distillers Company.

to the court, with its obeisance to establishment values: 'I accept that a free press has responsibilities not only to its source but also to the Government.' He also referred to the paper's 'anxiety not to act irresponsibly,' insisted that publication of the first document had 'no national security implications', and pleaded that 'there was nothing in the memorandum which was published in the *Guardian* which could not easily have been gleaned by any person sitting in the public gallery at the House of Commons.'

These lines reflect one of the more timid of the *Guardian*'s several souls as well as the ambivalence of Preston and the principal editors towards the Campaign for Nuclear Disarmament—an ambivalence mirrored in a passage from Peter Cole's official history of the affair, published on 24 March:

> Inevitably there was some considerable discussion of what sort of person the source might be, and there were differing views. The non-coincidence, as it seemed, of the delivery of the document and the Hyde Park CND rally raised uneasy questions. It was certainly not axiomatic that the leaker would have acted out of altruism.

What can this mean? No payment had been involved. How can Cole cast such shameless aspersions when the *Guardian* itself had hurried its 'scoop' on to the streets in time for the CND rally of 22 October?

On 15 December the *Guardian* went in front of the Master of the Rolls, Sir John Donaldson, and his two colleagues of the Court of Appeal. The resemblance between the political profiles of Sir John Donaldson and the *Guardian*'s counsel, Lord Rawlinson, was a striking one. Both were pillars of the Conservative establishment. Rawlinson had served as Heath's Attorney General from 1971 to 1974, while Donaldson became President of Heath's ill-fated National Industrial Relations Court. And now they were confronted by a memorandum from a Tory Defence Secretary to a Conservative Prime Minister concerning an issue—nuclear weapons—which deeply and bitterly divides the political parties. In addition, Sir John Donaldson himself had only recently been the subject of an article in the *Guardian,* based on yet another leaked document, describing his political consultations with a senior civil servant on the subject of trade unions and the courts—consultations that had been set up by the then Chancellor of the Exchequer, Sir Geoffrey Howe.[2]

Thus the *Guardian* and its solicitors had reached deep into the antique Tory cupboard in search of a counsel. As for the judiciary, a comparison of British and American practice merely reminds us that British judges regard any challenge to their impartiality as contempt of court.

3

Three legal issues had to be decided: (1) did the Crown enjoy proprietory rights over both the document and the spoiled markings? (2) was handing over a document from an unknown source tantamount to revealing a source (i.e. was it covered by Section 10 of the 1981 Contempt Act)? (3) did national security factors apply in this case?

The latter was the decisive factor. All three Appeal Court judges argued that the national security factor precluded a successful defence under Section 10. The Appeal Court *seemed,* in the main, to be stressing not so much the security risk involved in the publication of this particular document as the future danger to national security if the source of the leak went undetected. Said the Master of the Rolls, Sir John Donaldson: 'Whether or not any harm has been done on this occasion, the next may be different.'

On 15 and 16 December the High Court and the Court of Appeal ruled that the *Guardian* must hand over the published document to the Government to assist the search for the 'mole'.

Leaving the court, Peter Preston complained that the judges had assumed the culprit would in future 'rob a bank' just because he or she had in the past 'whipped a tube of Smarties.' This was disingenuous for at least two reasons. First, the Crown and Appeal Court, though emphasizing future dangers if the mole went undetected, did not dismiss as negligible the national security damage

[2]Ten years earlier, Howe had served as Solicitor General when Rawlinson was Attorney General in the Government of Edward Heath.

involved in the publication of the Heseltine memorandum about cruise missiles. Three months later an element in the prosecution's case against Sarah Tisdall was precisely the damage-assessment on the leaking of that document. Second, and much more important, Mr Preston was well aware when he spoke of banks and Smarties that the unknown Whitehall source had leaked to him not one document but two—the second being, according to his own criteria, too dangerous to publish verbatim.

This brings us to a crucial question. Mr Preston obviously knew about the second document, but how much did the Government and the Appeal Court know? Equally interesting, how did they gain their knowledge? By reasonable inference and guesswork, or by something more conclusive?

The Government had demanded the return of only one document, the memorandum published by the *Guardian* in full on 31 October. As the Attorney General explained in a written statement on 12 April this year, 'When the *Guardian* published the secret minute...it was appreciated for the first time that the paper must have the document, or a copy in its possession.' Clearly no such certainty attached in the Government's mind to the second document; whatever his suspicions, the Attorney General did not care to go fishing in the dark. Indeed the Treasury Solicitor's correspondence, and the subsequent writ, made no mention of the second document.

The Government obviously had good reason to suspect that the *Guardian*'s reports from 22 October to 1 November had been inspired by both documents. Were their suspicions—and hence the Appeal Court's—confirmed advertently or inadvertently from the *Guardian* side? Mr Preston flatly denies it: there was, he says, absolutely no collusion. He writes to explain that he formed the opinion in court 'from what Simon Brown, the Treasury Counsel, said tangentially at two points, that the Government knew (or strongly suspected) that we had had a second document.'

Journalists who attended a meeting in Preston's office immediately after the Appeal Court's ruling, on 16 December, believe that the truth about the second document had been conveyed through lawyers representing the *Guardian* to lawyers representing the Government. They explain this as a conscious act of plea-bargaining by the *Guardian* in an attempt to prove its patriotism and avoid a subsequent criminal prosecution under the Official Secrets Act. Mr Preston is adamant in his denial: 'But there is all the difference in the world between deducing on the one hand and telling/dealing/conniving on the other.'

According to another view, Preston let it be known privately that the Government had learned the truth about the second document from the *Guardian*'s counsel, Lord Rawlinson, during the trial. Hugh Stephenson, editor of the *New Statesman* (and perfectly well disposed towards Preston) is clear in his mind about this: 'I did have a conversation with Preston in a pub at someone's leaving party and the Tisdall case came up. I had been talking about the case to people on the *Guardian,* and I am, therefore, clear that I "know" that Preston's view is that he had bad legal advice in general and from Rawlinson in particular and that Rawlinson made an "unforced error" in relation to the second document.' Mr Stephenson then adds: 'I could not say—for I kept no notes—that Preston said all this to me in those terms at that pub meeting. It may be that he said something that confirmed what I already knew from someone else to be the case.'

Mr Preston is again unequivocal. Asked whether he had confided to friends that Rawlinson had made an 'unforced error', he replied: 'I confided nothing of the sort to friends or anybody else because none of it bears any relationship to the facts.' It is of course unknown what instructions Preston gave Rawlinson or what advice Rawlinson gave Preston.

I have in essence put only one question to the lawyers involved in the case: did the *Guardian*'s lawyers, whether solicitors or counsel, ever privately tell the Government's men the truth about the second document? The *Guardian*'s solicitors, Lovell, White & King, refused to grant me an interview despite a written request and an oral one to the editor himself. The deputy Treasury Solicitor is Mr J.B. Bailey; it was he who actually asked after the second document at about 1.00 p.m. on 16 December when Preston finally handed over to him the published document. Mr Bailey denies having learned anything from the *Guardian*'s lawyers. Treasury Counsel in the case, Mr Simon D. Brown, writes to deny that Lord Rawlinson said 'any such thing to me and I shall be very surprised if he suggests the contrary.' Lord Rawlinson writes that he 'cannot possibly comment—either by way of refutation, admission, rejection, acceptance, elaboration, explanation or what you will.'

The recollections of the principal editors at the *Guardian* do not in fact coincide. While Preston and Peter Cole deny knowledge of any exchanges between lawyers concerning the second document, deputy editor David McKie remembers that the second document 'had been mentioned in informal discussions between lawyers.' This coincides with the recollections of *Guardian* journalists who, sadly but I suppose inevitably, wish to remain unattributed.

And what of the Appeal Court judges, what did they know, if anything, of the second document? When they referred to future dangers was this perhaps a code for something they knew about the past but could not, within the conventions of the specific legal action, express? Asked whether the Court of Appeal, in assessing the national security factor, had knowledge that the same source had given two documents to the *Guardian,* the Master of the Rolls, Sir John Donaldson, writes: 'My recollection of the details of the *Guardian* newspaper case is quite insufficient to answer the question you ask.' Mr Justice Slade writes: 'I can do no more than echo what he says....' Mr Justice Griffith answers that convention prevents him from commenting.

Can the judges have been in ignorance of something which the Government considered vital to national security?

4

Following the Appeal Court's ruling, an ad hoc emergency meeting of journalists was held in the editor's office. This meeting was not mentioned in the crisis-report published the following day, nor indeed was the existence of the second document. Whether or not the purpose of the meeting was to compromise the staff by binding them to the editor's decision, that was certainly the outcome: they emerged convinced that handing back the document was awful, repulsive—but inevitable. By all reports only Aidan White, Father of the Chapel of the National Union of Journalists, kicked against it; the majority of those present listened, groaned and swayed like the women of Argos in lament for a royal nemesis. Morally associated with Preston's decision thereafter, the Chapel was reduced to searching for scapegoats outside the paper, notably Lovell, White & King, but also Rawlinson, the judges, the Government.

His distress palpable, the editor explained that if he were thinking only of himself and his own sense of honour, he would tear up the document there and then; but he had a duty to the paper, our paper, so suddenly wealthy and so vulnerable to a Government itching to bite off this awkward liberal thorn in its side.

Those present listened in awe as the spectre of huge, pulverizing, escalating fines was advanced. It was whispered that lawyers spoke of £100,000 a day. As one of those present later put it to me: 'We would have been subject to mounting fines and the *Guardian* couldn't have stood it. If we'd destroyed the document a judge might have gone crazy.' There was also the strong feeling, perhaps communicated by deputy editor McKie, that the rest of Fleet Street would make no move in support; the gallant *Guardian* would rapidly sink with the loss of all aboard and Mrs Thatcher would attend the funeral dressed in pink.

All of which was nonsense, of course, provided the editor resolved the dilemma by publicly destroying the document with a photographer to hand. Such an irreversible act of defiance might, according to the legal opinion I have consulted, have resulted in a fine of £50,000 or £100,000—but even a quarter of a million would scarcely have dented the paper's buoyant finances, with its rising circulation and 1.5 million readers. The company's shares in Reuters are worth millions; it also owns a hunk of Blackpool tower.

If any person having in his possession or control any sketch, plan, model, article, note, document, or information which relates to munitions of war, communicates it directly or indirectly to any foreign power, or in any other manner prejudicial to the safety or interests of the State, that person shall be guilty of a misdemeanour . . . .

If any person receives any . . . sketch, plan, model, article, note, document, or information, knowing or having reasonable ground to believe, at the time when he receives it, that the . . . sketch, plan, model, article, note, document, or information is communicated to him in contravention of this Act, he shall be guilty of a misdemeanour.

From **Section Two, 1911 Official Secrets Act**

However, make no mistake, these practicalities were totally outweighed in Preston's mind by an overriding principle: 'All my working life I have preached respect for the law.' This commanded respect, too: many convinced themselves that once the paper had embarked on the legal process it had to abide by the outcome. But supposing the court had commanded one of those present at that meeting to name a source who was known to him: what then? Should journalists abide by the provisions of the Internal Security Act in South Africa, out of respect for the law and the courts?

Those present were acutely aware that in recent weeks one *Guardian* editorial after another had attacked the printers' union, the NGA, for flouting court injunctions against 'illegal secondary picketing' (forbidden under the Tory Employment Act of 1980). They were equally aware that the *Guardian*'s management was simultaneously invoking this same Tory legislation by making itself a party to a three-million-pound action for damages against the NGA brought by twelve national newspapers. Thus the paper's editorial principles were far from being disinterested: the scent of profits wafted through the ink. On 10 December a new *Guardian* leader, 'Back at the brink of the abyss', had again attacked the NGA and also the TUC; simultaneously, as if to confirm the marriage of principle and profit, the paper's management became a party to a new legal move to prevent the union ordering a national printers' strike for 14 December. This was the day the *Guardian* began its defence in the High Court against the Government's demand for the return of the published document. On 15 December a *Guardian* leader writer, again brandishing principled respect for the law, advised the NGA and its members to 'climb down as best they can'.[3]

The need to be consistent with the paper's stand against the NGA's defiance of the courts was stressed at the meeting in Preston's office during the fatal hour before lunch on Friday, 16 December. Enter now the sinister shadow of the second document (which had been seen by no more than a dozen members of staff, perhaps less,

[3]In February 1984 the Fathers of the eight *Guardian* union chapels, including the NUJ, wrote jointly to Peter Gibbings, chairman of the company, urging him to withdraw from the legal action undertaken against the NGA on the basis of Tory legislation which the paper itself had condemned. This was not reported in the paper.

and whose contents, it was hinted, could not be fully divulged). One journalist comments: 'There were only about six in the know: Preston, Cole, McKie, Ian Wright, Ken Dodd, Fairhall, though a few others had glimpsed the document. They behaved throughout in a secretive way, timid, frightened, engaging in an elaborate dance with the Ministry of Defence. There had been no consultation and they had bungled.'

It was McKie who introduced the second document into the discussion now, and with the definite purpose of further bending all those present to acquiescence in handing over the published document to the Government. Here we may quote Peter Cole's account (24 March):

> It wasn't even, as the deputy editor noted, as if the destruction of the [published] document would bring the whole miserable story to a close. If we destroyed the first document now, the attack on the paper was likely to be renewed on the basis of the second document. The Government might well argue that this document had indeed been a direct threat to security...and our decision not to print it and destroy it constituted our recognition that this was so.

McKie repeated this argument to a staff meeting on 29 March, after Sarah Tisdall's trial.

But wait: how could the Government punish the *Guardian* for *not* having published the second document? The answer must be that Preston, McKie, Cole and Dodd feared that if they defied the Court of Appeal then the Crown might turn on its criminal engines and prosecute the paper for having used both classified documents in stories published between 22 October and 1 November. (This danger would be all the greater if the Government had private confirmation that the newspaper had received and quoted the second document.)

The principal editors were clearly intent on convincing the journalists that the court order had to be obeyed. It was *sauve qui peut*—and that meant saving the *Guardian*'s skin, not Sarah Tisdall's (or whoever), even though the paper would no doubt have increased its circulation still further if Preston had spent a week in Wormwood Scrubs (not that the Director of Public Prosecutions would have been so foolish as to seek his martyrdom).

The meeting in the editor's office offered the assembled journalists an image of democratic discussion, but in reality the decision had already been made. To quell the natural revulsion of decent journalists at the prospect of betraying a source, two further ideas were implanted.

The first was introduced obliquely: might it not be the case that an unknown source did not merit the same protection as one who took a journalist into his or her confidence? After all, what do we know of this mysterious and possibly sinister source who foisted dangerous documents upon us before vanishing into the twilight? When this was first mentioned to me, some weeks later, I was sceptical: given the fact that the *Guardian* had exploited these two documents so energetically between 22 October and 1 November, surely no decent man could advance so insidious a proposition. It would also suggest a disconcerting overlap between Preston's reported position and *The Times*'s leader of 17 December, which said:

> The recipient's obligations towards an informant who does not trust him with his identity can hardly be one of the same kind as those in a genuine confidential relationship. No explicit or implicit contract exists, and it is almost quixotic to act as if it did.

Far from repudiating this position, Mr Preston embraced it as his own. The words printed above were prominently displayed in the *Guardian*'s major 'Tisdall' issue of 24 March (the day after her trial); four days later *The Times* published a letter from Preston gratefully acknowledging the 'sympathetic' leader of 17 December and one sentence in particular: 'No explicit or implicit contract exists, and it is almost quixotic to act as if it did.'

But perhaps it was the second item implanted at the editorial meeting of 16 December which was the basest: that the unknown source of the two documents was possibly not 'so white after all'. Given the fact that the source had leaked such sensitive material on the eve of the CND march of 22 October, what kind of a person might the paper be protecting? Peter Cole's later comment is worth repeating: 'It was certainly not axiomatic that the leaker would have acted out of altruism.' A journalist who was not present at the staff meeting of 16 December recalls: 'Even before the case came to court we'd been made to feel that the second document was a genuine breach of national security and therefore the source was a security risk.'

The meeting broke up. 'There were,' as one of those present recalls, 'many churning stomachs.' Preston walked down to Holborn Viaduct, retracing the steps taken by Sarah Tisdall exactly eight weeks earlier, on another Friday, and handed over the document to the deputy Treasury Solicitor, Mr J.B. Bailey—who promptly and confidently inquired about the second document. According to Peter Cole, 'He was assured it did not exist.'

Sarah Tisdall was now doomed. Preston had to face public criticism but was determined to limit it by erasing any mention of the second document. This involved not only hoisting a huge D-Notice[4] over 119 Farringdon Road, but also a rapid intervention at the *Observer.*

On 17 December the *Guardian* published a front-page story and a leader lamenting the great document disaster. No mention was made of the second document. Heseltine had sent '*a* memo'; someone had photostatted '*the* memo' and '*it* was delivered to the *Guardian* that evening.' David Fairhall had contacted the Ministry of Defence without disclosing the existence of '*the* memo'—my emphasis throughout. Who would suspect from this relentless singular that the *Guardian* had based its stories on two documents from the same source? Preston had only to lift a Ricardian eyebrow to ensure that the young *Guardian* reporters chronicling the case never mentioned the second document.

But this curtain of secrecy was threatened by the alert *Observer* journalist, David Leigh, who had worked for the *Guardian* until July 1981. There may have been a personal edge to Leigh's interest when he learned from a senior member of the *Guardian*'s editorial staff the contents of the second document.[5] Leigh's source may well have been frustrated that Preston had shrunk from publishing the second alongside the first.

---

[4]An official prohibition on the disclosure of specified information.

[5]In 1979 Leigh and a colleague had written a story based on an interview with a juror in the Jeremy Thorpe trial. Warned by his favoured legal adviser, Geoffrey Grimes of Lovell, White & King, that the Attorney General might bring a test case, Preston had shrunk from the possible consequences of publication. The story eventually appeared in Bruce Page's *New Statesman.*

Learning that Leigh intended to publish the facts in the *Observer,* Preston telephoned the paper's editor, Donald Trelford. Both newspapers are prominent critics of governmental secrecy and information laundering, but are capable of practising the same techniques when expedient. The styles of the two editors, however, are far from identical. Where the *Guardian* may seem sedate and cautious, the *Observer*'s way is brash and buccaneering; Trelford is at ease with the front-page headline which may well be forgotten by the following week, whereas Preston peers at the world from the dark recesses of the centre-fold with an almost donnish reserve. Preston's freedom of manoeuvre throughout the five months between the arrival of the two documents and Sarah Tisdall's incarceration in Holloway partly reflected his exceptional freedom from management interference and pressure; Trelford on the other hand, conscious of the *Observer*'s precarious circulation and finances, would not lightly kill a front-page 'exclusive'.

Neither Preston nor Trelford will disclose what was said, or demanded, or granted, during their telephone conversation of 16 December. But there can be little doubt that Preston wanted David Leigh's second-document story dead and buried, citing his own embarrassment and that of his lawyer, Lord Rawlinson, whose formal defence in court had made no reference to the second document.

Equally clearly, both Trelford and David Leigh preferred a little surgery to an outright burial. Leigh had a good story and he was keen to twist Preston's tail: he was convinced that the *Guardian* had come clean about the second document to the Government behind the scenes. Preston's attitude towards the truth resembled that of a landlord towards a vacant property—if he chose not to occupy it that didn't give anyone else the right to squat in it. But Leigh, with Trelford's consent, decided that if the *Guardian* didn't 'want' the second document, the *Observer* might as well lay claim to it. Preston was furious; so were Cole and Dodd: the counterfeiter had been robbed of his wallet.

Doctored, the *Observer* story appeared on 18 December under the headline, 'New Heseltine secrets leak':

> Details were obtained yesterday by the *Observer* of a secret minute by the Defence Secretary Mr Michael Heseltine,

> which outlined for senior colleagues how British troops were to be deployed to stop the political risk of US servicemen opening fire on Greenham Common women. This document is potentially more explosive than the *Guardian* document, also written by Mr Heseltine.... The new document's nature explains both Mr Heseltine's fear at what political damage the Whitehall 'mole' might still do, and the manner in which the Defence Secretary behaved in Parliament last month when the issue of shooting the peace protesters came up. The document is a minute on 'contingency security arrangements' at Greenham Common once the US cruise missiles arrive. It was circulated to Ministers and the Chief Whip's office along with the *Guardian* memo of October.... During last week's hurried appeal by the *Guardian* against a High Court ruling that it must hand over the document, the Defence Secretary's lawyers emphasised the hypothetical dangers to 'national security' if the mole should leak other documents.

These extracts from the unsigned article would surely lead any intelligent reader to the conclusion that *the same 'mole' had leaked both documents.* But it would also lead the reader to conclude that the two documents had been leaked to different newspapers. Thus the doctored story, as it emerged after Preston's telephone call to Trelford, protected the *Guardian* but not the person who turned out to be Sarah Tisdall. The *Observer* story brought Chief Detective Superintendent Ronald Hardy of the Serious Crimes Squad rapidly on to the scene; he also called on the *Guardian*'s solicitors, for Hardy was in little doubt that, if the *Observer* actually had possession of the second document, then it had received it from a source inside the *Guardian.*

Trelford's leader column of 18 December also repays study. Although he knew that the *Guardian* had received a second document which the paper had considered too sensitive to publish, his editorial suggested there had been only one, and that of a political rather than a military nature.

5

An NUJ chapel meeting was held at the *Guardian* on 21 December. At the same time Preston issued new guidelines about the destruction of documents, the implication being that a system had been at fault rather than an individual: structuralism instead of sodomy. 'Any confidential document that comes into our possession is at risk the moment legal proceedings for its return are initiated. This can happen with frightening rapidity so nothing should be left to chance,' he advised all departments. Frightening rapidity? Fully eleven days had elapsed after publication of the document on 31 October before a letter arrived from the Treasury Solicitor; and a further eleven before a writ was issued.

'It has been a horrible blow,' Preston told his staff. 'But the paper goes on and, I hope and believe, in a way that shows it can't be squashed or intimidated.'[6] Resentful of an Early Day Motion in the Commons by Brian Sedgemore, MP, calling for Preston's resignation, the chapel meeting of 21 December expressed its respect for 'the editor's painful decision' and reaffirmed its 'total support for the editorship of the paper.' Grief and wrath were diverted on to the hapless Lovell, White & King: two months later the chapel unanimously passed a motion of no confidence in the Holborn Viaduct solicitors.

The national executive committee of the NUJ, meeting on 3 February, took a less charitable view of what the Hon. General Treasurer described as Preston's 'odious lapse'. The union's president, Eddie Barrett, commented: 'The fact is that the *Guardian* editor has shat on a principle we hold dear, and shat on the informant.' David Thompson, Father of the Chapel at the *Daily Mirror,* expressed complete disgust: 'I don't know of a case of anyone who cracked like Preston.' Feelings ran high now: Sarah Tisdall had

[6]This reminds me of the letter I received from an indignant *Guardian* journalist who assured me that the possibility of sending the editor to prison for 'a probably long term' had been considered at the 16 December editorial meeting 'hard and hopefully', as an alternative to handing over the document.

been charged at Bow Street magistrates' court on 11 January. The act of betrayal had yielded a real victim, young, female, helpless. Early in April Preston was condemned by the annual conference of the NUJ meeting in Loughborough. The motion was passed overwhelmingly after it was moved by the City of London branch, whose Father declared: 'The editor of the *Guardian* did not only betray Sarah Tisdall. He betrayed every one of us here.' The *Guardian*'s NUJ Father of Chapel, Aidan White, quoted words written about the most illustrious of *Manchester Guardian* editors, C.P. Scott: 'If it came to the point, he was perfectly ready to sacrifice the commercial success of his newspaper to its journalistic integrity... better extinction than a failure of principle.'

Some measure of courage may be required to protect a source in the face of the threat of legal sanction, but not courage of heroic proportions. The role of honour is an ancient one. E.D.G. Lewis of the Manchester *Daily Despatch* published an article in 1937, drawing on a confidential circular issued by the Chief Constable of Southport—who was livid. Lewis was charged and fined after refusing to name his source. In the 1960s two journalists went to prison rather than divulge confidential information to a tribunal investigating security matters. In 1980 Granada TV was sued by British Steel after screening a report highly damaging to the Corporation and based on documents leaked by an employee. Despite adverse rulings in the High Court, the Court of Appeal and, finally, the Lords, Granada made no attempt to persuade its researcher, Laurie Flynn, to disclose the identity of the British Steel employee who had leaked the documents—not that Flynn would have done so in any event.

If we are tempted to take seriously Peter Preston's principled respect for the law, rather than believe that he simply lost his nerve, the *Guardian*'s editorial of 18 August 1980 makes instructive reading. Praising Granada and Mr Flynn for their 'courage throughout the ordeal,' for having stood firm 'at a high cost and considerable personal risk,' the *Guardian* concluded: 'now there will be no need for disclosure or broken promises.'

A source is a person who should enjoy the status, if not the sentiment, of a friend. 'If I had to choose between my sources and my country,' E.M. Forster might have said, 'I hope I'd choose my sources.' This was apparently the attitude of Samuel Popkin, a Harvard expert on Asian affairs and Vietnamese village life who found himself suddenly caught up in the investigation into the leak of the 'Pentagon Papers' in 1971. A grand jury wanted to know which US Government officials had helped him in his research. Popkin refused to name them. Judge Arthur Garrity jailed Popkin—a verdict upheld on appeal by the Supreme Court. Clearly the Harvard professor did not regard 'the law'—the moral authority and awesome ritual of the courts—with the same terror that Peter Preston seems to have discovered in the Royal Courts of Justice.

Despite the First Amendment and the Freedom of Information Act, American reporters have several times been forced to rub their principles on the whetstone of personal courage. In 1972 the Supreme Court affirmed the obligation of journalists to testify fully, like other citizens, to courts and grand juries. In one of the cases under review, a *New York Times* reporter, Earl Caldwell, had refused to disclose to a grand jury information about his contacts with Black Panthers. In 1982 a television reporter declined to inform a New York grand jury how he had obtained the jury's own secret report on a case of illegal gun sales. Not until this year was New York's 'shield law' upheld in a test case, protecting journalists from contempt charges for refusing to disclose information or sources. But whatever English or American law says or allows, the need for personal courage among journalists remains inescapable.

Of the lessons to be drawn from the *Guardian*–Tisdall case, the need for individual courage and civil disobedience in the face of oppressive laws is a relatively simple one. Far more complex and problematical is the web of secrecy. We tend to focus our indignation on governmental instruments of censorship: the Official Secrets Act, D-notices, the kind of manipulative disinformation briefings offered by the Ministry of Defence during the Falklands conflict. We view the Tisdall case as a battle lost in the war against the Ministry of Defence's proven aim of processing public information: Heseltine's memorandum to Thatcher about cruise missiles is of the same order as the recent Rhine Army exercise in which selected journalists were subjected to methodical, man-to-man muzzling by so-called 'minders'—as *The Times*'s correspondent noted, under such conditions his distinguished predecessor could never have reported the Charge of the Light Brigade. This being so, we naturally focus our hopes on the Campaign for Press Freedom and other initiatives which promise to open the valves of official secrecy to some degree.

But we deceive ourselves if we imagine that the principal threat to freedom of information emanates from Whitehall; it emanates from Fleet Street. This was brought home to me when I tried to establish the existence of the second document during the period, extending to five months, when it was not once mentioned in the *Guardian.* The journalists I spoke to avoided any reference to it; others, when questioned, simply lied:

'I can't comment.'

'I didn't personally see a second document.'

'I don't actually know if there was one.'

'No comment.'

'You're free to read between the lines.'

'Officially I can tell you there was only one document. Anyone who saw a second document is probably old enough to keep silent about it.'

A departmental editor said: 'All knowledge of a second document is surmise. What leads you to imagine two documents arrived in the same envelope? Aren't you aware the police believe that a second document was leaked to the *Observer,* not the *Guardian*?' A few minutes later he said: 'If we *did* receive two documents,' adding, 'I'm trying not to confirm the existence of a second document.'

When colleagues say, 'No comment,' I feel depressed. On 7 February, waiting to be admitted to Bow Street, I asked the *Guardian*'s managing editor, Ken Dodd, about the second document. He shot back: 'What are you talking about? I don't know about any second document...and I wouldn't tell you if I did.' He did, however, declare that Sarah Tisdall had been detected and identified as the culprit by the police without resort to the document returned by the *Guardian.*

The game of truth plays second fiddle to the game of secrecy and, if necessary, of lies. Processing a secret is a comfortable feeling, like having money in your pocket. The journalist is pleased to escape from his customary role as scavenging hack: at long last it's his turn to say 'No comment.' Yet Fleet Street is no worse than the society that sponsors it—we are all, in our weak moment, Peter Preston. We do not need governments to teach us secrecy, lies, deception; in our private and professional lives we liberally dispense embargoes and injunctions, some explicit, some coded.[7]

The government lives within ourselves. We cherish 'privacy'; the breaking of an oath of secrecy (like Sarah Tisdall's) touches a sensitive spot; we may admire her at a distance but would we employ her? There is certainly a sexual fear in our high regard for taciturnity and our suspicion of the wagging tongue; the secrets of the bedroom are only thirty minutes on the underground from the Official Secrets Act.

Following Sarah Tisdall's trial I was for the first time granted interviews with the principal editors: McKie and Cole on 26 March, Preston and Dodd four days later. McKie seemed genuinely anxious to help and was very kind. I learned little that was new to me. When asked why the *Guardian* had deleted all mention of the second document from its pages for three months, Preston answered: 'The priorities were to defend the unknown source against further damage and consequence.' Believe this if you must: Sarah Tisdall had signed a confession that she had leaked both documents on Monday, 9 January, yet *Guardian* reports during the following ten weeks maintained the fiction that she had been charged with leaking *one* document, even though nothing was said at Bow Street magistrates' court to support such an improbable outcome. 'The truth wasn't going to help anybody,' Preston added; perhaps this motto should replace 'one of the world's great newspapers' on the letterhead.

Not content with suppressing the truth in his own pages, Preston had on 16 December intervened to try and suppress it in the *Observer* also. I again asked Mr Preston what he had said on the telephone to

[7]I recall sessions of the Executive Council of the Writers' Guild, a body in favour of Freedom of Information but not disposed to publish the minutes of its own meetings. And there are always good reasons. Disclosure would discourage members from 'speaking freely'. And if it were recorded how each of the councillors voted, that would pose a threat to their 'independence'.

Donald Trelford, what he had requested, and why. I got no answer. Both Preston and Dodd inveighed against 'investigative journalists with one-track minds' and demanded to know what David Leigh had told me. The tone was sarcastic and furious. Preston insisted that his conversation with Trelford had been 'confidential'; Dodd snapped that Preston had every right not to answer me. 'There was no plot,' Preston said, 'you're dancing on the head of a pin. Why don't you ask Donald Trelford?' (This advice was repeated but in vain, for I received no answer from Trelford despite two letters and a series of telephone calls extending over three weeks.)

Long ago I made a private vow never to sue in the rough business of journalism; and I'll try to hold to that view now. Others involved, of course, may have no such hang-ups. But if you would like to sue me on my considered view that (in this instance) you are a devious, sloppy and malevolent operator with a rare disregard for fact and a rare talent for obsessed distortion, then that would be a different matter.

Letter from Peter Preston to David Caute, 14 May 1984

This seems to be the style of the custodians of the Fourth Estate when their actions are investigated. Nor is the Chicago touch entirely missing—take the following minor incident. I asked the *Guardian*'s news editor, Peter Cole, why he had publicly criticized David Leigh (*Guardian,* 24 March) for having implied that the *Observer* had seen a copy of the second document, when in fact Leigh's version of the second document story, as it appeared on 18 December, was a direct result of Preston's intervention with Trelford. Cole looked blank: he said he knew nothing of that. Soon after I took my leave, however, Cole apparently took the short walk to his editor's office and Preston once more went to Trelford—who then had a word with David Leigh.

By convention we remain silent about such incidents: it is from this fear-induced silence that the gaps in our knowledge are fashioned. Of necessity this report must depend partly on unattributable sources within the *Guardian*—no one wants to be the paper's Sarah Tisdall, particularly in view of Preston's visceral and threatening reaction after this article was submitted to the *Guardian* for publication. But that is another story.

On 12 April the Attorney General attempted to explain why only Sarah Tisdall, and not the *Guardian* also, had been prosecuted. He spoke of 'evidential difficulties...and there was also the fact that the evidence against [the *Guardian* staff] had been obtained by a compulsory civil process.' This is nonsense: the paper had published a classified document in full and admitted to continuing possession of it. No, the lesson here is quite different: Mr Preston had played ball. By the time the Serious Crimes Squad interrogated Sarah Tisdall, it knew for certain that she had leaked two documents. Although the second document was apparently played down by prosecutor and judge at her trial, the Lord Chief Justice made a meal of it at her appeal. She got six months. The *Guardian* was spared not only prosecution but also the odium of being subpoenaed to appear in court as witness for the Crown; spared the public humiliation of betraying Miss Tisdall yet again, in public, and under the cool, disgusted gaze of the young woman in the dock.

GRANTA

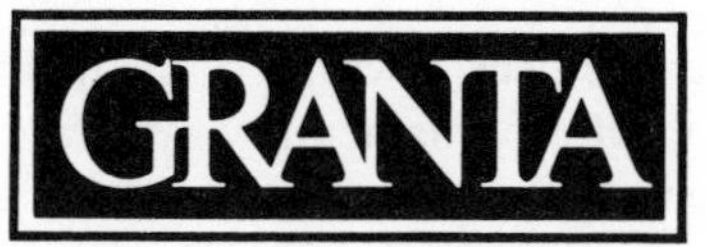

GÜNTER GRASS
RESISTANCE

They are here: against the wishes of the majority of the people, by the wishes of a parliamentary majority. They are referred to as weapons, but they are instruments of genocide. They are here ostensibly for our security, but they increase the risk of a nuclear holocaust in Europe. Though they are stationed here, decisions regarding their deployment and possible use are taken far away, where we have no say. They are supposed to strengthen our defences, but they have been designed for an aggressive first strike. Their presence here is explained by the need to 'close the gap', but the deployment of corresponding systems in the other Germany and in Czechoslovakia is also called 'closing the gap'; so that on both sides the 'gap' will go on being 'closed'—far beyond the threshold of madness already. They are called medium-range missiles. Representative of all the other accumulated power of destruction, they give a picture of the condition of mankind as it spends billions on preparing an end for itself; the deadly logic of self-destruction spares no expense.

I am not sure if this terminal development can still be arrested. After last November's debate in the *Bundestag,* the Lower House of the German Parliament, which was concerned less with the criminal dangers of the new missile-systems than with 'loyalty to NATO' and keeping our word to the United States, my doubts hardened into fear: the people governing us are fools. Overtaxed by the gritty day-to-day of politics, they take refuge in a majority decision that hands the responsibility for life and death to our major allies, and commits us to silence and acquiescence. The stance of this parliamentary majority is one that I can only condemn as pathetic or insane.

They clearly don't know what they're doing. Accustomed only to following matters of detail, they have become criminals acting out of conviction. And when they cry, 'There is a price to pay for freedom!' then one begins to worry seriously about both freedom and its price.

But who can protect us from those who will protect freedom to death? How can a process be arrested, when its terminal tendency appears virtually pre-ordained? Isn't it already apparent how the peace movement is slowing down, flagging, impotent? Do we still have the exact words to express our horror? Are we not faced daily with the cynicism (and the submissive kowtowing to government statements) of the press and television which credit the government's security forces for the failure of the peace movement and the non-appearance of the promised 'hot autumn' of protest? And medium-range missiles? Nuclear warheads? They're all old news—fish-and-chip paper, in the journalists' slang. But is it true? Are we learning to live with them, as we've learned to live with the poison-gas stockpiled in the Pfälzer Wald, and with over five thousand tactical nuclear weapons that have been on West German soil for years? And—I ask myself—am I not sated too by all these protests, by the almost identical appeals, the recurring lists of the names of protesting public figures—my own name always among them?

For that reason, because exhaustion and weariness were to be anticipated, our motto must now be 'Learning to Resist'. There are people—the Poles, for instance—who don't need to learn, because their history is a history of resistance. But the Germans have time and again failed to resist. German history is a history of the failure to resist. But can it be learned? Can it be drummed into people through lessons? Do we in Germany—since we are so helplessly smitten with pedagogy—have to make resistance a special subject?

It cannot simply be prescribed. But whoever sees non-violent resistance as the only way of opposing the prevailing insanity (which even includes genocide in its calculations of nuclear fatalities), will decide on that course for himself, and carry it out himself. Like me too. That is why I must talk about myself and my own experience, my hopes and disappointments, and insights which I can no longer evade.

In the summer of 1944, aged sixteen, I became a soldier. I arrived at the barracks in shorts, with a cardboard suitcase. When my training was completed—seventeen by now—I was sent to the Eastern Front. After several days of seemingly pointless to-ing and fro-ing, and after we had finally withdrawn, the whole company came under fire from a battery of Soviet rockets (known as 'Stalin's organ-pipes'). The company—consisting only of jeeps, small tanks and light artillery—had retreated to a forest of young trees. The Soviet barrage lasted for about three minutes. When it was over, half the company had been killed or maimed. Most of the dead and injured were seventeen, like myself.

Ever since, I've known what fear is. Ever since, I've known that it's only by chance that I am alive. Ever since, any war has appeared conceivable to me. And after the war, my generation found it easy to say the imploring words, 'No more war!'

But this 'No more war!'—this attitude of include-me-out—wasn't enough. The decision to re-arm was taken, first in the Federal Republic, then in the German Democratic Republic, despite the voices of opposition, despite the lessons of history. The division of the country was deepened as the West German Army over here, the Federal Defence, and the 'The People's Army' over there, were incorporated into the military alliances of the two great power-blocs. This reality is part of the postwar history of both German states. In each case, it was justified by the constitutional imperative of national self-defence. (Article 26, paragraph 1 of the *Grundgesetz* forbids a war of aggression and any preparation towards such a war.) Many citizens who had spoken out against re-armament accepted the Federal Defence and the membership of NATO, because they believed the assurances that the weapon-systems, the army-manoeuvres and the war-strategies would be exclusively for the purpose of defence. I too was satisfied with such explanations, and put my hopes in disarmament and a reduction of tension.

Only now, too late, and to my horror, do I realize that I should have been alerted—and reminded of Orwell's 'Newspeak'—by the strategical 'concepts' of the military: like that of so-called 'forward defence'. But it was only when it became transparently clear that the United States and NATO claimed the right to an atomic 'first strike' that I understood the deception, and reverted to my original 'No': 'no more war!'

The Pershing II nuclear missile is a first strike weapon. Accepted by the West German government (as a member of NATO), the new missile transforms the theoretical basis of the Federal Defence. It no longer serves to protect us, as a defence; it has been harnessed to a strategy of aggression. We are therefore talking about a breach of the Constitution. Since the deployment of Pershing IIs began, the Federal Defence is no longer engaged in defensive duties; transgressing Article 26 of the *Grundgesetz,* it is outside the law. We are obliged by the Constitution to resist this perversion.

Not indiscriminately, though. Without violence. It is not blanket opposition but specific and targeted resistance that is needed. This must be directed against a Federal Defence which has been cheated of its defensive mission: because it has been put in the service of NATO's first strike strategy, because the soldiers of the Bundeswehr are being improperly used, because they are already being discounted as casualties in the Pentagon's war-offensive plans.

In the same way that thousands of doctors refuse to prepare emergency services in readiness for a nuclear war, so in future I shall practise what is termed 'demoralizing the armed forces'. I will call on my sons and their friends to refuse to do their military service. In my writing and my speeches, I will introduce and reiterate, unambivalently, the same unwillingness to support an unconstitutional force. In answer to questions from foreign journalists, I will henceforth deny West Germany's commitment to peace, because, through the NATO twin-track decision, through the deployment of first strike weapons, it has again become possible that for the third and last time, war can be started from Germany.

This is the resistance I intend to learn. I will resist, and encourage others to resist, until West Germany is free from nuclear weapons—both tactical and strategic—and free from agents of chemical and bacteriological warfare. Only in this way is it possible for me, and for us, to help the Federal Defence to return to its constitutional duty, exclusively to defend West Germany. It is not new weapons and additional nuclear warheads that we need, but radical democrats, who will stand by West Germany's Constitution, and, still more, who will protect this Constitution from the idiocy of our rulers.

Twice now, writers from the two Germanies have met, first in East Berlin, then in West Berlin. The meetings were heated, because the mania for armaments has gripped both East and West, occupying minds and militarizing thought. But all of us realized that SS 20s and Pershing II missiles are equally horrifying. In the end our talks failed because each side expected the other to take the first step out of the vicious circle. Nevertheless, the Academy of Arts in Berlin sent out invitations for a third meeting, this time in Heilbronn, one of the sites of this accursed development. The writers from the German Democratic Republic did not show up; some didn't want to, others were not allowed to. For the present, then, we will have to learn how to resist without them.

Translated from the German by Michael Hofmann

GRANTA

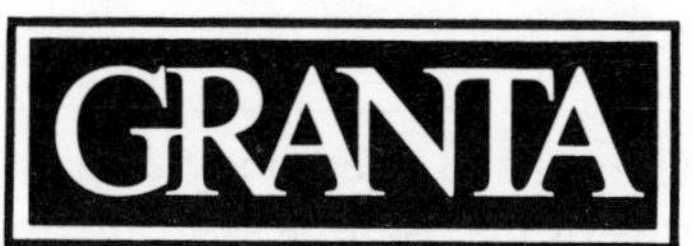

Breyten Breytenbach

Prison-Scribe

Breyten Breytenbach

I was the scribe. In prison everybody eventually finds his own function in terms of his usefulness to the inmate community. You may be the one 'sticking' the others, meaning that you decorate them with tattoos; you may be only a cleaner of cells and a washer of clothes; you may be making cakes illegally, or 'boop-puddings' as they are called, and selling them for a measure of tobacco; you may be a 'grocery rabbit', flogging your dubious sexual charms in return for some tinned food; you may be a 'boop lawyer'—often after having been a real one outside, to counsel the legally-obsessed; you may be, if I can call it that, an interior decorator—decorating people's artificial teeth by drilling small holes in them and inserting bits of coloured glass filed down smooth; you may paint and sell your pictures, using coloured toothpaste as pigment, or you may be a sculptor, carving little objects from the prison soap and staining them with prison polish; you may do needlework, embroidery, or patiently build boats and houses from matchsticks; or you could be the bookmaker, running a gambling school.

But I was the scribe. At the outset it was strange that people should approach me, asking me to answer their letters—it impinged upon my sense of privacy. I soon learned that a letter in prison is public property. Those who do not get any mail, even the poor 'social cases', can thus vicariously have an outside dimension to their lives. No major decisions in love or in family problems are made without their being discussed widely among the prisoners. (One could also be a love-consultant.) Often this brings about an amount of degradation. I heard one prisoner, Dampies, lying in the 'bomb'

Since deciding to live abroad, Breyten Breytenbach has returned to South Africa only twice. Once was in 1973, a trip he was allowed to take with his wife and which occasioned the writing of *A Season in Paradise*, describing not only the experience of his visit, but why he could never again enter South Africa, legally. Two years later, however, he returned: alone, in disguise, and with the cooperation of an underground organization. He was followed by secret agents, and, as he was about to board a plane for France, he was arrested and brought to court on eleven charges of 'terrorism'. He was sentenced to nine years' imprisonment.

(the punishment section), sell his fiancée for three packets of tobacco to another prisoner lying in the next-door cell.

Nothing in prison is free. (If a fellow strolls by your cell giving you a broad smile, he is sure to be back within the hour to ask you a favour in return.) You cannot render a service for free either; you must observe the customs or else you're very suspect. So I had to submit—I objected strenuously—to being given fruit in return for the writing I did for my fellow-prisoners. Once I even scored a dictionary from the deal. It was left as payment by an old man whom I had helped, composing his appeal for mercy when his case came up for review. Can you not understand that a man wants to go home and die in peace, Mr Investigator? (This was my line of attack.) He was one of my most successful clients. He left for court. It was near Christmas and the judge, perhaps succumbing to the spirit of the season, released him immediately.

Among my more noteworthy successes I must cite two instances where writing bore tangible fruit. One was an old lag, 'Pirate', who came to ask if I could refer him to anyone outside. He was due for release and he was, he said, in need of some money to buy tools. Tradesmen must have their own equipment. I wrote a poem, requesting (in rhyme) that the unknown addressee help the bearer out with fifty rand. This he 'bottled' (you must know, Mr Investigator, that 'arse' in Cockney slang becomes 'bottle and glass'). He was duly discharged and, after giving birth to the poem, presented himself to a patron and collected immediate royalties.

The other instance was more problematical. Another prisoner, Bames, approached me, asking for a hand with a translation. He was starting a new gang (a difficult undertaking) and he wanted its members to have tattooed on their backs the Praying Hands of Dürer—an evergreen favourite among the pious lifers—and the Latin version of *live and let live.* But no, man! I protested—I don't know Latin. But yes, Professor Jail-bird, he insisted. Was I to lose face? I warned him that the best I could come up with would be an approximation in corrupt Italian (not even the vulgar form). Good enough for Bames. And before I left I could see his acolytes circling the exercise-yard, with respectfully folded hands on their bare backs, and written large and indelibly underneath: *vivere e lascare vivere.*

People came and asked for love-letters; for poems—

particularly for poems—or they wanted me to write requests to the Boere warders for this or for that; or to help them apply for jobs outside when the time for release became imminent and parole depended on their having employment. So I was continuously inventing their lives too, Mr Investigator. Imagine: here I am, so-and-so, applying for this responsible position, entirely rehabilitated you see, having understood the errors of my ways, a trustworthy and honest man willing to break my balls for my prospective employer who would be missing the chance of his life if he passed me up. And, while I'm writing this, I have in front of me a poor bugger who has no intention of working and no temperament for it either . . . . I wrote requests for parole, for release, for transfer, for interviews. You name it. I am the writer. I wrote the personal histories of men, which they then had to submit to their social workers. A prisoner would come and say: well, *you* know, just write that I'm OK, you know what to put in, I'm sure you know better. In fact, they were quite convinced that whatever life I could invent for them would be far better than the one they had. Some, the saddest cases, came wanting me to write a letter of contrition to a loved one. They always spoke of having broken a mother's heart and of having seen now, now that it was too late, their evil ways. And some came wanting me to write their life-stories. One small-statured 'robaan' (slang for robber), said to me, laughing with a big toothless purple mouth like the fig's overripe burst: 'If only I had the time to tell you my life, what a novel it would make!' And I'm sure it would have been true too. There were as many novels in there as there are human beings going to hell.

One tall distinguished multiple-murderer named Jakes claimed that he'd gone through every possible trick to get to the same prison I was in. Because, he said, he had had these incredible experiences as a mercenary in the Congo: surely all it needed was for me to help him divide the material in paragraphs and, you know, pop in the commas, and we would have a masterpiece on our hands. It was all there, ready to be poured out. It needed only my say-so. Eventually he showed me the manuscript. It was clear that, judging only from the handwritings, it had already been written by five different people—all giving free rein to their diverse fantasies.

What people wanted was always the same thing. What they believed of themselves and of others was along the same lines. If I had to typify the genus 'prisoner', I'd say he is weak, socially; he cannot control his desires and impulses; he has no means of separating the real world from imaginary ones. He is also of course someone without the slightest sense of responsibility, and no feeling for 'property'. 'Look here,' one of them said to me seriously, 'I've decided to be a writer too. I'm going to take all those old books people no longer read and re-write them, just changing the names.' I was most impressed, though, by Skollie, another prisoner, who, just before being hanged, sent me a poem of quite outstanding originality. It was addressed to God—a simple conversation in which he announced that he was looking forward soon to making acquaintance. The poem, hidden and re-hidden, survived with me for years. I was going to do something for the defunct killer's literary reputation. I was disappointed when some time after my release I came across the identical verse written by an American soldier in Vietnam.

I was the scribe not only for my fellow-inmates, but also for the Boere. Brigadier Dupe, very soon after I started doing my time, came to ask if I would translate a certain number of French texts into Afrikaans. I was only too glad to do so, basically because in this way I could obtain paper which I could hide away for my own writing needs. And reading French, any French, was like being 'back home'. These texts turned out to be reproductions of articles published during the Boer War in the International Red Cross reviews of the time: reports written by their envoys in the Transvaal and the Orange Free State. They described not only the nature of the wounds found among the warriors and their rudimentary medical care, noting that far more people died of dysentery than wounds—but they also contained reflections on the conduct of the forces in the field. They pointed out the anarchistic way in which the Boere forces went to war and their lack of discipline: there was bravery, very often, but also abject cowardice, with people inflicting wounds upon themselves in an attempt to opt out. They emphasized the marksmanship of the *burgers* of the time: the majority of casualties among the English apparently had head wounds between the eyes. Most of the fatal wounds inflicted upon the Boere were in the back!

I learned that the material was a subject of dispute between the South African authorities and the Red Cross. Brigadier Dupe and his colleagues were hurt by demands made on them by the International Red Cross Committee on behalf of political prisoners, and true to their own nature accused the Swiss delegation of being biased, of being anti-Afrikaner. ('The whole world is against us. The world is sick.') To the disgust of Dupe my translations bore out the Swiss position.

I had to write love-letters for the Boere too, or applications for promotion. Another one of my successful cases, Mr Investigator: I managed to have a Boere transferred from the sections (looking after us in the building) to the workshops where at least he could be taught a trade. And sometimes I was even asked to write essays for their kids.

But there are two instances of my profession as scribe of which I'm not very proud, Mr Investigator. They remain etched in my mind. In one, a Boere brought me a request from Johan, one of the prisoners due to be hanged. I was being asked to answer a letter from his girlfriend. How does one deny somebody who's going to be dead soon? So I sat down and I composed a letter, trying to put myself in his position. I must buck the girl up. Encourage her. Invent a future for us together—which all the time I knew was impossible. A second letter came. Johan sent it along to me—and gradually it was as if he fell away. I grew into his skin. The contact between me—the Johan on the page—and the girl, living in poverty with her parents on some small farm in the back of beyond, became direct. And then came the time to die: the moment to take leave. How far, Mr Investigator, can one push duplicity? I was doing something filthy, surely, and yet at the same time I was extending a last hand of human solidarity to Johan, the shadow, who called me 'the Professor'. Don't think that the possibility of playing a mirror-game of chess with death never crossed my mind. What if I should continue writing to her, still pretending to be Johan? Communicating from beyond the grave? Or would it have destroyed the memories glowing in her, that one major event in her life perhaps, when a man, with the black taste of daybreak already on his lips, poured out his last thoughts and sentiments—his last protestations of innocence and his deep commitment to a pure life ahead?

The other instance was even stranger. I was approached by the head of the prison, asking if I would help him write a letter, in

English: he did not trust his own skill. The letter had to answer an imperious demand he had received from the Clerk of the Transkei Supreme Court (the Transkei had seceded not very long before) to produce, before a certain date, two accused and convicted persons before the said bench. The hitch, Mr Investigator, the slight technical fuck-up, was that these two gentlemen were no longer with us. They had arrived here condemned to death a month or so before Christmas. Things happen rather quickly immediately before the season of love and peace on earth, and hanging services are meant to close down over the festive period. The High Courts too. And, according to the letter I was asked to transcribe, these two natives had refrained from informing the prison authorities of the names of their legal representatives, and since they were quite illiterate and did not leave the addresses of their next-of-kin (we all know what complicated and unusual family-ties these people entertain), nobody knew whom to inform when their demise became imminent. It is with much regret, the letter was to continue, that we now learn that an appeal had been lodged against their convictions and that the said appeal is to be heard by Your Honour, the Judge President of the Transkei Supreme Court. But it wasn't really our fault, Your Honour. You must understand that there are language barriers and the warrant-officer, on duty the day these two men were booked in, perhaps forgot to do the necessary checking. And so, inasmuch and herewith notwithstanding, with all our respect, sir, we the undersigned etc., always your willing servant....

Mr Investigator, I often lie here thinking that these two men who had jerked their heels could still have been alive. I dared not show the depth of my revulsion to the head of the prison and the warders. I don't remember that they themselves were particularly affected. When you process humans by paper, a wee slip 'twixt last breath and noose is, alas, always possible. To err is human. And I could not then make any notes of the event, but for a long time I remembered the two names. Then one slipped away and now I have only one name left: Sizwe Bethani he was called. I repeated it to myself: this you mustn't forget—*Sizwe*. Just think of Athol Fugard's play. And *Bethani*—wasn't Jesus also reputed to have been to a certain Bethany? Ah, Mr Investigator, with all due respect we regret that writing can be used as topsoil for burying mistakes. Notwithstanding, I'm sorry if I sometimes forget that it is at the same time the maggots which lay bare the structure....

Peter Davis
Christmas in Nicaragua

On a blasted corner in Managua, a city which effectively ceased to exist after the earthquake in 1972, three white buildings continued to stand until 1978, over a year before Somoza was overthrown. The buildings were white not because it's popular and cheap in the tropics—yellow, beige and pink resist the dust better—but because the buildings performed a singular medical function that required a hygienic veneer. Nicaraguans came to them to bleed into small transparent bags. The product was then shipped north, a contribution to the raw materials Nicaragua exported to the United States. Surely this must be the kind of 'illuminating detail' writers are supposed to look for, the part that reveals the whole? What greater exploitation can there be than for an impoverished people to have their own blood extracted for the benefit of their imperial masters?

Well, yes. But the trouble with everything in Nicaragua is that one detail leads to another, and then another, and another, forming a series of contradictions and paradoxes that threaten to engulf the sanity of anyone trying to observe them. A clear case of capitalist imperialism or communist oppression, of social progress or economic decline, need only be turned slightly on its axis in order to be seen as its opposite. It is not that nothing is true in Nicaragua—for a start I would say that, unlike the American policy towards Nicaragua, the revolution is succeeding more than it is failing—but that the truth seems to dissolve into a collection of meanings whose common thread is their ambiguity. The only antidote is an attitude of certainty. If you go to Nicaragua committed to the revolution, you will find plenty to strengthen your commitment. If you go opposed to the regime, you will find a satisfying amount to criticize. But if you go with an ambivalent attitude, you may return with an ambivalence whose depth is oceanic.

A priest says the Sandinistas who control Nicaragua are trying to crush the church; a nun swears she found God in the revolution. One industrialist says the government stifles free enterprise; another claims the revolution has been good for business. A US State Department official condemns the 'asphyxiating' atmosphere—guns are seen everywhere—but Nicaragua is the only Central American country in which the US Ambassador can go anywhere without bodyguards. The Ambassador himself is available to a wide range of reporters, and is genial, informative and surprisingly unprejudiced.

But he refuses to be quoted in the American press, insisting on being referred to as 'a Western diplomat', summoning an image, for anyone raised on cowboy movies, of a Texas sheriff not unduly shy about reaching for his equalizer. But—again *but,* always *but*—the Ambassador gamely appeared on Nicaraguan television in a brisk policy debate with Sandinista officials who outnumbered but politely did not overwhelm him. This took place in December 1983, when it was devoutly believed by many Americans and by most of the 2.9 million Nicaraguans that the United States was preparing to invade the country and replace its government.

Putting many of its meagre resources into education, the revolution is on the verge of a triumphant conquest of illiteracy among peasants and workers, but the middle class complains that the newly literate are taught history, sociology and economics along strict Marxist lines. *An Americas Watch Report: Human Rights in Central America* concludes that 'Nicaragua shows no signs of evolving in the direction of a democratic society in which freedom of expression is respected.' With a pride in their civil liberties that approaches smugness, Americans in general point confidently to the Bill of Rights as freedom's touchstone for the world. But Nicaraguans are not buying American these days. 'America's freedom, sir,' said Daniel Ortega Saavedra, head of Nicaragua's revolutionary junta, as we talked alone late one hot December night in Government House, 'America's freedom is a monster.'

Soaring and plunging, the revolution is like a kite in an uncertain wind. People live normally, ordinarily—and also on the edge of sanity and peril. The cast of characters might be from one of those Renaissance canvases that seems to include everyone in Florence: the Jinotega coffee-grower who pays the state more taxes than it requires because he wants the country strong for the anticipated US invasion; the union organizer from Rivas, giving the revolution credit for rescuing Nicaraguan labour from serfdom; the banana-plantation owner who sees in the revolution the death of democracy; the chemical executive who sees the Sandinistas as Nicaragua's determined greenhorn saviours; the lawyer from the United States, his life in what most of us would consider splinters, cheerfully finding his best self by working for Nicaragua; the Gold Star Mother from Los Angeles, her son killed in Vietnam, helping with the Nicaraguan rice harvest, putting her life in jeopardy as a witness for peace on the Honduran border; the Managua newspaper editor who does not know from one day to the next what he will be permitted to publish; his brother, a rival editor, who sees the revolution as a mission of national reconstruction; the textile worker whose misery under the old regime has been transformed to something beyond hope: he talks of a revolutionary sunrise that inspires in him and his family expectations as fond as their memories are bitter.

In this riddled context, one asks questions. Is Nicaragua the first mainland domino in the Americas, falling long enough after Cuba to make Castro's revolution an antecedent rather than a precedent? What is the Soviet role? Given US actions as well as Nicaragua's momentum, what are the revolution's prospects? What might an appropriate US response to Nicaragua be? Is there a point, in terms of libertarian expectations, where the Sandinista revolution could be said to have betrayed itself?

Who validates Nicaraguan history? A secret US State Department memorandum has a clarifying passage: 'Central America has always understood that governments which we recognize and support stay in power, while those which we do not recognize and support fall. Nicaragua has become a test case. It is difficult to see how we can afford to be defeated. Usually it has been sufficient for us to intervene on the sole pretext of furnishing protection to American lives and property.' This memorandum, which was declassified in the 1960s, was written in 1927. Does current thinking—that of the State Department and the Kissinger Commission on Central America—repudiate this attitude as oppressively anachronistic? Or does it reaffirm America's manifest hemispheric destiny? The questions seem pertinent. In Nicaragua they recede dizzyingly before new questions—before a socialism, for instance, hopelessly married to capitalism.

What a relief to return for a moment to the simplicity of the the Managua blood bank, draining the malnourished pre-revolutionary Nicaraguans for the benefit of a rich United States, swollen like a tick from sucking up the life substance of its subjects to the south. Except it was not exactly a blood bank. It was essentially a plasmapheresis centre, where the donor's blood, after removal, was centrifuged to separate out the plasma. The packed red cells and other blood components were mixed with saline solution and reinfused into the donor. The plasma was shipped to the United States. According to a haematologist who received the plasma in New York City and a research chemist who inspected the plasmapheresis process in Managua, the centre's health standards were the highest in the world. The plasma produced was superior (with less risk of infectious hepatitis, for example) to what could be obtained from any comparable centre in the United States. The three buildings in Managua contained one hundred and eighty beds and were capable of handling 1,000 donors a day. When the operation was at its peak, 20,000 litres of plasma were shipped to the United States every month, approximately seven times as much as that produced by the average centre in a big American city.

Then everyone was served: Nicaraguans and Americans each got something they desperately needed. But there is one more detail. The Managua centre was owned by an exiled Cuban doctor and by Anastasio Somoza Debayle, dictator of Nicaragua and third in his family, after his father and brother, to hold that post with the economic and military support of the United States. Although Somoza and the Cuban doctor, whose name is Pedro Ramos, did pay the donors between five dollars and ten dollars for each unit of plasma, they sold it for at least three times that amount. For 20,000 litres per month at approximately fifty dollars per litre, the income was around twelve million dollars a year. Somoza, bleeding his own people, had turned his country into the ultimate family business. When *La Prensa,* the Managua newspaper that opposed the Somozas then and opposes the Sandinistas now, ran a series of articles in 1977 denouncing the traffic in blood, Dr Ramos sued its editor, Pedro Joaquin Chamorro, for libel. Ramos lost the suit and moved to Miami. In January 1978, Chamorro was assassinated, and a captured hit man identified Ramos as having put out the contract. Managua erupted. A full year and a half before the triumph of the Sandinista revolution, enraged Nicaraguans stormed the plasmapheresis headquarters and burned it down. Somoza lost a business, and his customers lost access to fifteen percent of the world's plasma supply. The Nicaraguans' name for the centre they destroyed was *casa de vampiros.*

Four and a half years after the victory of the Sandinista revolution in July 1979, Nicaragua presents the United States with a midlife crisis. Old enough to know better, they used to say, young enough to do it again. The United States looks to Nicaragua, as it once looked to Vietnam, to test its illusions (the situation is infinitely improvable) or to confirm its disillusionment with everything (the situation is only hopeless, not serious). While the United States supports a government of murderers in El Salvador, it opposes one of independence and progressive ideals in Nicaragua. Its policies towards Central America have edged the Soviet Union into its own contradiction. In El Salvador the Russians connive to overthrow a government that suppresses its opposition as they themselves do, only less effectively. In Nicaragua the Russians support a government committed to a pluralism they would never tolerate.

A mirror is almost the first object a visitor sees entering Nicaragua. Above each customs booth at Sandino International Airport, it perches, tilting down over the heads of arriving passengers, enabling the customs officer to look at people's feet if that is what he wants to do. The mirror is from East Germany, which has provided training and techniques for the Sandinista security apparatus. But the customs officer is not East German. He is smiling, he is puffy with midnight sleepiness and he is, if ethnic generalizations can still be applied without insult, very Latin. '*Bienvenido.* Enjoy,' he says, even though an impression of surveillance is further fortified by a sign on his booth quoting General Augusto César Sandino's advice to be on the lookout for '*los imperialistas Yanquis*'.

Above the baggage inspection ramp a sign in English said, 'Welcome to Nicaragua. You'll love it.' An official was inspecting a porn magazine he had found in the luggage of the passenger ahead of me, a Nicaraguan returning from Miami. After he gave the magazine back to its owner, he conscientiously searched my belongings before waving me through. Suspicious that everyone was an agent for us or them, and apprehensive—no, terrified—that the widely predicted US invasion would begin as soon as I arrived, I glanced furtively at the night sky for planes or parachutes, then shared a cab with two Americans who spoke with slight Spanish accents. They said they were businessmen from Iowa, tyre retreaders come down to do some merchandizing in Nicaragua. Can't the CIA think up a better cover than that? Still, all the way into town they kept up their chatter about the Nicaraguans needing retreads since they could not afford to buy new tyres. Who knows?

It is to a pre-revolutionary, pre-earthquake trapezoidal hive called the Intercontinental—the 'Intair' as it is pronounced locally—that almost everyone in the international-information-gathering community turns. The Intercontinental buzzes with journalists, photographers, TV crews, putative agents, visiting US officials in-country for a quick briefing but not important enough to stay with the Ambassador, town gossips, Marxist theorists delivered straight from La Coupole along with their Gauloises, revolution groupies, Sandinista press officers and poets, black marketeers, idealists gathered for one more chance to remake the world.

On the night I arrived, Orson Welles was crowding out all other objects on the small television screen in the bar. Like TV in most other bars, the set stayed on for the sake of the pictures, providing the comforting illusion of more people in the room having a better time than was actually the case, but the sound was turned off. Orson Welles was followed by a trailer for a forthcoming *Lou Grant* episode.

Two young men came in from the pool, where there was a big party with spirited dancing. The music from the loudspeakers around the pool almost drowned out the Nicaraguans as they asked what I was doing in their country.

'*Periodista,*' I said.

'Oh, a journalist.'

'*Si,*' I said.

'Yes,' they said. 'Did you come to see the revolution?'

'Isn't that why everyone comes now?'

'Do you like it?'

'I don't know. I've only been here ten minutes. Do you?'

One of them was crying. 'No,' he said. 'it's not for me. It's good for some people, not for me.'

He was eighteen, or thirty. It was dark in the bar, but the tears shone on his face and he tried to sniff them back.

'Why isn't it good for you?'

'It's not mine, it's not my own, this revolution. I want to love it and I can't.'

On the television screen, *Lou Grant* was replaced by the FSLN (Frente Sandinista de Liberación Nacional) logo: *TODAS LAS*

ARMAS AL PUEBLO. 'All arms to the people' is the literal translation. Learn to live with contradiction is the looser construction. The old mixed signal.

Outside by the pool, young Nicaraguans were flinging themselves around with what I thought to be rather reckless abandon. Where were the bomb shelters, the trenches? Where was the country under siege? Is this what I was so scared of? For these people it was graduation night, maybe a Christmas ball. It was hot, at least eighty degrees, and the sound system blared 'Maniac' from *Flashdance* while the poolside party jumped and swarmed. Behind the dancers a wall, perhaps twelve feet high, protected the Intercontinental from what used to be Managua. An NBC News crew came out on the terrace and briefly filmed the dancers, throwing their shadows up against the wall with a Sun-Gun light that gave the cameraman the exposure he needed. 'Meanwhile, in beleaguered Managua at the centre of the political storm, pre-Christmas revels go on as usual among the dwindling middle class.' Elvis came on with 'Hound Dog'—'You ain't never caught a rabbit and you ain't no friend of mine'—and the dancers' silhouettes kept rhythm with one another on the wall. I wondered what the US Army Rangers would look like climbing over that wall in assault force. They would be followed by the Marines, of course; twelve-foot walls are nothing to those guys. Together again, the same winning team that brought you Grenada. NBC News went up to bed, the dancers oblivious, grinding Latinly on.

Fantasies disappear at the Intercontinental's front door. Managua is not exactly patrolled by soldiers, but the country is on a wartime footing, and armed police or militia or members of the regular army are posted in various spots around town, some obviously strategic, others apparently random. A block from the hotel on my first day in Nicaragua, I was halted by a soldier with a rifle. The rifle was strapped loosely around his shoulder and he was smiling, but unaccustomed as I am to being stopped by people with guns, I put my hands up. He fiddled with the rifle barrel playfully as he asked for my identification, sticking a finger down the muzzle. For a reason I did not then understand but would shortly, I had an impulse to tell him to be careful, that thing was not a toy. But I shut up and produced a passport and a press card. The soldier fingered his rifle some more and called over his superior, who was standing a few yards away. The commander looked at the identification, smiled and told me I could go.

The crisis behind us, I asked them how old they were, and then I understood why I had wanted to warn the soldier about the lethal quality of his weapon. The one who stopped me was thirteen, the one in charge seventeen. The thirteen-year-old was carrying a Russian BZM-52; the seventeen-year-old had an AK-47, the standard Russian weapon of the Nicaraguan Army, known to everyone as an *Ahka.* Francisco, the younger one, was eager to be liked and seemed almost ready to ask me for a candy bar. He had had his uniform and rifle a little less than a year. Javier, the senior authority, had been practising with his *Ahka* for two years and hoped someday to become a carpenter. 'When President Reagan lets us study and work,' he said, 'instead of defending our homes.'

This theme, sounded first by a seventeen-year-old, was repeated to me often enough to become more than a refrain. It is a tenet of the national faith that the reason for Nicaragua's slow advance in education and industry is the militarism forced on its population by the United States. Extending the tenet, many Nicaraguans blame US economic and military policies for virtually all the country's problems—whether product shortages, poor distribution, bad crops or unrest among the Miskito Indians and other minorities. The United States, they feel, is trying to strangle them. In a crowning paradox, however, they are able to like Americans while hating its government. It is as though they believe the American government is not an expression of the national will but something imposed on Americans from without, as earlier governments in Nicaragua had been imposed by the United States. In talks with hundreds of Nicaraguans, I met only one, a professional army man from the North, who felt Americans were responsible for their government. Everyone else blamed the Administration, generally Ronald Reagan himself, for policies that have placed as many as 5,500 US military personnel in Honduras, Nicaragua's northern neighbour, hostile armies of counter-revolutionaries on both their Honduran and Costa Rican borders, American warships patrolling their Atlantic and Pacific coasts, mines in their harbour and have created an economic squeeze that not only cuts off Nicaragua's credits from the United States but denies it the opportunity to borrow from the International Monetary Fund and regional banks. Everyone else, beginning with these two teenagers, Francisco and Javier, exonerated the American people, with whom they wanted only to be friendly, for the acts committed in their name by their leadership. Francisco and Javier left me wondering how much longer the US was going to be able to get away with that.

Outside Managua it is easier to get a sense of how the revolution is doing in its struggle against both poverty and the tenacity with which some Nicaraguans cling to their pre-revolutionary ways. Nicaragua is a little larger than New York State and about half the size of Great Britain. More than ninety percent of the country's population lives in the western provinces and is descended from the Spaniards, who first settled the area in 1524 and ruled until 1821. But 30,000 Miskito Indians, never assimilated into the Spanish society of the West, live on the East Coast, along with several thousand Caribbean blacks and other Indians. If that section of Nicaragua acknowledged a colonial master it was England, which traded and pirated along the East Coast, not Spain, which periodically tried to conquer it.

The Sandinistas admit mistakes in their treatment of the Miskitos. These were due, they claim, largely to their overzealousness in trying to integrate the Indians into the revolutionary process, and to American propaganda and military pressure designed to alienate the Miskitos from the government and drive them into the arms of the counter-revolutionaries. Radio broadcasts and leaflets from Honduras tell the Miskitos the Communists are coming to kill them and send all their children to Russia. While I was in Nicaragua, the Sandinistas made a peace offering to the Miskitos, granting amnesty to those who had gone to Honduras and releasing three hundred who had been imprisoned for fighting the government. Meanwhile, the CIA was arming the Misura, a dissident faction of Miskitos and other East Coast groups, for the purpose of leading thousands of Indians away from Nicaragua. Propaganda from Honduras increased, with promises of American-style housing for Miskitos who cross the border.

From a CIA perspective, the Miskitos and the East Coast are the Vietnamese Montagnards and the Central Highlands redux. The area in northeast Nicaragua where most of the Miskitos live is even called the Highlands. The Miskitos have always been alienated from whatever government was in Managua, just as the Montagnards always ignored Saigon, and they are perfect targets for an enemy intelligence agency to recruit and run for a while, then drop when they are no longer useful. Through their revolutionary excesses, ignorance of Miskito ways and undoubtedly some prejudice against aborigines, the Sandinistas have helped the CIA make friends among the Miskitos. Last December, the government was trying to correct its mistakes, or at least was making overtures to the Miskitos. Several new villages were opened, old villages were being resettled and the land reform programme was being significantly extended to benefit the Miskitos.

One morning during my first week in Nicaragua a woman from the government press office, which the Sandinistas have shrewdly located, like a fishnet, in the Intercontinental, asked if I would go to the East Coast the following day with the three hundred Miskito Indians who were being repatriated. She said their villages were protected by government troops, secure from attacks by the counter-revolutionaries, *los contras.* The Indians would be free to build new lives for themselves. I felt too busy to join what smelled like a press junket to what sounded like a bunch of strategic hamlets, so I turned the trip down. An American lawyer, however, visiting Nicaragua to investigate human rights violations, went along and remained eight days on the East Coast with the Miskitos.

When she returned to Managua, the lawyer told of a thinly populated, exotic Miskito coast, where coconut palms sway over villages of houses on stilts. The lawyer was able to reach some of the settlements only by boat. In several of them, books and doctors were unknown until recently. The older communities are filthy, she said, and people often defecate upstream from where they do their laundry. There is a kind of random farming but almost no other organized economic activity. Into these conditions the Sandinistas were trying to insert themselves, introducing a little hygiene here, a few modern crop techniques there, rectifying their earlier errors where they could.

One village had been previously evacuated by the Sandinistas in order to deny a haven to the *contras.* The Miskitos the lawyer accompanied were glad to get home, and their new government-built houses were better than the shacks and lean-tos they had left. But a number of them were afraid of the government because of its past treatment of them, and the lawyer found that when she used a Sandinista interpreter who spoke Miskito, the Indians were far less communicative than when she used a Miskito interpreter who spoke English. The Miskitos told the lawyer of harassment and arrests by the government. In a small settlement along the coast called Walpasixa, the Sandinistas apparently arrested half the men and just carted them away. No one knew why the Sandinistas left the other half alone. Many Miskitos once worked for US lumber companies, which arrived in the 1930s, took all the pine they could find and got out in the 1960s. Some have not been employed since the lumber companies left. In successive villages the lawyer met Miskitos named George Washington and Abraham Lincoln. Washington hated the Sandinistas; Lincoln was satisfied with them. This part of Nicaragua, the Miskitos and the government agree, is a war zone, and no one is safe from roving bands of *contras,* down from Honduras, up from Costa Rica. The lawyer returned to Managua with her sympathy for the Sandinistas tested but intact.

The East Coast remains fickle. Just before Christmas, an American bishop accompanied several hundred Miskitos north into Honduras, presenting the counter-revolutionaries with a considerable public relations victory. Some of the Miskitos were said to be armed members of the anti-government Misura; others were said to have gone north reluctantly, bewildered at being moved one more time. In Managua the rumour was that the Misura had got lost in the jungle on their way to raid one village and wound up in another. This village contained the bishop and an American Catholic priest, who said later they were there by coincidence when the Misura arrived and took everyone north. In any case, the bishop, whom the Sandinistas initially reported killed by counter-revolutionaries, was evacuated to the United States in time to spend the holidays with his mother and receive the winning-coach-in-the-locker-room phone call from President Reagan on Christmas Day. Over the enterprise there hung confusion, missed opportunities for both sides, conflicting loyalties, and the whiff of a bungled CIA operation that accidentally succeeded.

American Indians have not neglected the Miskitos, with somewhat mixed results. An American Indian Movement official breezed into the Intercontinental one day early in December, took a quick briefing and emerged to declare that the Sandinistas are the best thing that ever happened to the Miskitos. The government treats the Miskitos, the AIM man said, far better than the United States has ever treated *its* Native American population. Then he breezed out again. He did not endear himself to the Miskitos and was regarded as unhelpful by the Sandinistas. Not many people, on the other hand, would go to the trouble of a 4,000-mile trip just to get better trajectory for a shot at the US Interior Department.

A few days later, a delegation of Vietnam veterans arrived. They looked around, talked to as many people as they could and decided that while Nicaragua was not Vietnam, the United States was behaving in a similar manner, blending cruelty with ignorance. 'We're not going to go through this again,' one of them said. The delegation included an American Indian, who asked stern and probing questions of the Sandinistas and the Miskitos about their intentions towards each other. He won the respect of both.

Since the western provinces hold most of Nicaragua's population, including 15,000 who have migrated from the East to find jobs, it is in the West that the revolution will stand or fall. After Managua, which has approximately 300,000 people, the largest cities are León, 63,000, and Granada, 45,000. Population figures in Nicaragua are rough estimates, since no census has been taken for more than a decade. One of the problems the government confronts in preparing for the elections scheduled for November 1984 is that no one has a clear idea of who or where the potential voters are, never mind how many of them exist.

Fifty-five miles northwest of Managua, León was the capital during a bizarre episode in the 1850s, when an American pirate named William Walker conquered Nicaragua and tried to have it annexed to the United States as a slave state. Walker made the mistake of confiscating a business owned by Cornelius Vanderbilt. For most of the decade Vanderbilt had been running a transit company that conveyed Americans hurrying from the Eastern states through Nicaragua to what they hoped was the gold in California. His profits were two million dollars a year, an irresistible lure for Walker. A coalition of Central American countries and the British Navy, helped by Vanderbilt, drove Walker out of his 'kingdom'. When he tried to return in 1860, he was executed by the Hondurans.

Walker and Vanderbilt prefigured an American attitude towards

Nicaragua that lasted more than a century. Statecraft was reduced to business, business to exploitation. Guided less by Thomas Jefferson's devotion to life, liberty and the pursuit of happiness than by his assertion, in 1813, that 'America has a hemisphere to itself', the United States made coffee and bananas the pedestals for its Central America policy. The US ambassador to Nicaragua became at times a virtual governor-general. When a nationalist leader cooperated with the British in a plan to build a trans-Nicaraguan railway that would compete with the then-unfinished Panama Canal, Washington declared him a 'destabilizing' influence and overthrew him in 1909. Thereafter, except for two brief periods, the United States Marines were in Nicaragua until 1933. Then came Somoza I, followed by Somozas II and III, lasting until the Sandinista revolution of 1979.

The fall of William Walker shifted the country's capital to Managua, but León still has dignity. Its eighteenth-century cathedral, the largest in Central America, is said to have been built by mistake after the Spanish design for an elegant cathedral to be constructed in the gold-rich capital of Lima, Peru, was mixed up aboard ship with the plans for a more modest church in León. The cathedral preens over its city with an opulence that refutes the revolution, and confirms it.

The morning I was in León, a public-address truck drove by the cathedral, blasting out instructions for a civil defence meeting where trench digging, fire-fighting and evacuation techniques would be taught in preparation for the Yankee invasion. The announcer, visible in the front seat of the truck, emphasized that the meeting would begin at 9 a.m. I looked at my watch and saw it was a little after 10.30. This is what is meant by *hora Nica,* Nicaraguan time. Meetings not only start late, they occasionally do not take place even on the day they are scheduled. The public-address truck proceeded around the city, past an open bazaar, the ancient university, shops, and signs advertising Pepsi, Coke, Black & Decker tools and 'Death to hoarding and speculating.'

Across the street on one side of the cathedral were two political statements typical of Nicaraguan cities. First, there were the gutted remains of a department store bombed by Somoza's Guardia Nacional during heavy fighting in 1978. Twisted metal girders were all that separate the earth from the sky. Next to this was a tiny plaza with enlarged photographs of the revolutionary heroes Sandino and

Carlos Fonseca, and of the martyr Rigobert o Lopez, the poet who shot Somoza I in León in 1956.

On the other side of the cathedral is Collegio La Asunción, formerly an élite parochial academy for girls, now a state comprehensive. The school no longer has its curriculum dictated by the church, but it has not embraced the revolution either. Two teachers and a school secretary I spoke with felt the Sandinistas were going backwards. One of them left shortly after we began talking—'Wait, I'll show you what I mean,' she said—and reappeared with a block of unrefined brown sugar. 'See, this is what we have to eat now.' It was no use telling her that current health-chic now stipulates raw sugar. The fact is that white sugar has always been a mark of the Nicaraguan middle class, and this science teacher could no longer buy it.

The two teachers described themselves as liberal but not of the left. They were pleasant and perplexed. 'Even with the hostility of the United States,' one of them said, 'there should be more progress four and a half years after the triumph. The government has good intentions, but it is on the wrong path. They give us no way to organize a campaign against their own mistakes.'

'When someone has told you three or four lies, the fifth time you don't believe him,' the other teacher said. 'Nothing good can come of the voting in 1985. There is not enough freedom. You can't even chop a tree down without their permission. This is no atmosphere for organizing elections. Their relationship with the Salvadorean guerrillas compromises us. They should be neutral. Why don't they behave better to get the economic aid from the United States restored?'

'We are not *contras,*' the first said. 'We want what is best for our *país,* our country, our *patria.*'

A nun sitting nearby looked up at the teachers and the secretary, then returned to her Graham Greene paperback, *La Fuerza y La Gloria.*

The secretary had been a student at the school, and her small, neat features drooped when she talked about the revolution. 'I can't complain myself,' she said, 'but the lack of freedom hurts the production of goods. You don't have to be an economist to see the economy is worse now than ten years ago. The US boycott hurts us too, prevents us from making progress. Because of the United States, we have to have so many people involved in defence we can't make what we need. The Sandinistas contribute to this with bad management. Their bomb shelters have broken more legs than they'd save in a raid. People run over the trenches and crack their knees. Some of our teachers have to go pick cotton on their holidays. That's not a proper activity for a teacher. I hated Somoza. The Sandinistas seemed like saints to me when they first came. I loved and supported them. But they let me down, and they don't show proper respect for the United States. They should change, be more friendly to your country, give no excuse for the United States to attack us.'

The nun looked up again as she turned a page.

'When the Pope was here in 1982,' one of the teachers said, 'it was a very painful experience.'

'It was *doloroso,*' the secretary said. 'He was insulted by Sandinistas waving their red and black flags right here in the cathedral square, while he was treated well at the university. How can you figure that? All right, some of my family are Sandinistas. We fight about it, but we're still a family.'

The teachers and the secretary left for lunch, and the school door was closed behind me for the midday break as I walked out. But there was a window in the door, barred with thin whitewashed wooden dowels. The little window opened. I had forgotten the nun. She appeared, spectral in the shadows behind the white bars. '*Por favor, señor,*' she said, 'we do not all feel like that.'

All I could see of her was white—her face, her nun's coronet, her plain T-shirt.

'First, the Pope,' she said. 'I love him, and the *campesinos* I work with were very happy to have him visit. But he was poorly advised. He should have said something about the *compañeros* who were killed on the border fighting against *los contras.* Just one word. No. He spoke only of the unity of the church. In the way the church can sometimes be, he was too dogmatic.'

Sister Ana Maria came to Nicaragua before the revolution. 'You could not go in the streets after 6 p.m. then,' she said. 'During Somoza's time, soldiers were everywhere and you could not look at them, not even a nun. They would do anything to you that amused them. At the time when Chamorro the publisher of *La Prensa* was killed, it could cost you your life just to walk past the headquarters of the Guardia here in León. Holy Week was full of terror. On the Monday before Easter, the Guardia killed three boys right in front of the church. The rest of the week, disappearances every day.

'But now, see the *vida nueva,* see the betterment. Priests and nuns in Guatemala and El Salvador are killed for doing the kind of work with *campesinos* I do here. The soldiers come up to me on the street and shake my hand. The agricultural co-ops bring us closer to providing for ourselves. There are shortages in some areas, but the revolution never promised Italian olive oil and French wine. The basic foods, the basic goods, we have. The poor people have the necessities they never dreamed of before. The Bishop of León understands this and favours the revolution. So do the Jesuits who come here from the United States. Some of them went home for a visit and were present when Jeane Kirkpatrick spoke at Georgetown. She gave her anti-Sandinista speech. We are all totalitarian pigs, or sheep, or wolves, or whatever beast was in her mind that day. The Jesuits protested quietly, politely, but they let her know how wrong she is about the Nicaragua they know.'

What Sister Ana Maria does not admire about the Sandinistas is the way they treat their opponents. 'I don't like the neighbourhood surveillance groups who harass people they don't agree with,' she said. 'I don't like the signs that say, "Counter-revolutionaries, 10,000 eyes are watching you." When people speak in disagreement with the government, they often try to make a joke about perhaps going to jail. The fact is, they do not go to jail, but the possibility is in the air enough so they have to make light of the possibility. I do not like this, but it is the tail of the revolution, not its body. The body is healthy and growing. Tell the United States government, *por favor,* it's all right not to help Nicaragua, but at least don't help the *contras.* Two of our boys from the farm have been killed on the border. We won't let them die in vain.'

I continued on to Corinto, Nicaragua's largest port, about thirty-five miles west of León. Before the revolution sailors would get off their ships, hire Nicaraguan bodyguards known locally as cowboys and make the rounds of bars, card games and brothels without fear of being rolled. Although the Sandinistas have tried to eliminate prostitution and gambling, Corinto is still a busy little city with a market in practically everything. The revolution has not changed the face of the port, but the CIA has.

Corinto is on an island and handles sixty percent of Nicaragua's foreign trade; both facts make it an attractive target for sabotage. The *contras* have tried to blow up the main bridge to the island but so far have failed. The CIA did not fail, however, in its night raid on Corinto's oil storage depot last October. The *contras* had been unable to penetrate the port's defences with either planes or small ships, so the CIA sent its own speedboat into the harbour. The oil depot was shelled from the speedboat for perhaps two minutes, after which the boat escaped. Four diesel-fuel tanks were hit directly. The explosions started fires which eventually destroyed eight tanks and their fuel lines, a loading crane, two molasses storage tanks, a concrete wall, two small buildings and a large warehouse with all its contents, which included coffee, beans and shrimps. Three million gallons of fuel were lost.

The following day, a group of counter-revolutionaries was captured near Corinto. They said that they had been trained for the job but when they could not accomplish it in several attempts, their CIA instructors did it themselves. According to the *contras,* the speedboat had a 325-horsepower engine and used 60-millimetre shells.

The fire burned for forty-eight hours. Mexico, Venezuela and Cuba quickly sent sophisticated fire-fighting equipment which helped keep the flames from leaping to the bordering residential neighbourhood. Diesel fuel is much less inflammable than petroleum. Port officials say that if the petroleum tanks had been hit, Corinto would have burned to the ground. Two of the destroyed tanks belonged to Exxon—business, too, must make its sacrifices for democracy—but the company will not say whether its insurance provides coverage against CIA operations. Although the fire was confined to the storage area, the 3,000 people who live nearby are being relocated to protect them from future US attacks.

In December, the storage depot was moonscape, with sheet metal twisted into five acres of pasta. Red and green paint lay in flakes on the ground, having passed through the stages of boiling and peeling. When I was there, planes from Honduras had come in low under the radar for three days in a row. They strafed the port and were driven away before they could do further damage to the oil tanks. In international law, that is known as repeated violations of airspace accompanied by unprovoked acts of war; in the intelligence community, it is called keeping in touch.

Irving Ramos, a nineteen-year-old with a primary school education, was piling rubble in the depot. Nicaragua can't afford to throw away any metal. 'What you have to try to understand,' Ramos said, 'is that the Nicaraguan government works for the *campesinos* now, instead of the other way around, like it used to be. Your war is good for nothing. If you can't send peace, at least don't send bombs. If you don't send bombs, maybe you'll send books. What about Salinger? I get off early if I go to night school.'

On the way out of Corinto, I drove past the statue of a boy holding the enormous letters A, B, C, D. The literacy campaign. Across the bridge, in the twilight, I was stopped by the blinking red lights of a slow convoy of Soviet tractors, unloaded that afternoon in Corinto. When I could pass them, I came to a caravan of Toyota pickups, also new. In front of the Toyotas were Soviet trucks and two Soviet ambulances. Just before the town of Chinandega, where I turned south to get back to Managua, I came to a field hospital built by the Russians, most of it under tents, staffed by Russian doctors, a gift to the Nicaraguans.

The way the United States and the Soviet Union were behaving towards Nicaragua was like the fairy tale about the wind and the sun. The wind and sun look down at the earth and see a freezing man wearing an overcoat. They devise a contest to see who can get the coat off the man first. The wind blows hard and almost whisks the coat right off the man's back, but the man grabs it and hugs it tightly around him. The wind swirls around, huffs and puffs some more, but nothing works. It is the sun's turn. He shines brightly for a few minutes. The man removes his overcoat and continues walking.

Why must the United States be the wind in this story?

Gabriel García Márquez

Julio Cortazar, 1914-84

Julio Cortázar 1914-84

The last time I went to Prague was fifteen years ago with Carlos Fuentes and Julio Cortázar. We were travelling by train from Paris—because of our common fear of airplanes—and had talked about everything as we traversed the divided night of the two Germanys, past oceans of beetfields, factories of all kinds, the ravages of horrific wars and violent loves.

Just when we were considering sleep, it occurred to Carlos Fuentes to ask Cortázar how, when and on whose initiative the piano was introduced into the jazz band. It was a casual question, intended to elicit at most a date and a name, but the answer was a brilliant performance, a lecture which, between hotdogs and crisps and enormous glasses of beer, lasted until dawn. Cortázar, who knew how to weigh his words, gave us, fluently and simply, an aesthetic and historical reconstruction of jazz that culminated, as the sun rose, in an Homeric apologia for Thelonious Monk. He spoke not only with his deep voice resonating with rolling r's but also with his large-boned hands, more expressive than any I can remember. Neither Carlos Fuentes nor I will ever forget the surprises of that unrepeatable night.

Twelve years later, I saw Julio Cortázar before a crowd in a park in Managua armed only with his beautiful voice and one of his most difficult stories: 'The Night of Mantequilla Nápoles'. It is about a boxer down on his luck who tells his own story in *lunfardo,* the dialect of the Buenos Aires underworld, which would have been completely incomprehensible to the rest of us mortals if we had not already had a taste of it listening to so many low-life *tangos.* Nevertheless, it was this story that Cortázar chose to read from a platform set in a vast illuminated garden, before a crowd made up of all sorts: celebrated poets, out-of-work bricklayers, commanders of the revolution and their adversaries. It was another brilliant performance. Although, strictly speaking, it was not easy to follow the meaning of the story, even for those well-versed in the jargon of *lunfardo,* one suffered with Mantequilla Nápoles and felt the blows he received in the solitude of the ring and wanted to weep for the false hopes and squalor of his life, because Cortázar had succeeded in communicating with his audience on such an intimate level that it no longer mattered to anyone what the words meant or did not mean, and the crowd seated on the grass seemed to float in a state of grace bewitched by a voice which did not seem to be of this world.

These two memories that touched me so much also seem to define him best. They represent the two extremes of his personality. In private, as on the train to Prague, he was seductive in his eloquence, his lively erudition, his millimetric memory, his subversive humour, in everything that made him one of the great intellectuals in the old sense of the word. In public, in spite of his reluctance to perform or entertain, he captivated audiences with an unavoidable presence that had something of the supernatural about it, tender and yet unfamiliar. In both instances I felt he was the most impressive person I've known.

Towards the end of the sad autumn in 1956, he used to go sometimes to a Parisian café that had an English name, and write at a corner table—as Jean-Paul Sartre did three hundred metres from there—in a school exercise book, using a fountain pen that stained his fingers. I had read *Bestiary,* his first book of short stories, in a cheap hotel in Barranquilla where, for one *peso* and fifty *centavos,* I slept among badly-paid fourth-division football players and cheerful whores, and from the very first page I knew that he was the kind of writer I wanted to become when I was older. Someone in Paris told me that Julio Cortázar used to do his writing in the Old Navy café in the Boulevard Saint Germain and there I waited for him, for several weeks, until at last he entered like an apparition. He was the tallest man one could imagine, with the face of a wicked child, inside an endless black overcoat that looked like a priest's soutane, and his eyes were set very far apart like those of a young bull, so oblique and diaphanous that they could have been the eyes of the devil, were they not so evidently ruled by his heart.

Years later, when we had become friends, I thought I saw him again as I saw him that day, for it seems to me that, in one of his finest stories, 'The Other Sky', he recreated himself in the character of a Latin American without a name who, purely out of curiosity, used to attend the guillotine executions. As if he had been writing while seated before a mirror, Cortázar described him thus: 'His expression was distant and at the same time curiously fixed, the face of someone who has become frozen in one moment of a dream and refuses to take the step which will lead him back to wakefulness.' This character wore a long black cloak wrapped about him—like the overcoat Cortázar wore when I first saw him—but the narrator of the story does not dare approach the man in the cloak for fear of the cold anger with which he himself would have greeted such an intrusion. The strange thing is that I didn't dare approach Cortázar either that afternoon in the Old Navy and for the same reason. I just watched him as he wrote for more than an hour without pausing for thought, drinking only half a glass of mineral water until it began to grow dark outside in the street and he put his pen into his pocket and left with the exercise book under his arm, looking like the tallest, skinniest schoolboy in the world. On the many occasions on which we met years later the only thing that had changed in him was the thick, dark beard; until scarcely two weeks ago the rumours of his immortality seemed true, as he had never stopped growing and had always stayed the same age all his life. I never dared ask him if the rumours were true, just as I never told him that in the sad autumn of 1956 I had watched him in his corner of the Old Navy, and I know that—wherever he is now—he'll be cursing me for my timidity.

Idols instil respect, admiration, affection and, of course, great envy. Cortázar inspired all those feelings in a way few writers do, but he also inspired something less common: devotion. He was, perhaps without meaning to be, the Argentinian who endeared himself to everyone. Nevertheless, I dare say that if the dead can die twice, Cortázar must be dying again of embarrassment at the world-wide consternation his death has caused. No one feared posthumous honours and funereal pomp more than he did—whether in real life or in books. More than that, I always had the idea that death itself seemed indecent to him. Somewhere in his book *Around the Day in Eighty Worlds,* a group of friends convulse with laughter on learning that a mutual friend has committed the folly of dying. For that reason, and because I knew him and loved him dearly, I find it hard to participate in the laments and elegies for Julio Cortázar. I prefer to go on thinking of him, as I am sure he would have liked me to, with an immense joy that he has existed, a deeply-felt pleasure that I knew him, and gratitude that he left to the world a work, albeit unfinished, as beautiful and indestructible as his memory.

Translated from the Spanish by Margaret Jull Costa

NOTES FROM ABROAD

Notes from New York
James Wolcott

In 1982 an Amarillo, Texas, oilman named T. Boone Pickens, top honcho at the Mesa Petroleum Company, threw a few high-stakes thrills into Wall Street by trying to take over an oil company twenty times bigger than his own...a classic case of a minnow trying to dine on a whale. Asked why he would risk the future of his own company to acquire a difficult, perhaps elusive giant, Pickens would only shrug and say, 'It's time to make a deal.'

The magazine scene in New York this summer seems antsy and acquisitive too; the big enchiladas, consulting their pocket calculators, are in a mood to cut a few deals. The T. Boone Pickens of the slick-magazine field is Mort Zuckerman, a Boston real-estate princeling who purchased the ailing *Atlantic* a few years back and appointed William Whitworth of *The New Yorker* as its editor, then caught fire with the magazine's first big coup—William Greider's examination of Reagan's financial whiz-kid David Stockman and the funny-money guesswork arithmetic of the budget-making process. (Greider has since gone to *Rolling Stone,* where he stews ineffectually about the evils of Reaganism.) Once the David Stockman story became the talk of editorials and TV-news broadcasts, Whitworth and Zuckerman were seen as wizards who had awakened a drowsing dragon with a single *poof!*

Whitworth, a courtly, self-effacing editor in the *New Yorker* manner, has remained in the wings since the Greider scoop, but Zuckerman has gone on to become a minor celeb., squiring Nora Ephron and Arianna Stassinopoulos to parties, playing softball on the Hamptons with the vacationing literati, making fact-finding missions to Central America. Yet it would be a mistake to see Zuckerman as a vulgar upstart, crowding into the gossip columns simply to bask in the aurora of exploding flashbulbs. He's a genial, intelligent, decent guy, who seems free of the malice that pits the New York literary scene like so many bomb-craters. Unlike Rupert

Murdoch, Zuckerman seems to be on the look-out for buyable properties not to add a few new scalps to his belt, but to widen his social world—to have new prizes to invite to his parties. Compared to the power-lust and ideological crusading of a Murdoch (or, for that matter, of a Sir James Goldsmith), Zuckerman's zeal seems rather harmless, even sweet. Hedonism can be humanizing.

Under the new regime, *The Atlantic* still loses money, but it loses money prestigiously. It's become a model for liberal, affluent, moral seriousness, a *New Yorker* without cartoons or antique quirks. Yet even with its layers of convention and crust, *The New Yorker* remains the more vital, unpredictable magazine—its editor, the elderly, famously mild William Shawn, has a knack of coming up with something spectacular just when the air seems most weighted with dust. (Last year, it was Janet Malcolm's two-part report on the skirmishes tearing apart the Freud archives.) Increasingly, *The Atlantic* has come to rely less on kicking up fresh stories on its own and more and more on plumping itself up with safe, big-name book excerpts from the likes of Gore Vidal, Jane Jacobs, and Studs Terkel.

Perhaps feeling that *The Atlantic* has been safely dispatched from port, loaded with acceptable cargo, Zuckerman has turned his eyes to other properties; rumours have surfaced in print regarding his attempts to woo *The New York Review of Books* and Washington's *US News and World Report,* and entice *New York* magazine away from Rupert Murdoch's clammy grasp.

Zuckerman is not the only big-game hunter stalking the bush: Martin Peretz, the publisher of *The New Republic,* has sent out feelers for *US News and World Report.* The gossip columnist Liz Smith aired speculation that *New York* might be spun into Condé Nast's orbit (Condé Nast publishes *Vogue, GQ, Mademoiselle,* and the magazine I write for, *Vanity Fair*), though it seems unlikely Murdoch would sell; and—well, let's just say the numbers are really jumping on those pocket calculators.

Why this sudden urge to acquire and consolidate? In a sense we are not so far from T. Boone Pickens and his stratagems, only in this case it's the whales devouring the minnows. One of the reasons that there are so many takeovers in the oil business is because it's cheaper to buy a rival company and take possession of its oil reserves rather than drill for new oil, and perhaps come up dry. Similarly, it's easier to take over an established magazine and revamp it for a more upscale audience than start a new magazine from scratch (particularly since an established magazine already has what advertising types call 'name-recognition').

Of course, there are ominous aspects to all this corporate trophy-hunting. A reliable story making the rounds in New York concerns a meeting at *The New York Times* in which two of its top Executives (only the upper case will do) asked members of the *Times Book Review* staff what they thought of the *Times* having a go at buying *The New York Review of Books.* 'But why would you want *The New York Review* when you've already got the *Times Book Review*?' asked one staff member innocently. 'Because then,' said an Executive, pitying the poor fellow's lack of vision, 'we'd control books.' And they would. It's not an accident that editors at the *Times Book Review* have been dropping out of the place recently as quickly as their parachutes will open. There's a gangster aura about the place, and not everyone has the knack (or the desire) for being an armed messenger—an enforcer. These evacuees prefer not to close the drapes, like Michael Corleone in *The Godfather,* but open them, and admit light. As long as there are other places to parachute, editors and writers can exercise their option to flee, but in an acquisitive time those other places will become ever more scarce. And right now the ground below seems to be shrinking.

Now and then it can appear that an entire magazine is opening up the silks, searching for a soft place to land. When Phillip Moffitt and Christopher Whittle, a pair of young entrepreneurs from Knoxville, Tennessee, took over *Esquire* magazine in 1979, the magazine had been rocked silly by the misguided dreams and whirlwind flamboyances of editor Clay Felker, who tried to make the magazine more newsy by turning it into a fortnightly. (For one thing, hardly anyone in America understands what 'fortnightly' means, hence readers didn't even know how often the magazine hit the newsstands—a confusion advertisers came to resent.) Although Moffitt tends to talk in Zen/psycho-pop riddles (he uses phrases such as 'long-term shifts in the paradigm' and 'recreative self-actualization'), he's a smart, tenacious businessman, and under his editorship *Esquire* has limped away from the Felker wreckage and healed itself. The magazine is now limber and prosperous, the darling of advertisers, the bible of the YUPpie (Young Urban Professional) élite.

To celebrate its plunge into black ink and kick off its special issue on 'the new American woman', *Esquire* recently organized an event at the Waldorf with the feminist monthly *Ms* entitled 'The Big Thaw', hosted by TV-news toughie, Mike Wallace, whose shoe-polish black hair looks as suspicious as Mr Reagan's.

'The Big Thaw', a twist on the recent film, *The Big Chill,* put forth the proposition that men and women were no longer engaged in an Apache dance of power (as in the bad old angry days of feminism), but were now engaged in reconciliation, learning to cha-cha as equals. If a consensus *was* reached at 'The Big Thaw', it was through yawns—a marriage of liberal platitudes. Equal pay for equal work...fathers should assist more in housework and childrearing...a woman in the White House as vice-president...stronger clamps on alimony-cheats.... Only Jimmy Breslin, the rumpled, gloomy reporter once immortalized by Philip Roth as 'that precinct house genius', cut through the cant when he said that women would get these things only when they demanded them—that men aren't going to give in and be nice because it's the right thing to do. Power isn't bestowed: it has to be taken—grabbed.

Oddly, no one, either before the 'Thaw' or after, noted that *Esquire*'s special issue was itself rather thick with cant and condescension. A special section on women as lovers begins pantingly, 'She loves with the passion of her body, the sparks of her mind. She is freer and more giving than the packaged goods that came before her....' (Their ellipsis.) Leaving aside all that bother about sparks and passion, by what measure do all women born before the baby boom get dismissed as 'packaged goods'? Isadora Duncan wasn't packaged goods; Rebecca West wasn't packaged goods. One of the problems with the YUPpie mentality is that it can't conceive that full, exploring lives were actually led before 1945. YUPpies think everything began with Chuck Berry...that humanity emerged from the primordial ooze in a duck-walk.

The one ungallant note of the evening was struck when Mike Wallace, acknowledging the upcoming fiftieth birthday of *Ms* editor and founder, Gloria Steinem, said in a come-off-it tone, 'Oh, she's been fifty for three or four years now.' From the female YUPpies around me came a chorus of hisses. Even liberated gals want men to show a little class.

Summer is also the season when there is a rolling out of the big, dependable guns. Gore Vidal, Saul Bellow, John Updike, and Norman Mailer are all publishing novels, and so far all have received splashy treatment. (I say 'so far' because the Mailer novel hasn't yet been reviewed.) The Bellow collection, *Him with his Foot in his Mouth,* which some have taken to calling *Me with my Foot in her Blouse,* has been given an especially cordial welcome—a welcome cued by Bellow's publisher, who issued photographs of the author *grinning,* thus informing reviewers that this wasn't a gloomy-gus sulk like *The Dean's December,* but a book in which Bellow removes his shoesies and enjoys a chuckle just like the next fella.

After the pounding Mailer took for *Ancient Evenings,* he too may be due for a light fanning, but his new book—*Tough Guys don't Dance*—is of a badness that makes waving of palm-fronds difficult, even by the most devoted. A highbrow pulp mystery, *Tough Guys* is a return to the genre of *An American Dream* (my favourite Mailer novel), but where *An American Dream* danced on an electric wire of tension, *Tough Guys* is swamped with turgid thoughts, turgid sex. In one of the book's more curious passages, Mailer's narrator reveals, 'I realized I had never looked at a pussy properly until I read Updike,' then launches upon his own description, which sounds rather like Henry Miller spitting out his mouthwash ('...the outer meat of her vagina—the larger mouth—reveals the sullen grease-works...'). And then there is the scene in which Madeleine, she of the sullen grease-works, tells our hero that her previous lover could bop her five times a night, and the last would be as good as the first. 'On the best day you'll ever have, you'll never come near Mr Five. That's what I call him.' And Mailer's narrator confesses, 'Against every intent of my will, there were tears in my eyes from the pain this speech gave me.' For, as Mailer's narrator puts it, 'Can you conceive of how deep he dived into Madeleine's treasure chest?'

Mailer's admirers are claiming that the book was dashed off for money (to pay tax assessments and his kids' college bills), and that it's all intended as a big, brilliant put-on—a hot libido *Torrents of Spring.* I'm dubious. If the transcendental bowel-movements of *Ancient Evenings* weren't a put-on, there's no reason to believe the delvings into Madeleine's treasure chest are, either. But it is happy to have Mailer back in the twentieth century again, after all that time in Egypt. The best line about *Ancient Evenings* was cracked by Saul Bellow, who called it, 'Marquis de Sade for mummies'. *Tough Guys don't Dance* is closer to a gynaecologist working without gloves.

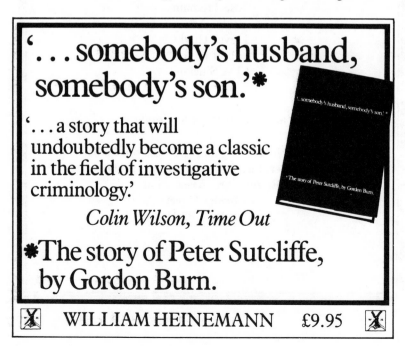

GRANTA

LETTERS

Whose Whale?

To the Editor

Salman Rushdie writes fiercely, funnily and justly about the comeback of the British Raj in television and literature [*Granta* 11]. But the second part of his 'Outside the Whale' suddenly lurches into an intemperate and inaccurate attack on Orwell. I've now read it three times (fast, slowly, and even closely), but I cannot see how it connects with Orwell's essay, except in its borrowed title.

I almost wonder whether Rushdie has read any of Orwell's other essays. 'Inside the Whale' is admittedly not one of his best, most mature, or coherent. To use it as representing Orwell's views on politics and literature and on commitment is very questionable. A serious critique would look to Orwell's later 'Why I Write', 'The Prevention of Literature', 'Writers and Leviathan', 'Politics *v.* Literature' and 'Propaganda and Demotic Speech'. However, even from reading only old 'Whale', it is quite false to conclude that Orwell believed that 'political commitment distorts an artist's vision,' that 'resistance is useless', and in the value of 'passivity'. This is an extraordinary *mis*reading, an inversion of Orwell's views. 'Where Orwell wished quietism, let there be rowdyism; in place of the whale, the protesting wail,' Rushdie urges. Yes, I'm all for rowdyism (as long as the rowdies have style); but so was Orwell.

Salman Rushdie seems to me to fall headlong into the trap against which Orwell so often warned: thinking that a bad man cannot be a good writer, or that a good man, especially an activist, should be granted some kind of artistic indulgence. He presents Orwell's praise of Henry Miller as a writer as an acceptance of Miller's passive, quietistic, indeed one might add, wholly cynical, attitude to the world. But Orwell praises Miller precisely to make the point that even such a bastard *can* be a good writer.

Orwell is quite clear that his own best writing (and most critics think he is right) is polemical; but the point he makes against the 1930s Communist view of 'the committed writer' is that it must be one's own polemic, no writer can write to order, and the consequences will not always please those who are happy to have writers on their side, but would be even happier if they would only bark in unison. Orwell joked that a 'writer cannot be a *loyal* member of a political party;' he never said that a writer could not be a member of a political party.

Orwell was attacking people to whom 'rowdyism' in literature was as abhorrent as to the bourgeois press when he wrote:

> What I have most wanted to do throughout the past ten years is to make political writing into an art. My starting point is always a feeling of partisanship, a sense of injustice. When I sit down to write a book, I do not say to myself, 'I am going to produce a work of art.' I write it because there is some lie that I want to expose...

> But I could not do the work of writing a book, or even a long magazine article, if it were not also an aesthetic experience. Anyone who cares to examine my work will see that even when it is downright propaganda, it contains much that a full-time politician would consider irrelevant.
>
> 'Why I Write' (1946)

'Irrelevant' was an understatement. Ever since *Animal Farm* some of the Left have denounced Orwell for speaking prematurely and, because his polemics against Stalinism got used by some anti-socialists, for giving them succour. That was the basis of Edward Thompson's essay directed against Orwell as the cold warrior, the ideologist of NATO: it, too, was called 'Outside the Whale' and Rushdie merely echoes it when he orates:

> I have no wish to re-open these old hostilities; but the truth cannot be avoided, and the truth is that passivity always serves the interests of the status quo, of the people already at the top of the heap, and...Orwell... is advocating ideas that can only be of service to our masters. If resistance is useless, those whom one might otherwise resist become omnipotent.

What 'passivity'? Does this word accurately describe the man who went to Spain to fight (not to bring his boyfriend home or attend a cultural congress) and who wrote the revolutionary tract *The Lion and the Unicorn* (1941)? Even on the grounds that 'Whale' is sandwiched between *Homage to Catalonia* and *Lion,* Salman Rushdie might have thought twice whether he (and Edward Thompson) had not misread it.

Rushdie quotes Orwell saying that 'On the whole, the literary history of the thirties seems to justify the opinion that a writer does well to keep out of politics.' He seems to be reading that far more literally than I do, completely missing the sardonic tone and the irony. Everyone knew that Orwell could not keep out of politics, and yet everyone at the time (and some younger mythics since) believed that there was a great Left wing literature of commitment in the 1930s. Where is it?

Orwell's argument in 'Inside the Whale' deserves respect for it is subtle—too subtle for some. Yes, he does say that politics will invade literature, not always as a stimulus or benefit; and he does say that even some fascists can produce great literature—he adopted this approach to Miller, Yeats, Eliot and Ezra Pound. But 'to lock yourself up in an ivory tower is impossible and undesirable.'

In political times a writer must distinguish between his artistic and his political responsibilities, but pursue *both.* If, for instance, he is asked to write propaganda (as Orwell was at the BBC):

> He should do so as a citizen, as a human being, but not *as a writer*.... To suggest that a creative writer, in a time of conflict, must split his life into two compartments, may seem defeatist or frivolous; yet in practice I do not see what else he can do.... To yield subjectively, not merely to a

party machine, but even to a group ideology, is to destroy yourself as a writer.

I find this 'dualism' far more sensible than demands for total commitment which, anyway, are usually rhetorical, most writers who talk thus showing substantial reservations in their actual behaviour (how Orwell would have relished the word 'trendy'). Orwell's defence of Miller, like his later defence of Pound, exhibits this dualism.

It is either political malice (the usual way of uniting the Left by first dividing it), or a gross misreading, to present Orwell as in any way a quietist. But I notice that Rushdie also says that *Nineteen Eighty-Four* is unrelieved pessimism, which seems to me a failure to recognize Swiftian satire. I do not go as far as Anthony Burgess in calling it 'a comic novel', but I am perpetually surprised that so many people can miss the black humour in it, and thus not be cheered by its savage mockery of the power-hungry, its assertion of liberty, equality, truth, language, by caricaturing their negations.

It is a pity, too, that in his rage against Orwell—which genuinely puzzles me, for the similarities of these two writers are evident—Rushdie actually misses the point of Orwell's flick at Auden's line in the first version of 'Spain': 'The conscious acceptance of guilt in the necessary murder.' Rushdie defends Auden's use of 'murder' as if Orwell wanted some more polite or heroic word. Orwell was in fact expressing disapproval of the word 'necessary'—which was the word that Auden subsequently removed. Orwell had no compunction about killing fascists, but he objected to the Marxist determinism of 'necessary'. The person who pulls the trigger should take the responsibility for it, not hide behind the iron skirts of history. That is the moral attitude the novelist Rushdie should approve; but the new activist Rushdie seems in too much of a hurry to notice such fine detail.

When a novelist, or a scholar, uses the authority or fame of his or her name for political polemic, it is essential that they at least get the facts right. Moreover, politically, it is a pity that such an excellent and respected new writer as Rushdie is reviving the sour anti-Orwell gripings of the old New Left, the ex-Communist generation who didn't like premature truth; especially at a time when most writers on the Left (see the work of the late Peter Sedgwick) now see Orwell as one of the leading voices of British socialism—certainly the only one who tried in all his writings (with wildly varying success) actually to communicate with the common man. Orwell's belief that the common man could be both common reader and citizen is central to any serious discussion of the relationship between literature and politics.

Bernard Crick
London

To the Editor

I enjoyed Salman Rushdie's polemic against the revival of the Raj on British TV, but neither he nor Stephen Spender (who seems to have given him the idea) can be allowed to get away with glossing the notorious line in Auden's 1937 poem 'Spain', 'The conscious acceptance of guilt in the necessary murder,' as a reference to death in battle. Nothing in the context licenses one to read 'murder' in any other than the literal sense, of premeditated and unlawful killing, which legal and ordinary English usage clearly distinguishes from killing of and by armed combatants in war. The stanza in question is conspicuously bare of metaphor:

> Today the deliberate increase in the chances of death,
> The conscious acceptance of guilt in the necessary murder;
> Today the expending of powers
> On the flat ephemeral pamphlet and the boring meeting.

Orwell's paraphrase is valid, and devastating:

> The...stanza is intended as a sort of thumbnail sketch of a day in the life of a 'good party man'. In the morning a couple of political murders, a ten minute interlude to stifle 'bourgeois' remorse, and then a hurried luncheon and a busy afternoon and evening chalking walls and distributing leaflets.

That Auden himself felt uneasy about it is implied by his 1939 revisions: 'the *inevitable* increase in the chances of death' and 'the *fact* of murder'. Later, of course, he repudiated the entire poem.

David Lodge
Birmingham

Against Stereotypes

To the Editor

Colin Harding's criticisms ['Letters', *Granta* 11] of the report produced by the Commission investigating the murder of the eight journalists in Peru allow me the opportunity of examining those criticisms and trying to clarify the facts for an international public who, because they are misinformed, often have confused ideas about such matters. First, I must express my regret that Mr Harding found it necessary to add some half truths, even lies—like his comic invention that 15,000 people demonstrated against the report's conclusions in the streets of Lima. This transformation of a march commemorating the anniversary of the killings into a protest meeting against me is typical of the distortions (by an artful use of syntactical ambiguities) from which Mr Harding's letter suffers. It merely confirms the impression I had when I discussed this matter with him in a BBC studio: his style of journalism is a tendentious one, more intent on defending a particular thesis than in getting to the truth.

His thesis, that the report was intended as a kind of cover-up, is one put forward both by some sectors of the far Left in Peru and by a newspaper linked to the former military dictatorship. The accusation does not deserve to be taken seriously since it rests not on concrete facts but on fanciful conjecture and flagrant distortions of facts, dates and evidence.

To make this quite clear we must return to the basic facts:

First. No evidence has emerged to alter the main conclusion of the report: that the journalists were murdered by the peasants of Uchuraccay and other Iquichan communities. Only days before, these people had murdered several guerrillas and were living in an atmosphere of extreme tension for fear of reprisals by *Sendero Luminoso.*

Second. Criticisms of the report do not object to this conclusion, as it is supported by the recorded testimony of the people responsible for the killings. The criticisms turn instead on this question: to what extent were the military and political authorities indirectly responsible for the murders? Did the Guardia Civil *sinchis* [counter-insurgency police] actively encourage the Iquichano peasants to murder the journalists? The thesis put forward by the far Left—and by Mr Harding, it seems—is that the Iquichano peasants murdered the journalists under orders from the politico-military command which had organized them into paramilitary groups with instructions to kill anyone who arrived in the peasants' territory on foot. Those who arrived in helicopters were to be regarded as friends.

It is not correct that the Commission failed to examine this possibility. On the contrary, it was, as the recorded tapes of our interviews prove, the matter which we investigated most closely and on which we did not comment until we had exhausted all possible evidence. A year later I do not know of one scrap of evidence which might alter the conclusions we reached. That is, it is true that in murdering the journalists the peasants believed that they were acting within the law: the Guardia Civil *sinchis* had told them—in the only visit by helicopter prior to the crime which the peasants admit—that if attacked the peasants should defend themselves and kill the *Sendero Luminoso* guerrillas. But there is absolutely no evidence to support the thesis that peasant paramilitary patrols existed in the area or that the authorities had systematically encouraged the Iquichano peasants to lynch strangers.

The people who propound this thesis forget essential evidence and, more than that, falsify the chronology of the events. When could these paramilitary patrols, which the peasants deny ever existed, have been formed? According to the schoolmistress in Uchuraccay, not one *sinchis* military patrol passed through in 1982 (although there had been one in 1981). The peasants were adamant that prior to the killing the *sinchis* had paid only one visit to the village, by helicopter. (It was not possible for us to ascertain whether this happened days or weeks before the killing as the Iquichano peasants' measure of time is, without a doubt, different from our own.) It has been conjectured that the peasant leaders could have gone to the city of Tambo to receive instruction from the military command there. However, the political authorities and the Guardia Civil had left Tambo in the middle of 1982 (more than six months before the killings) and the government only installed a politico-military command on December 29.

The infantrymen arrived in the city of Tambo the second week in January. Military communiqués examined by the Commission do not indicate that any patrol crossed or encroached on the Iquichan region in the days preceding the killing of the journalists (on January 25). When, then, could those paramilitary patrols have been organized and trained to kill strangers?

When the Guardia Civil *sinchis* arrived in the region days before—shortly after the peasants had killed members of the *Sendero Luminoso*—the first thing they did was to take away the guns which the peasants had seized from the guerrillas. Why disarm the peasants if the politico-military command wanted them organized into paramilitary groups? In the hearing that the Commission set up in Uchuraccay, the Iquichan peasants complained to us that 'el señor Gobierno' neither gave them arms to defend themselves nor offered them protection and they asked us insistently to send them at least three rifles in case the *Sendero Luminoso* guerrillas attacked (as in fact happened). Are these not persuasive arguments? There is no doubt the Iquichan peasants thought they were acting with the support of the military authorities. However, there is still nothing to suggest that the military authorities directed or planned that particular crime.

Third. Mr Harding omits to mention that the report roundly denounces and condemns many of the abuses committed by the armed forces in their struggle against *Sendero Luminoso.* For my part I have, in the Peruvian press, on radio and television, repeatedly criticized the violations of human rights—crimes, tortures and disappearances—perpetrated by the counter-insurgency forces, and I have demanded that the government ensure that the fight against terrorism and insurrection be carried out within the law. Otherwise the democracy we recovered four years ago will be shown to be a mere fiction. Mr Harding's suggestion that the report was written to serve President Belaúnde and not the truth merits only contempt. Although it is true that I respect Belaúnde, this has never stopped me from criticizing his government or even him personally, as I did when he made a disparaging reference to Amnesty International, an organization which (though it occasionally makes mistakes) is wholly deserving of respect.

My criticisms of Mr Harding do not proceed from his insinuation that I am a fanatic intolerant of the slightest criticism of my country's system of government. I know very well that the Peruvian democratic system is fragile and defective and needs constructive criticism if it is to improve. But I also believe that it needs to be defended because a

Pinochet-type military dictatorship or the Marxist-Leninist dictatorship that the *Sendero Luminoso* would like to establish would be worse, and would only increase the sufferings of the Peruvian people. Certainly I am engaged in the struggle to defend democracy in my country, but that is not the same as defending the government. It is a difficult and problematic struggle and to those of us involved it is painful to discover that those determined to destroy democracy in Peru—and in all of Latin America—can sometimes count on finding allies among those journalists of the great democratic newspapers of the West who, through blindness, ignorance, ingenuousness or prejudice, contribute to the discredit and defamation of those democracies—like the one in Peru—which are trying to survive in extremely difficult conditions.

Mr Harding seems to be an example of this phenomenon. I would not be concerned that his statements and writings about Peru echo all the most demagogic exaggerations, distortions and inventions of the enemies of democracy in my country—except for the fact that he is a journalist for *The Times*. If such opinions appear in a newspaper like *The Times,* they acquire a respectability and weight which they would never have if they appeared in other publications in Great Britain whose political bias would at least contextualize if not invalidate them (as is the case in Peru). In any event, it is not an unusual occurrence. There are many journalists in Western Europe like Mr Harding who, consciously or not, caricature Latin America and help to reinforce the image of barbarous countries for which there exist only two alternatives—military dictatorship or totalitarian revolution. Happily, the reality does not conform to the stereotype.

Mario Vargas Llosa
London

Translated from the Spanish by
Margaret Jull Costa

Politics and Literature?

To the Editor

I have forced myself to read through Martha Gellhorn's 'Testimonial' [*Granta* 11] for a second time, and I feel sick and very angry. I want first to speak for 'that lost country' of El Salvador, but what is there to say? Recent television documentaries suggest that this is not unusual and that El Salvador exists in a state of 'they do it to us: we do it to them.' Worse, Martha Gellhorn herself implies that this disgusting behaviour reflects the state of our species. But surely there was a time—I am thinking of Castro's introduction to Che Guevara's *Diary*—when humanity co-existed with revolution?

But I am also concerned that a literary magazine, like *Granta*, can even publish this sort of writing. You have upset me, you have made me angry, but you haven't offered me any outlets through which to express my anger or my grief. Such an outlet would have been simple: an address to which I could send money or offers of help—even just details of the unfortunate young man today. Gellhorn would presumably say that the young man is only one among many, but the events depicted happened two years ago and this reader, at least, is interested in specifics. Is he still in prison?

Can a literary magazine put writing of this sort to the political use it clearly requires? I am concerned that the context of this article—a literary magazine—detracts from its serious political and humanitarian implications.

Carole Ann Cotter
Leicester

The individual whose testimonial was published in Granta 11 *is believed to be living in exile in Costa Rica. More information can be obtained from Frances Crook at Amnesty International (British Section, 5 Roberts Place, London EC1R 0EJ), which in April 1984 launched 'A Campaign Against Torture', and from the El Salvador and Guatemala Committee on Human Rights, 21 Compton Terrace, London N1.*

Proffessionalism

To the Editor

The narrator of Jayne Anne Phillips's 'Rayme—A Memoir of the Seventies' in *Dirty Realism* [*Granta* 8] claims to have lived in a house with 'a West Virginian, who'd worked in the doomed McCarthy campaign.' Surely, given the time and social milieu, the campaign in which her housemate worked was that of Senator George McGovern whose latest assault on the presidency so recently came to grief. I hope the error is *Granta*'s rather than Ms Phillips's, if only to prove that the magazine is not the slickly proffessional publication it would seem to be. Otherwise, I don't much care for the name, the price, the presentation, and rather resent the success, but think the stories are terrific.

Roy Thompson
Wolverhampton

Jayne Anne Phillips replies:

The reference in question is indeed to the 1968 campaign of Eugene McCarthy—whose campaign was considerably more doomed than McGovern's, given the fact that he lost the Democratic nomination to Hubert Humphrey amid the riots and political wrangling of the Chicago convention. The point is that the West Virginian mentioned is six or seven years older than the narrator, and by the time of McGovern's candidacy in 1972 he, like many of his contemporaries, had finished with politics. I would suggest to Mr Thompson that 'time and social milieu' do range rather more than he suggests in his 'slickly proffessional' letter. I don't much care for Mr Thompson's complaints against *Granta,* but I do think his interest in literature is terrific.

Jayne Anne Phillips
Boston, Massachusetts

Notes on Contributors

'The True Adventures of the Rolling Stones' is from a book that **Stanley Booth** began writing fifteen years ago and which he will complete this summer. Heinemann publish it in January. **Raymond Carver's** most recent book is *Cathedral.* **Richard Ford's** previous contribution was in *Granta* 8 *Dirty Realism: New Writing from America.* **Carolyn Osborn** lives in Texas; 'Cowboy Movie' is her first published work in Britain. **Jayne Anne Phillip's** 'Danner, 1965' is from her first novel, *Machine Dreams* to be published by Faber and Faber in the autumn. **David Caute's** most recent books include *Under the Skin,* a documentary history of the war in Rhodesia, and *The K-Factor,* a novel. **Günter Grass** is currently completing a new novel. **Breyten Breytenbach's** most recent book is *Mouroir,* a novel. 'Prison-Scribe' is from his new book, *The True Confessions of an Albino Terrorist,* to be published by Faber and Faber at the end of October. Longer extracts are due to appear in the *Observer* on 9 and 16 September. **Peter Davis** is a writer and film-maker, whose work includes *Hearts and Minds.* **Gabriel García Márquez** has been a regular contributor to *Granta.* He won the Nobel Prize for Literature in 1982. **James Wolcott** is an Associate Editor at *Vanity Fair.*

Photo credits (in order): Jim Marshall, Dezo Hoffman, Jim Marshall, Popperfoto, ABC Television, Michael Putland/LFI, Michael Putland/LFI, John Hillelson, Yves Coatsaliou/John Hillelson, Camera Press, Popperfoto, Michael Cooper Estate, Dezo Hoffman, *The Sunday Times, The Sunday Times*, Owen Franken/John Hillelson, the *Sun*, William Collins and Sons. Photo research: Tracy Shaw.